I0755803

Empty Admiration

Empty Admiration

Robert Lewis Dabney's Expository Homiletic

Russell St. John

FOREWORD BY
Scott M. Gibson

PICKWICK *Publications* • Eugene, Oregon

EMPTY ADMIRATION
Robert Lewis Dabney's Expository Homiletic

Pickwick Publications
An Imprint of Wipf and Stock Publishers
199 W. 8th Ave., Suite 3
Eugene, OR 97401

www.wipfandstock.com

PAPERBACK ISBN: 978-1-7252-6439-7
HARDCOVER ISBN: 978-1-7252-6440-3
EBOOK ISBN: 978-1-7252-6441-0

Cataloguing-in-Publication data:

Names: St. John, Russell, author. | Gibson, Scott M., foreword.

Title: Empty admiration : Robert Lewis Dabney's expository homiletic / by Russell St. John ; foreword by Scott M. Gibson.

Description: Eugene, OR: Pickwick Publications, 2020 | Includes bibliographical references.

Identifiers: ISBN 978-1-7252-6439-7 (paperback) | ISBN 978-1-7252-6440-3 (hardcover) | ISBN 978-1-7252-6441-0 (ebook)

Subjects: LCSH: Dabney Robert Lewis—1820–1898. | Preaching—United States—History—19th century. | Clergy—United States—Biography. | Presbyterian Church—Clergy—Biography. | Presbyterian Church in the U.S.—History.

Classification: BV4208 S75 2020 (print) | BV4208 (ebook)

I dedicate this book to the Reverend William Hewes Bell (1940–2015), whose preaching was never flashy but ever faithful. He served the Triune God and his people with kindness, homespun wit, and a self-effacing manner that belied deep troves of biblical knowledge. If ever a faithful shepherd of sheep ascended a pulpit, it was Bill. I miss him dearly, and I look forward to the reunion that is coming.

Contents

Foreword

The nineteenth century had its share of homiletical luminaries. These preaching legends and educators included Charles H. Spurgeon of Great Britain, Phillips Brooks of Boston, Austin Phelps of Andover Theological Seminary, John A. Broadus of Southern Baptist Theological Seminary, Samuel Miller of Princeton Theological Seminary, and notably Southern Presbyterian, Robert L. Dabney of Union Theological Seminary in Virginia. If explored, each one of the lives of these titans would undoubtedly yield surprising insights.

Such is the case with Russell St. John's study of the homiletical teaching and the practice of preaching of Robert L. Dabney. St. John's thoroughness, insightfulness, thoughtfulness, and gentle critique provide a homiletical portrait of one of the nineteenth century's neglected preachers and teachers of preaching.

This study explores Dabney's life in light of his expository homiletical theory and classroom teaching and the conflict between the two. St. John engages with original resources, including Dabney's own teaching notes and the actual sermons he preached. In the process, St. John discovers a manifest structure for Dabney's expository sermons and the tension between the way he taught sermons to be preached and the way he himself preached them—and even the way his students preached sermons.

St. John illuminates that although Dabney advocated the preaching of expository sermons, Dabney actually did not practice what he taught. This is highlighted in Dabney's sermons and in the sermons of students whom he taught to preach.

This book will provide readers with a fair evaluation of Dabney, although surprising and possibly uncomfortable at times. The contours of this preacher's life are at one moment unpraiseworthy and at another interesting and even frustrating. Dabney's ministry was to train preachers. As an educator and as a practitioner, Dabney seemed to miss the mark. Although hailed in some circles as a master pedagogue, this classroom teacher seemed to produce a disparate homiletic.

Contradiction is not an easy term to apply to preachers, for their lives or for their homiletical practice. We live in an age of idols, propping up the cult of personality, venerating the skills of preachers as they communicate or even entertain their listeners. We expect preachers to be consistent in lifestyle and in practice. Yet what one says may markedly contrast with what one does. This study of Robert Lewis Dabney's expository homiletic is an insightful, honest examination of a life and its consistencies and inconsistencies born out in the practice of the classroom and pulpit life.

Russell St. John is to be commended for this work on Robert Lewis Dabney. And I recommend it to you with confidence and admiration—not empty admiration, but wholehearted admiration, for Russell St. John is an exceptional scholar and writer and brother in Christ.

Begin the journey of exploring the homiletics of a noted nineteenth century teacher and preacher, recognizing that faint praise may not be the best or most suitable praise one can receive, especially if the praise ends up to be hollow.

Scott M. Gibson

David E. Garland Chair of Preaching
George W. Truett Theological Seminary, Baylor University

Acknowledgements

I am grateful to the LORD for his manifold mercies in Christ.

My wife and our six children deserve hearty thanks for their patience, grace, and encouragement. Absent their support this book would not exist.

The leadership and members of Twin Oaks Presbyterian Church could not have offered greater backing or more constant prayer, and I am keenly aware of their contributions to this work. Likewise, Heritage Presbyterian Church, Grace United Reformed Church, Oakwood Presbyterian Church, and Grace Coastal Church each encouraged and shaped me in ways both subtle and profound.

Scott Gibson ("Doctor Father") merits high praise for his careful contributions to my research and writing, and Jeffrey Arthurs, who is both mentor and friend, encouraged me to persevere, faithfully prayed for me, laughed with me (and sometimes at me), and met my setbacks with calm assurances of future success. Both are dear brothers in Christ, without whom I could not imagine completing this work.

I am grateful to Bryan Chapell for teaching me to preach, to Craig Davis for teaching me to think, and to Bill Myers for teaching me to shepherd.

Without Merlin Whitman, my able and eager proofreader and formatter, this book never would have made it to print. I am grateful beyond words for her assistance.

The gracious people at Wipf & Stock bore patiently with me as this book came together, and I am thankful for their professionalism and care.

1

Biography

Introduction

Overview

Offering a brief biographical sketch to acquaint the reader with the outlines of Dabney's life and ministerial labors,[1] this chapter demonstrates that Robert Dabney is a consequential figure in American Presbyterian history, worthy of ongoing attention. Throughout his lifetime, Dabney proved dutiful, theologically and socially conservative, and devoted to unchanging principles. He also demonstrated lifelong, inveterate racism, mixing the chaff of his personal support for slavery and segregation with the wheat of his homiletical and theological labors. Over the course of five decades of teaching, writing, and preaching, Robert Dabney profoundly shaped Presbyterianism in the American South, and his legacy demands continuing research.[2]

The Plan of This Chapter

This chapter describes Dabney's life and work in five stages. The first section traces Dabney from birth until he enrolled at Union Theological Seminary in Virginia. The second recounts his seminary experience, labors as

1. It is not the scope of this paper to offer a full-fledged biography. Dabney has two biographers: Johnson, *Life and Letters*; and Lucas, *Robert Lewis Dabney*.

2. The Presbyterian Church in America, which is the daughter denomination of the church to which Dabney belonged, continues to engage his legacy. See Duncan, "Defending the Faith." Duncan addresses Robert Dabney at length.

a home missionary, and pastorate at Tinkling Spring Presbyterian Church. The third describes his early years teaching at Union Theological Seminary and his involvement in the American Civil War. The fourth recounts Dabney's struggles in postbellum Virginia and his decision to leave Union Seminary for the University of Texas in 1883. The final section outlines Dabney's closing years and death, offering the reader a sampling of memorials to Dabney, which demonstrate his significance to Presbyterianism in the American South and his continuing worth as a subject of historical and homiletical research.

Early Years

Heritage

Robert Lewis Dabney was born in Louisa County, Virginia on March 5, 1820, the sixth of eight children. His parents were "land rich but cash poor"[3] Virginia gentry, devout Presbyterians, and slaveholders. Thomas Cary Johnson suggested that "[t]he people of this region were marked for their high spirit and keen sense of honor. They were conscious of a good heritage and self-respecting."[4] Noting that most of Dabney's kith enjoyed the benefits of sound education, Johnson contended: "[T]hese people were a reading people. They had books. These books were old-fashioned but good."[5] He summarized the character of the Dabneys by asserting that "they became a people of education and culture."[6] Robert Dabney's great uncle was a Revolutionary War hero. His father fought in the War of 1812 and served the Virginia Legislature, while his mother's lineage embraced the Randolphs of old Virginia. His was a respected heritage.[7]

This Virginia gentry of Dabney's youth was conservative, socially and theologically, and aristocratic.[8] David Overy noted that "Dabney was

3. Thompson, *Her Walls*, 181.

4. Johnson, *Life and Letters*, 21.

5. Johnson, *Life and Letters*, 22.

6. Johnson, *Life and Letters*, 22. Johnson taught with Robert Dabney at Austin Theological Seminary and the University of Texas from 1888–90, later filling various faculty positions at Union Theological Seminary in Virginia. A personal friend and protégé of Dabney, Johnson is an excellent source for the basic outlines of Dabney's life and work but often presents a hagiographic picture of Dabney's character and accomplishments. See Moore and Scherer, *Centennial*, 123, and Moore et al., *General Catalogue*, 39–40.

7. See Dabney, *Sketch of the Dabneys*.

8. See Snay, *Gospel of Disunion*, 71–73. Francis Simkins described Dabney's people as "the aristocracy of Piedmont Virginia. It was a society of homespun ladies and

not so much a Southerner as he was a Virginian, and a particular kind of Virginian at that," for he was "a member of the old Tidewater-Piedmont gentry,"[9] which Carter Turner described as a society founded on "clear racial and gender distinctions."[10] David Coffin dubbed Dabney a "Southerner *par excellence*,"[11] while Johnson opined: "It may be doubted whether many more perfect products of the civilization of his section can be found than Robert Lewis Dabney."[12]

Education

Dabney's elder brother, Charles, oversaw Robert's early education. He stressed a few subjects deeply, which inculcated in the younger Dabney a lifelong penchant for analytical thinking. Johnson argued:

> [H]is studies at this period of his life seem to have covered no great number of topics, but . . . they were extensive in the classics. Two advantages naturally followed from this: concentration of energies along a few lines enabled him to put more force out along those lines, and accomplish relatively great things in those studies; he was also preserved from falling into the habit of skimming over the surface of things.[13]

Other tutors followed, preparing sixteen-year-old Robert Dabney for Hampden-Sydney College, in which he enrolled in June of 1836 as a partially advanced sophomore.[14] Turner noted that "[Dabney] already possessed an ethic of duty,"[15] and he gained a reputation for hard work and academic excellence. Johnson recorded: "He seems to have put forth painstaking effort on every branch of his studies, and to have applied himself closely," so much so

gentlemen who lived in modest homes, were uncorrupted by wealth, emphasized kinship and the laws of hospitality, took intelligent care of their slaves, stressed Presbyterianism and classical education, and ruled their communities through an aristocratic type of representative government." Simkins, "Dabney, Southern Conservative," 393.

9. Overy, "Apostle," 318

10. Turner, "Causes Lost and Found," 27. These distinctions formed the mental and moral architecture within which Dabney furnished his intellectual world.

11. Coffin, "Reflections," 9 [emphasis original].

12. Johnson, *Life and Letters*, 24. Johnson was more correct than he knew. Dabney did indeed represent "his section," both in the manner Johnson intended, and also in the stark racism and provincialism of that section.

13. Johnson, *Life and Letters*, 28.

14. Johnson, *Life and Letters*, 30.

15. Turner, "Causes Lost and Found," 32.

that "his notes were widely copied by his fellow-students."[16] Completing his courses in physics, mathematics, Latin, and Greek, Dabney left Hampden-Sydney in September of 1837 to care for the family estate.[17]

Disposition and Faith

When Robert Dabney was thirteen his father had died, and given that his elder brother Charles had already left home, the younger Dabney assumed responsibility for the family home and holdings. He was suited to a patriarchal role, and his family members lovingly referred to him as "the old gentleman."[18] Thomas Jenkins recognized that Dabney was in fact an "old man in personality,"[19] while Johnson suggested that for Dabney, to be called "old-fashioned" was a compliment.[20] He worked for a year to quarry stone to rebuild the family mill and oversaw the planting of the farm,[21] caring for the family interests. At the same time, he opened a small grammar school, teaching the children of local landowners, and found that the classroom suited him.[22]

More significant than any academic achievement Dabney earned at Hampden-Sydney was his conversion to the Christian faith during a campus-wide revival in the late summer of 1837.[23] Writing that "[t]he most important event of this period to me was my profession of faith in Christ," Dabney recalled that "the college was visited by a powerful and genuine awakening."[24] Prior to his conversion, Dabney had resolved to become a learned man,[25] and thereafter he also resolved to become a learned minister, writing: "[M]y mind was made up to preach the gospel."[26]

16. Johnson, *Life and Letters*, 31.

17. Johnson, *Life and Letters*, 30.

18. Johnson, *Life and Letters*, 41, 44.

19. Jenkins, "Character of God," 326.

20. Johnson, *Life and Letters*, 84.

21. Johnson, *Life and Letters*, 44–45.

22. Johnson, *Life and Letters*, 45.

23. Johnson, *Life and Letters*, 42.

24. Dabney, unpublished autobiography, 3. Dabney notes within the manuscript that he prepared his autobiography in 1895.

25. Johnson, *Life and Letters*, 31.

26. Dabney, unpublished autobiography, 7.

During his brief stay at Hampden-Sydney, Dabney had forged a friendship with Anne Rice, the widow of John Holt Rice, founder of Union Seminary.[27] In a letter dated February 13, 1838, Rice exhorted Dabney, writing:

> I trust you will make your religion serviceable to you in every thought and action. It is of little avail if our religion is not in continual practice, if it is not interwoven in our very system. Oh! how much Christians lose by not being more entirely Christian . . . I wish you to take a higher stand than the common Christians.[28]

Taking her counsel to heart, Dabney professed faith and joined the local Presbyterian congregation in which his father had once served as a Ruling Elder.[29] He thus united himself to a theologically conservative, Old School[30] branch of Presbyterianism, never to depart from it. Overy observed that "Dabney was no innovator,"[31] and in fact he shunned theological novelty.[32] Turner captured Dabney's theological conservatism, writing: "Old School Presbyterianism, Dabney believed, was the only American denomination based entirely on the Bible."[33] Dabney was just 18 years old, but for the next sixty years he never departed from or altered the conservative theological stance of his youth.

To the University

When the family estate recovered a firm financial posture, Dabney returned to his studies, choosing to continue his education at the University of Virginia in December of 1839. He appreciated the education, complained about foreign professors, whom he believed ill suited to teach Virginians,[34] and showed

27. Lucas, *Robert Louis Dabney*, 27.

28. Johnson, *Life and Letters*, 46.

29. Dabney, unpublished autobiography, 4. See also Lucas, *Robert Lewis Dabney*, 36.

30. In 1837 American Presbyterians divided into Old and New School branches, the former pursuing doctrinal purity according to the Westminster Standards, while the latter embraced doctrinal latitude, including a more open stance toward revivals. See Hart and Muether, *Seeking*, 121–27.

31. Overy, "Apostle," 317.

32. Noting that Dabney's theology consistently defended the Westminster Standards, Johnson contended: "Dr. Dabney shows his great power while walking in old paths." Johnson, "Sketch," 9.

33. Turner, "Causes Lost and Found," 65.

34. Johnson, *Life and Letters*, 51–55. Dabney harbored a lifelong conviction that Southern students learned best from Southern teachers, and he especially distrusted foreigners. Overy aptly contended that Dabney "never outgrew the extremely narrow provincialism" of his youth. Overy, "Apostle," 318.

a willingness to pursue duty in the face of controversy. During Dabney's second year a student rally[35] turned violent, and a student shot and killed a faculty member. The student body appointed Dabney an investigator, and he pursued his work diligently. Writing to his brother, William, Dabney stated that he "was determined to stop at nothing in discharging what I thought the trust reposed in me by my fellow-students required," and reflected:

> If a man is certain that it is a *duty* which calls him into danger or disagreeable circumstances, he will turn neither to the right hand nor to the left, for fear of any evils which may threaten him, from the injustice of public opinion, or from personal violence.[36]

Dabney felt that the defense lawyers behaved unscrupulously by defending a man they knew to be guilty, and he noted that two key witnesses refused to testify.[37] The trial never materialized and the suspect took his own life the following year, but Dabney had proven himself willing to face public opposition to pursue duty. Describing Dabney's resolve as predictive of his future course, Johnson admired Dabney's commitment to duty, contending:

> [W]hen his judgment had once approved a course, when he heard the clear call of duty, he was going to answer, no matter what the obstacles in his way. This incident is typical of his whole life, and prophetic. He was preparing himself to uphold the right in the face of a disapproving world.[38]

Noting that "Dabney had little patience for dishonesty, inaccuracy, or even vagueness," Turner aptly observed that he "was always attracted to clear-cut positions,"[39] and Dabney's formative years demonstrate his resolve to live according to "clear-cut"[40] principles and the dictates of duty. Dabney graduated with the Master of Arts in July of 1842.

35. The students had gathered to commemorate the anniversary of the 1834 student "rebellion," in which students protested against and successfully abolished a nightly student curfew. Johnson, *Life and Letters*, 56.

36. Johnson, *Life and Letters*, 60 [emphasis original], from Dabney's December 7, 1840 letter to his brother, William.

37. Johnson, *Life and Letters*, 59.

38. Johnson, *Life and Letters*, 60.

39. Turner, "Causes Lost and Found," 39.

40. Turner, "Causes Lost and Found," 39.

To Union Seminary and Back

First Labors

Once again returning home to help his mother,[41] Dabney resumed teaching local children, including his younger sister Betty, for whom he wrote a Latin grammar.[42] He was offered and refused the editorship of a Richmond, Virginia newspaper, and also declined a teaching position.[43] Dabney aspired instead to preach, and in November of 1844 enrolled in Union Theological Seminary at Hampden-Sydney, Virginia, one of just eighteen students.[44] Completing three years of studies in two years, he graduated in May of 1846. Hanover Presbytery[45] licensed him to preach, and Dabney began a year of missionary labor in Louisa County, Virginia.[46] He earned a reputation for powerful preaching and theological acumen, and Johnson suggested:

> His preaching was duly appreciated by the little flocks to which he ministered. Moreover, he commended himself to all classes, by his blood earnestness, and uncommon honesty of word and behavior, by his unaffected and thorough-going interest in the well-being, both temporal and spiritual, of his parishioners, and by his genuine sympathy for all the weak and the suffering.[47]

Sean Lucas recognized that Dabney was ever "aspiring to places of higher usefulness,"[48] and when he caught the attention of a prominent congregation—the Tinkling Spring Presbyterian Church in Augusta County, near Staunton, Virginia—Dabney was intrigued. After visiting the

41. Johnson, *Life and Letters*, 77, and Turner, "Causes Lost and Found," 43.

42. Johnson, *Life and Letters*, 78.

43. Turner, "Causes Lost and Found," 44.

44. Moore and Scherer, *Centennial*, 61–63. See also Lucas, *Robert Lewis Dabney*, 37. For a full history of Union Theological Seminary, see Sweetser, *Copious Fountain*.

45. Presbyterian polity recognizes local, regional, and national "courts" within the church. The Session represents the local, the Presbytery the regional, and the General Assembly the national court.

46. On the origin of Dabney's Louisa County evangelistic ministry, Johnson recalled that at his licensure Dabney "looked so thin and pale that the Presbytery thought his life would probably be a short one, and that he needed the care of interested friends. A few weeks before, the church of Providence and the South Anna and Green Springs neighborhoods, in Louisa county [*sic*], had been thrown together, thus constituting a missionary field. As his mother's home was in this field, and as the field was vacant, the Presbytery assigned Mr. Dabney to it." Johnson, *Life and Letters*, 95.

47. Johnson, *Life and Letters*, 99.

48. Lucas, *Robert Lewis Dabney*, 49.

congregation in April, he accepted a call to serve as its pastor, beginning in July of 1847.[49]

Tinkling Spring

Dabney served Tinkling Spring Church for six years, shepherding what he believed to be a hardheaded Scotch-Irish congregation. He considered the Scotch-Irish "of all people in the world" to be "the most inflexible and obstinate,"[50] and complained to his mother about quarreling congregational factions, for whom the construction of a new sanctuary provided opportunity for rancor:

> I fear . . . that by the time the house is finished there will be no congregation to worship in it. They seem to be, a part of them, possessed with the desire to quarrel about every trifle in the arrangement of the matter. I have been fretted until I heartily wished the old trap standing still, with all its defects. Both parties in these altercations are to blame, some for meddlesomeness, and some for repelling that meddlesomeness in too rash a manner . . . The Scotch-Irish are the most inflexible people in the world when they are right, and the most vexatiously pig-headed and mulish when wrong.[51]

Nevertheless, Dabney also recognized that "the persons really active in the evil-doing are few," while many in his congregation were "moderate, forbearing, and forgiving Christians, whose pious endurance . . . honors the gospel as much as the conduct of others disgraces it."[52]

By his own testimony, Dabney's greatest accomplishment during his pastorate at Tinkling Spring was his marriage to Margaret Lavinia Morrison. Writing, "I found the wife appointed for me by Providence,"[53] Dabney described Lavinia as "the most charming lady in that region—for her piety,

49. Dabney recalled that during his visit to Tinkling Spring Church he had no symptoms of the digestive difficulties that normally plagued him, and he ascribed his improvement to "the limestone water" of the spring. Dabney, unpublished autobiography, 11.

50. Johnson, *Life and Letters*, 109, from Dabney's March 8, 1849 letter to his mother.

51. Johnson, *Life and Letters*, 109, from Dabney's July 30, 1849 letter to his mother. Dabney, who was himself often rigid and inflexible, betrayed a lifelong lack of self-awareness.

52. Johnson, *Life and Letters*, 109, from Dabney's July 30, 1849 letter to his mother.

53. Dabney, unpublished autobiography, 11.

good sense, and the best of daughters."[54] Coming to admire her skills on horseback, he referred to her as "remarkably graceful,"[55] and stated: "Mine was very nearly a case of 'love at first sight' . . . Then began the first and last love affair of my life."[56] Dabney married his beloved "Binny" on March 28, 1848 and fathered two sons while at Tinkling Spring—Robert Lewis, born February 19, 1849, and James Morrison, born April 1, 1850.[57]

During these years Dabney also honed his skills as a preacher. Lucas suggested: "[I]f later testimonials are any indication, Dabney's preaching was memorable,"[58] and contemporary appraisals united in describing Dabney's "pulpit intensity, his lack of polished oratory, and his didacticism."[59] Possibly conceding that Dabney's intensity served as a barrier to fruitful evangelism, Johnson suggested:

> He was, perhaps, better fitted to edify God's saints than to win the unrepentant to God. He was preeminent, even in these early days, for instruction in the teachings of Scripture. He broadened, and deepened, and built up his people in their knowledge and understanding of the Scriptures.[60]

The same "blood-earnestness"[61] that Dabney displayed as a missionary in Louisa County, he also showed as pastor of Tinkling Spring, and he confessed: "My charge hangs on my hands like a growing burden, heavier and heavier continually."[62] Dabney despaired that his preaching seemed "to human eyes to be utterly without effect; bad for me, bad for them."[63] His sense of duty sometimes led Dabney to criticize himself, for he took his responsibilities seriously. In a March 5, 1853 letter to Dabney, his friend, C. R. Vaughan, wrote:

> You do not know how much I value you, Dabney; and I value you mainly because I think you are the most honest—almost the only honest—and the least selfish man I know in the ministry. I

54. Dabney, unpublished autobiography, 12.

55. Dabney, unpublished autobiography, 13.

56. Dabney, unpublished autobiography, 14.

57. Dabney, unpublished autobiography, 14.

58. Lucas, *Robert Lewis Dabney*, 50.

59. Lucas, *Robert Lewis Dabney*, 51.

60. Johnson, *Life and Letters*, 110. Chapter 5 of this paper demonstrates that Dabney frequently "built up his people" in knowledge of the doctrines and duties of the Bible rather than the text of the Bible itself.

61. Johnson, *Life and Letters*, 99.

62. Johnson, *Life and Letters*, 110, from Dabney's January 9, 1849 letter to his mother.

63. Johnson, *Life and Letters*, 110, from Dabney's January 9, 1849 letter to his mother.

> mean the younger ones. I preach for show . . . I hate myself for it; but I still do it; and I speak what I believe when I say that you are the only young minister in my acquaintance of whom I do not feel the suspicion.[64]

Johnson boasted that Dabney's friends uniformly felt him to be "honest to the back-bone,"[65] and Dabney's preaching enjoyed the refreshment of a brief revival, which Tinkling Spring experienced during the summer of 1850.[66]

The Seminary Calls

Dabney also wrote. Even as a seminarian, he composed articles for Presbyterian papers and magazines,[67] and his pen waxed prolific during his Tinkling Spring pastorate.[68] Addressing politics, popery, the use of musical instruments in worship, and other topics, always endorsing a conservative, traditional stance, Dabney's writings garnered him regional renown,[69] and in May of 1853 his alma mater, Union Theological Seminary, called him to serve as Chair of Ecclesiastical History and Polity. He debated whether to accept.

The position had been offered to several notable pastors, each of whom had declined. Dabney remembered: "It was indeed rather hawked about and declined by all," for "the general opinion was that the Sem[inary] had poor prospects and was nearly dead."[70] Union Seminary boasted just two professors, twelve students enrolled for the fall term, and a small endowment.[71] Dabney had, moreover, recently built a house, of which he was fond. His church was prospering, and his health, which he knew to be unsuitable to Hampden-Sydney, flourished at Tinkling Spring.[72] Stating, "I was 33 years old," and "I was not a candidate—did not desire it—and

64. Johnson, *Life and Letters*, 114.

65. Johnson, *Life and Letters*, 114.

66. Johnson, *Life and Letters*, 112–14 provides a history of the revival and of Dabney's response to it.

67. Johnson, *Life and Letters*, 89.

68. Merrill Matthews suggested that Dabney possessed the "ability to move easily in a number of academic disciplines," and Dabney seemed to justify Matthews's observation, writing in theology, homiletics, philosophy, economics, and politics. Matthews, "Conservative Thought," 4.

69. For a sampling, see Johnson, *Life and Letters*, 127–30, and Turner, "Causes Lost and Found," 48–55.

70. Dabney, unpublished autobiography, 17.

71. Moore and Scherer, *Centennial*, 68–69.

72. Dabney, unpublished autobiography, 18.

knew nothing of the movement,"[73] Dabney was nevertheless gratified to receive letters urging him to accept, not only from friends and trusted advisors, but also from Drs. Sampson and Wilson at the seminary. Dabney respected Sampson in particular, later writing that he was "the best scholar and teacher I ever knew, and the purest Christian."[74] The opportunity to labor alongside Sampson tipped the decision in favor of leaving for the seminary. Dabney stated: "The belief that I should have him as a colaborer, was the one thing which reconciled me to undertaking an almost helpless enterprise."[75] Dabney nevertheless submitted the matter to his presbytery, which encouraged him to accept.[76] He moved in August of 1853, and remained at Union Seminary for thirty years.

Teaching and Fighting

Starting at Union

Shortly after Dabney arrived at the seminary, Samuel Wilson, who taught both systematic theology and sacred rhetoric, began to suffer the effects of age and ill health. While a student at Union, Dabney had studied sacred rhetoric under Wilson,[77] and in the 1855–56 academic year Dabney assumed from Wilson responsibility for teaching homiletics.[78] From 1855–59, Dabney taught church history, polity, and preaching, but beginning in the fall term of 1859, he transferred from Church History and Polity to Systematic, Polemic, and Pastoral Theology, while retaining responsibility for homiletics.[79] This move reconciled a rift in Dabney's mind, for Dabney felt that the teacher of systematics, not of church history, should teach homiletics. He suggested: "It is most natural and facile for the professor who has just shown how to systematize the truths of redemption, to show the proper mode of their presentation to the human mind."[80] Dabney continued to teach homiletics until he left the seminary in 1883.

73. Dabney, unpublished autobiography, 17.

74. Dabney, unpublished autobiography, 8.

75. Dabney, unpublished autobiography, 21. Sampson died on April 9, 1854, only eight months after Dabney arrived at Union. See Dabney, *Memorial*, iv.

76. Johnson, *Life and Letters*, 134.

77. Moore and Scherer, *Centennial*, 34. See also Trotter, *Always Prepared*, 198. *Always Prepared* is a revision of Trotter, "Blasting Rocks."

78. *Catalogue of the Officers*, 6.

79. Moore and Scherer, *Centennial*, 34, and Johnson, *Life and Letters*, 195.

80. Johnson, *Life and Letters*, 153.

Dabney's work as a theologian and homiletician excelled his work as an historian, and Johnson raved: "His success in his new chair was greater than in that of history. It was not only emphatic, decided and distinguished—it was huge. He had found his most appropriate sphere."[81] Attention followed Dabney's success, and in 1860 Fifth Avenue Presbyterian Church in New York offered him the pulpit, but he refused.[82] Later that year, he also received an overture from Princeton Seminary offering him a faculty position in church history.[83] This too he declined. In offering an explanation for his decision, Dabney wrote:

> By the time I would get settled in Princeton, the abolitionists would have forced the country into a war between the sections. And it would be impossible for me to side with the fanatics and usurpers against my own state and people.[84]

This blanket condemnation is typical of Dabney. To his mind, all Northerners were abolitionists and thus "fanatics and usurpers." Charles Hodge nevertheless tried to persuade Dabney to accept, and while Dabney agreed with Hodge that "[t]he true question, as you have correctly stated, is, In which position shall I be likely to effect most for Christ and his church?" Dabney answered, writing:

> I cannot avoid the conviction that, so far as our fallible wisdom can judge, the post of superior usefulness for me is here. My reasons for this conclusion may be briefly summed up in this statement: that by going away I shall inflict an almost fatal injury on a minor interest of the church in order to confer a very non-essential assistance on a major interest of the same church.[85]

Princeton persisted, and Dabney exchanged a series of increasingly tense letters with Hodge and other Princeton faculty, ultimately standing firm in his refusal.[86] Dabney later recalled that while his rejection was clear, "[A]pparently [Hodge] and the Princeton people could not conceive how

81. Johnson, *Life and Letters*, 197.

82. Johnson, *Life and Letters*, 198.

83. Dabney was a highly regarded theologian and teacher. The January 12, 1898 edition of the *Presbyterian Banner* of Pittsburgh, PA stated: "Several times we have heard the late Rev. Archibald Alexander Hodge, D. D., say that he regarded Dr. Dabney as the best teacher of theology in the United States, if not the world." Cited in Johnson, *Life and Letters*, 534.

84. Dabney, unpublished autobiography, 27–28.

85. Johnson, *Life and Letters*, 203, from Dabney's April 10, 1860 letter to Charles Hodge.

86. Johnson, *Life and Letters*, 198–211.

any little Southern man could do otherwise than hanker in his heart after such a place."[87] In point of fact it appears that Hodge and Princeton's faculty genuinely strove to understand Dabney's decision, and continued to admire his talents[88] despite his refusal. Dabney remained in Virginia.

Family and Grief

While his academic labors flourished and his reputation grew, Dabney's family experienced both blessing and tragedy. His third son, Charles William, was born on June 19, 1855, but in November and December of that same year Dabney's two eldest sons, Robert and James, died from diphtheria.[89] Dabney was crushed, writing, "I have learned rapidly in the school of anguish this week,"[90] and admitted to his brother:

> To see my dear little one thus ravaged, crushed and destroyed, turning his beautiful liquid eyes to me and his weeping mother for help, after his gentle voice was obstructed, and to feel myself as helpless as he to give any aid—this tears my heart with anguish.[91]

Dabney confessed that when Robert died only a month after James, he was "not only wounded, but [also] benumbed,"[92] and feared to show affection to his infant son, Charles. Decrying his own heart, Dabney lamented: "Death has struck me with a dagger of ice."[93]

Grief changed him, and thereafter Dabney demonstrated great tenderness toward those who suffered. In an undated letter to Thomas Cary Johnson, Margaret Babcock described Dabney's care in weeping with those who wept:

87. Dabney, unpublished autobiography, 25–26.

88. Ten years later, Hodge positively reviewed Dabney's *Sacred Rhetoric*. See Hodge, "Notices of Recent Publications," 147–48.

89. Dabney, unpublished autobiography, 19. Three more sons followed: Thomas Price on April 5, 1857. He too died of diphtheria in September of 1862. Samuel Brown was born on June 8, 1859, and James Meriwether on August 11, 1865. Dabney, unpublished autobiography, 19–20.

90. Johnson, *Life and Letters*, 168, from Dabney's November 15, 1855 letter to his brother, Charles.

91. Johnson, *Life and Letters*, 169, from Dabney's November 15, 1855 letter to his brother, Charles.

92. Johnson, *Life and Letters*, 172, from Dabney's December 12, 1855 letter to his brother, Charles.

93. Johnson, *Life and Letters*, 172, from Dabney's December 12, 1855 letter to his brother, Charles.

> About the year 1859, Dr. Dabney came to our house . . . [O]ur near neighbors were Mr. and Mrs. Offutt and their little boy, an only child. This child was ill with fever. One morning, I told Dr. Dabney of their grief, and my fears that he would die, asking him if he would not go over with me. This was soon after he had buried two dear boys at Hampden-Sidney [*sic*]. He, without hesitation, granted my request. Without ringing, we gently walked through the house to the back parlor, where the child was lying. Mrs. Offutt was on her knees near her child; Dr. Dabney stood erect, between the wide folding-doors, with his arms crossed, silently taking in the whole scene. Soon he walked to the bed, and kneeling near the mother, gave way to a flood of tears such as I then thought I had never seen a man weep. Then he offered such a prayer as you can well imagine that great tender heart, so recently bereaved, would offer for the afflicted parents, and the precious child then almost in the Saviour's[94] arms.[95]

Dabney's confidence in the fidelity of the Lord likewise grew through his grief. A seminary student, noticing a change in his professor, wrote:

> I remember vividly how impressed I was with the change in question, by his comments on one of the first hymns he had us sing at the first preaching service he conducted in the Seminary Chapel after his sad bereavement, beginning, "Come humble sinner in whose breast." The emphasis he laid upon the word "perhaps" caused my nerves to tingle as he recited these stanzas:
>
> "All to the gracious King approach,
> Whose sceptre pardon gives;
> Perhaps he may commend my touch,
> And then the suppliant lives.
>
> Perhaps he will admit my plea,
> Perhaps will hear my prayer;
> But if I perish, I will pray,
> And perish only there."
>
> He looked as if this word "perhaps" was suggestive to him of a very realistic apprehension of the ever-present power of the serpentine, satanic accuser of Christ and his would-be brethren. The preacher turned partly around, he fixed a piercing downward

94. This book retains the original spelling in cases in which that spelling was, in nineteenth-century America, acceptable. Some spellings that Dabney and his peers employed, such as "labour," reflect what today would be considered a British over against an American spelling.

95. Johnson, *Life and Letters*, 177–78.

> gaze, his eyes flashing with indignant, fiery emotion, his heavy right heel smiting the floor with rapid, startling stampings, he, in the meanwhile, exclaiming, with an intonation that of all the speakers I have ever heard, only Dr. Dabney could voice: "There is no *perhaps* about it. It is a libel on the promises, which are yea and amen in Christ Jesus. There is no *perhaps* about it, for the gracious King will admit the humble sinner's plea, and will hear his prayer. There is no *perhaps* about it."[96]

The Peculiar Institution

In the midst of Dabney's professional success and personal heartache stood the question no educated person could ignore: slavery. In a January 22, 1840 letter to G. Woodson Payne, written during his studies at the University of Virginia, Dabney suggested that abolitionist rhetoric had, in recent years, hardened the views of his fellow Virginians. He wrote:

> I do believe that if these mad fanatics had let us alone, in twenty years we should have made Virginia a free State. As it is, their unauthorized attempts to strike off the fetters of our slaves have but riveted them on the faster. Does this fact arise from the perversity of our natures? I believe that it does, in part. We are less inclined to do that which we know to be our duty because persons, who have no right to interfere, demand it of us.[97]

Nevertheless, Dabney insisted also that the shift in Southern opinion toward the continuation of slavery resulted from "free discussion," which led most Virginians to conclude that emancipation was "dangerous."[98] Dabney repeated an indefensible Southern claim, stating that blacks, as a race, bore no capacity for self-government. His twisted conclusion thus argued that emancipation would comprise an act of hatred toward slaves rather than love. He opined:

> If we had hastened on to give the slave his liberty at once, as I believe public sentiment was tending, we might have done irreparable injury. I am no Abolitionist. I do not doubt that liberty would ruin the African race in the Southern States; that they would wane away, like the unfortunate Indians, by the effects of their own vices and from the pressure of a more

96. Johnson, *Life and Letters*, 174 [emphasis original]. Johnson offered no information about the provenance of this letter, stating only that it came from a student.

97. Johnson, *Life and Letters*, 67.

98. Johnson, *Life and Letters*, 67.

> powerful and more enlightened race. I cannot conceive of any duty arising from the command to love my neighbor as myself which compels me to inflict a ruinous injury on that neighbor, and such would be immediate freedom to our slaves. But yet I do not believe that we ought to rest contented that slavery should exist forever, in its present form. It is, as a system, liable to most erroneous abuses.[99]

In listing those abuses, Dabney offered an honest evaluation of slavery's evils, but he also defined those evils as abuses of a morally justifiable system rather than intrinsic to a morally indefensible system.[100] Seeming to sense the contradiction, Dabney asked:

> Do you think that there will be a system of slavery, where the black is punished with death for an offence for which a white man is only imprisoned a year or two; where the black may not resist wanton aggression and injury; where he is liable to have his domestic relations violated in an instant; where the female is not mistress of her own chastity; where the slave is liable to starvation, oppression and cruel punishments from an unprincipled master—that such a system can exist in the millennium? If not then, it is an obstacle to the *Prince of Peace*, and if we would see his chariot roll on, among the prostrate nations, it is our duty to remove this obstruction.[101]

Offering no practical steps to implement such reforms, Dabney instead addressed slavery in the abstract, asking, Does the Bible endorse slavery as a legitimate human relation or reprobate it? Convinced of the former, Dabney urged Southerners to argue the slavery question from the Bible. Writing to his brother Charles on January 15, 1851, Dabney revealed that he had already formed his conclusions about the supposedly "infidel" motives and aims of any person who supported abolition. He stated:

> [T]he proper way to argue this ethical question is to put the Bible arguments . . . If we want to effect the general current of national opinion on this subject, "Is slave-holding intrinsically immoral or unjust?" we must go before the nation with the Bible as the text, and "Thus saith the Lord" as the answer. This policy is the wiser, because we know that on the Bible argument the abolition party will be driven to unveil their true infidel

99. Johnson, *Life and Letters*, 67–68.

100. This became Dabney's conviction throughout his lifetime, and it represents the fundamental argument in Dabney, *Defense of Virginia*.

101. Johnson, *Life and Letters*, 68 [emphasis original].

> tendencies. The Bible being bound to stand on our side, they will have to come out and array themselves against the Bible . . . Here is our policy, then, to push the Bible argument continually, to drive abolitionism to the wall, to compel it to assume an anti-Christian position.[102]

Dabney nevertheless acknowledged that no biblical argument would secure broad public support if Southerners refused to mitigate abuses of the slave system. He argued:

> [T]o enjoy the advantages of this Bible argument in our favor slave-holders will have to pay a price. And the price is this. They must be willing to recognize and grant in slaves those rights which are a part of our essential humanity . . . These are the rights of immortal and domestic beings.[103]

Despite his exhortation to "push the biblical argument,"[104] Dabney offered other justifications for slavery that boasted no origin in Scripture. Dabney believed blacks incapable of exercising individual freedom, and thus he insisted that slavery was both necessary and beneficial to society. Attempting to veil his racism in the guise of this supposedly civic concern, Dabney argued:

> [T]o confer on those who are incompetent to use them, the same privileges granted to others who can and will use them rightfully, would be essential inequality; for it would clothe the incompetent and undeserving with power to injure the deserving and capable, without real benefit to themselves . . . If the society contains a class of adult members, so deficient in virtue and intelligence that they would only abuse the fuller privileges of other citizens to their own and others' detriment, it is just to withhold so many of these privileges, and to impose so much restraint, as may be necessary for the highest equity to the whole body.[105]

However unjust and unjustifiable Dabney's views appear today, his sentiments regrettably reflected a common opinion among Southern whites. Turner summarized this Southern position, writing:

> [I]t was common for southerners to argue that slavery was the only way to properly order society. By God's decree, they

102. Johnson, *Life and Letters*, 129.

103. Johnson, *Life and Letters*, 129.

104. Johnson, *Life and Letters*, 129.

105. Dabney, *Defense of Virginia*, 256–57.

> believed, blacks and whites developed different qualities over time, and slavery was the only way for the two races to exist harmoniously.[106]

Dabney continued to defend Southern slavery until the day of his death, claiming that by virtue of his *Defense of Virginia*, the righteousness of Southern chattel slavery was "absolutely established."[107]

Clouds of War

Throughout the tumultuous years that preceded the Civil War, Dabney painted himself a staunch advocate for federal union.[108] Lucas noted that Dabney sought to "moderate passions among Southerners,"[109] while Turner recounted Dabney's public appeals for peace, which he offered as late as March of 1861.[110] Dabney showed little patience for hawkish Southerners, feeling that the South stood ill prepared for war, even though he believed war inevitable.[111] In a December 28, 1860 letter to his mother, he confessed: "I feel sick at heart at the state of the country. I have been attempting, in my feeble way, to preach peace, and to rouse Christians to their duty in staying the tide of passion and violence," but he lamented that "Christians seem to have lost their senses with excitement, fear and passion; and everything seems hurrying to civil war."[112] He continued, writing:

> [T]hree-fourths of the people there are for peace; but we seem to be given up of God, and the violent ones have it all their own way. As for South Carolina, the little impudent vixen has gone beyond all patience. She is as great a pest as the Abolitionists.

106. Turner, "Causes Lost and Found," 129. Mark Noll offered a thoughtful analysis of pro and anti-slavery arguments prior to the Civil War in Noll, *Civil War*. For a thorough understanding of Dabney's own views, see Dabney, *Defense of Virginia*.

107. Dabney, unpublished autobiography, 48. Dabney was so convinced of the justness of the Southern cause that he insisted on being buried in his Confederate uniform.

108. Johnson, *Life and Letters*, 223.

109. Lucas, *Robert Lewis Dabney*, 105.

110. Turner, "Causes Lost and Found," 113. Turner offered a helpful overview of Dabney's public writings in favor of preserving the federal union. See Turner, "Causes Lost and Found," 110–14.

111. Dabney, unpublished autobiography, 31, and Turner, "Causes Lost and Found," 80.

112. Johnson, *Life and Letters*, 214.

> And if I could have my way, they might whip her to her heart's content, so they would only do it by sea, and not pester us.[113]

Stating, "I was a constitutional union man as long as honor permitted,"[114] when war finally erupted, Dabney committed himself wholeheartedly to the Confederacy and the Southern cause. In reality, Dabney's appeals for peace and federal union ended at precisely the moment those appeals became socially unacceptable in Virginia. In an April 20, 1860 letter to his friend, S. I. Prime, Dabney therefore parroted the now unanimous sentiment of his state, writing:

> [T]he Constitution of the United States has been rent in fragments by the effort to muster new forces, and wage war without authority of law, and to coerce sovereign States into adhesion, in the utter absence of all powers or intentions of the Federal compact to that effect. Hence, there is now but one mind and one heart in Virginia . . . In one week the whole State has been converted into a camp.[115]

During the summer of 1861 Dabney served as Chaplain for the Eighteenth Virginia Regiment, returning to the seminary for fall term. In the interim, he renewed his acquaintance with Thomas "Stonewall" Jackson. The two men were related by marriage: Dabney's wife was third cousin to Jackson's. Both men embraced Presbyterianism of the Old School stripe, and Jackson judged Dabney a competent man, so much so that in the spring of 1862 Jackson offered Dabney the position of Adjutant General on his staff.[116] Dabney accepted,[117] served with Jackson during the Shenandoah Valley Campaign, and succumbed in late summer to "camp fever," noting with regret: "My constitution and health were wholly unfit for campaigning such as Jackson's."[118] Dabney resigned his commission, returned to the seminary, and fought with his pen, writing *A Defense of Virginia*.[119] After Jackson's death, his widow asked Dabney to author her late husband's

113. Johnson, *Life and Letters*, 215.

114. Dabney, unpublished autobiography, 31. Merrill Matthews noted that Dabney was "one of the major voices in Virginia for the maintenance of the Union." Matthews, "Conservative Thought," 45.

115. Johnson, *Life and Letters*, 226.

116. Dabney, unpublished autobiography, 36.

117. The Confederate government passed a conscription law in the spring of 1862 that effectively closed Union Seminary and freed Dabney to serve with Jackson.

118. Dabney, unpublished autobiography, 38.

119. Dabney, *Defense of Virginia*.

biography, which he did.[120] Dabney accompanied the army as an informal chaplain in late 1864 into the spring of 1865,[121] fleeing the army after Lee's surrender at Appomattox.

Despite the war, the Old School Presbyterian Church initially held together, meeting in Philadelphia in May of 1861 for its General Assembly.[122] That Assembly, however, passed the Spring Resolutions, which called Presbyterians to support the federal government, by inference accusing Christians in the South of rebellion. The offending resolution read:

> *Resolved*, That in the judgment of this Assembly, it is the duty of the minister and churches under its care to do all in their power to promote and perpetuate the integrity of these United States, and to strengthen, uphold, and encourage the Federal Government.[123]

Dabney insisted that this resolution overstepped the proper sphere of church authority, and he, along with Presbyterians throughout the Confederacy, began planning for a new denomination.[124] Stating that Northerners "designed to usurp the spiritual authority of the church of Christ, and wield it in support of the sectional faction to which they belonged," Dabney dubbed the Spring Resolutions a "popish usurpation."[125] The Presbyterian Church in the Confederate States of America, which came to be known colloquially as the Southern Church, formed on December 4,1861.[126]

120. Dabney, *Life and Campaigns*.

121. Dabney, unpublished autobiography, 41–42.

122. Johnson, *Life and Letters*, 243.

123. *Gardiner Spring Resolutions*. Johnson contended that "[t]he Spring Resolutions of the Old School undertook to decide for all members of that church, North, South, East, and West, the legal and political questions by which the country was divided, and to give to the Federal Government at Washington the active allegiance of them all, at the cost of overt treason on the part of the Southerners." Johnson, *Life and Letters*, 243–44.

124. Lucas, *Robert Lewis Dabney*, 111–14.

125. Dabney, "Presbyterianism," 6.

126. Johnson, *Life and Letters*, 244–45. Dabney did not attend the new assembly. He was confined to bed, suffering a bout of "camp fever." When the Civil War ended the new denomination changed its name to the Presbyterian Church in the United States, but retained the informal moniker, the Southern Church.

Postbellum Virginia

The "Epitome of Virtue"

Dabney believed that antebellum Virginia represented "the epitome of virtue and holiness,"[127] and its ruin appears to have hardened Dabney's heart. Johnson conceded that after the war Dabney was "a grimmer man," for "iron had entered his soul,"[128] while Lucas aptly observed that for Dabney "[t]he war was the dividing line of his mental history."[129] For several years Dabney considered emigrating in an attempt to transplant the antebellum South to new soil, but ultimately abandoned the idea.[130]

Dabney loathed and feared the Reconstruction years, believing that while the war had left many destitute, "[T]he tyranny of reconstruction could make us far poorer than the most sweeping warlike plunder."[131] Offering a lament for postbellum conditions in Virginia, Dabney argued: "The dreadful war was less dreadful than yankee peace,"[132] and Dabney expressed his fear that such conditions might degrade his people and his children. He explained:

> Every downtrodden people is compelled almost irresistibly to seek escape from the injustice which can no longer be resisted by force, through the agency of concealments, of duplicity, of lies, of perjuries. The government of the oppressor is therefore a school to train its victims in all the arts of chicanery and meanness.[133]

In an August 7,1865 letter to his brother, he wrote: "To my children, life under a mean, brutal despotism must be a gradual school of lax principle and degraded aims. If history teaches anything, it teaches that the subjects of such governments always become a mean people."[134] Dabney therefore blamed the supposed moral inferiority of antebellum slaves on their race, but stood ready to blame any moral bankruptcy on the part of postbellum white Virginians on Northern oppression. Dabney's fears never materialized,

127. Groce, "New South Critique," 42. James Farmer argued: "[T]he typical Old South clergyman often came to feel that his society had attained a religious ideal unmatched elsewhere." Farmer, *Metaphysical Confederacy*, 286.

128. Johnson, *Life and Letters*, 294.

129. Lucas, *Robert Lewis Dabney*, 130.

130. Johnson, *Life and Letters*, 302–26.

131. Dabney, unpublished autobiography, 42.

132. Dabney, unpublished autobiography, 44.

133. Dabney, "Duty of the Hour," 113.

134. Johnson, *Life and Letters*, 304.

and his categorization of postbellum government in Virginia as "brutal despotism"[135] reflected Dabney's antipathy toward his circumstances more than political reality.

Sanctioning Segregation

Dabney's foreboding nevertheless remained, and he feared for his church as well as his family. In the aftermath of the Civil War, the Southern Church faced the question of what to do with free blacks. Some argued that black Presbyterians should create separate churches. Others contended that black churches and presbyteries should stand under the oversight of white leaders. Still others argued for full ecclesiastical integration of blacks and whites within the Southern Church.[136] In 1867 the Synod[137] of Virginia debated a resolution, which, if passed, would have asked the General Assembly to extend ecclesiastical equality to black members, allowing blacks to serve as officers within the Southern Church. The resolution passed while Dabney was absent from the Synod proceedings. When he returned, the delegates voted to reconsider the measure, and Dabney rose to denounce the resolution. Years later he frankly admitted:

> I was outraged and about desperate. I knew that this negro amalgamation would ruin our church. I felt that it was a moment of life or death for the church. I therefore resolved to strike like a man fighting for life or death, to drop every restraint, and to give full sway to every force of argument, emotion, will and utterance.[138]

Stressing that "when once political equality is confirmed to the blacks, every influence will tend towards that other consummation, *social equality*," Dabney asked:

135. Johnson, *Life and Letters*, 304.

136. Lucas, *Robert Lewis Dabney*, 143–45. Dabney sometimes struggled to acknowledge the intelligence or integrity of those with whom he disagreed, instead assigning their opinions to a lack of judgment, an abandonment of principle, or an overmastering emotion. When his faculty colleague, Thomas Peck, supported ecclesiastical equality of blacks within the Southern Church, Dabney suggested that Peck was "influenced . . . by [a] spirit of romantic magnanimity and self-sacrifice [rather] than by sound logic." Dabney, unpublished autobiography, 79.

137. A Presbyterian synod is comprised of the churches of two or more presbyteries, usually in geographic proximity, which work together in matters of regional impact.

138. Dabney, unpublished autobiography, 81.

> [W]ho does not see whither all this tends, as it is designed by our oppressors to terminate. It is (shall I pronounce the abhorred word?) to *amalgamation*! Yes, sir, these tyrants know that if they can mix the race of Washington, and Lee, and Jackson, with this base herd which they brought from the pens of Africa; if they can taint the blood which hallowed the plains of Manassas, with this sordid stream, the adulterous current will never again swell a Virginian's heart with a throb noble enough to make a despot tremble. But they will then have, for all time, a race supple and grovelling enough for all the purposes of oppression . . . Such is the danger which is now before us."[139]

While Dabney theologically confessed that blacks possessed the image of God no less than whites, and were thus theoretically co-heirs with Christ by faith, his description of black humans as comprising a "herd" from the "pens of Africa" exposed the unbiblical inhumanity of his racial views. Racial amalgamation was, to Dabney, a self-evident evil, and he opposed it fiercely despite offering no biblical warrant for so doing. A. C. Hopkins remembered:

> His voice trembled with emotion, his frame shook, his eyes snapped fire . . . His audience was held in the agony of suppressed emotion. It was difficult to judge which were more stifled by suppression, those who agreed with him or those who differed from him. Some of the visitors were fairly alarmed. When he finished, we felt as men feel when a tornado has just swept by them. We drew a long breath to relieve the lungs.[140]

Dabney later bragged: "One of our leading elders said to Dr. McIlwaine, 'That was the finest speech I ever heard from any man, on any subject.'"[141] When offered the chance to speak again later in the debate, Dabney declined, saying: "I have shot my bolt, and I think it will stick."[142] It did.

139. Dabney, *Ecclesiastical Relation*, 8 [emphasis original]. Dabney's speech was so widely lauded in the South that it was subsequently published as a pamphlet. For a point-by-point analysis of the speech, see Lucas, *Robert Louis Dabney*, 145–48. Prior to the Civil War, Dabney insisted that segregation via slavery represented a legitimate biblical institution. After the War, however, he argued for continuing segregation by playing on fears of racial amalgamation. If Dabney had held consistently to a biblical argument, his postbellum rhetoric would have insisted that Providence had terminated slavery and the segregation it enforced just as his antebellum rhetoric insisted that Providence endorsed it. Instead, his postbellum arguments reveal the underlying racism that his antebellum "biblical" arguments attempted to conceal.

140. Johnson, *Life and Letters*, 321n6.

141. Dabney, unpublished autobiography, 81.

142. Dabney, unpublished autobiography, 82.

Dabney's speech persuaded the Synod, and Johnson attested: "The speech made a powerful impression, and probably began the turning of the tide for the whole church."[143] As a result, the following year the General Assembly adopted a resolution maintaining racial segregation within the Southern Church. Johnson thus noted that Dabney's speech "sounded the key-note which regulated the subsequent legislation of the Assembly, providing ultimately for a separate but affiliated African organization."[144] Dabney had provided ecclesiastical sanction to ongoing, unbiblical racial segregation, spearheading "the 'racial orthodoxy' of the Southern Presbyterian church for the next hundred years."[145]

Ecclesiastical Isolation

Dabney was just as opposed to reunion with the Northern Church as he was to racial integration in the Southern Church. After the war, Old School Presbyterians in the North desired reunion with the Southern Church, but the South did not reciprocate. The 1865 and 1866 Northern Church General Assemblies reaffirmed the Spring Resolutions, embracing increasingly political statements. Harold Parker explained, writing:

> [A]s the successive assemblies made more progressively radical political announcements both as the war progressed and as Reconstruction began, reaction set in. The Old School General Assemblies of 1865 and 1866 drove out of the fold large numbers of Presbyterians, many of whom ultimately ended up in organic relationship with the Southern Church.[146]

Dabney had opposed the Spring Resolutions, not only because they accused him of rebellion, which he personally resented, but also because he believed that the church should shun political affiliations.[147] Fealty to the federal government became a *de facto* requirement for membership in the Northern Church and Dabney fought tenaciously to protect the Southern Church from the same.[148]

143. Johnson, *Life and Letters*, 320.

144. Johnson, *Life and Letters*, 320.

145. Lucas, *Robert Lewis Dabney*, 149. This episode stains Dabney's legacy, revealing that he was far from immune to the passions and prejudices of his day.

146. Parker, *Studies*, 196.

147. This commitment is known as the doctrine of the "spirituality of the church." For the most concise treatment of this doctrine within the Southern Church, see Robinson, *Church of God*.

148. See Dabney, "Offered in General Assembly." Dabney opposed any participation

When the 1870 General Assembly of the Southern Church debated taking steps toward ecclesiastical fellowship with their Northern brethren, many spoke favorably of the measure. Dabney, prodded by friends, rose to answer. He was livid. E. M. Green recounted Dabney's words:

> I hear brethren saying it is time to forgive. Mr. Chairman, I do not forgive. I do not try to forgive. What! Forgive these people, who have invaded our country, burned our cities, destroyed our homes, slain our young men, and spread desolation and ruin over our land! No, I do not forgive them. But you say, "They have changed their feelings towards us, are kind." And why should they not be kind? Have we ever done anything to make them feel unkind to us? Have we ever harmed or wronged them? They are amiable and peaceful, are they? And is not the gorged tiger amiable and peaceful? When he has filled himself with the calf he has devoured, he lies down in a kind, good humor; but wait till he has digested his meal, and will he not be fierce again? Will he not be a tiger again? They have gorged themselves with everything they could take from us. They have gained everything they tried to get, they have conquered us, they have destroyed us. Why should they not be amiable and kind? Do you believe that the same old tiger nature is not in them?[149]

Green concluded: "In that way, he went on for an hour. I never heard such a philippic. I was frightened. I believed every word he said, but I thought I had never encountered before such a terrible man."[150] Johnson conceded that "there was something almost awful in his passion," and recalled: "Men held their breath while the torrent rolled. It appalled them like the sweeping of the incoming waves of the Galveston storm, or the belching of Mount Pelee; yet the reason of it wrought in them respect."[151] Dabney's speech ended the debate. Johnson recorded:

> Rarely has there ever been seen in a deliberative body such a sudden wave of apparently refluent feeling and opinion. As Dabney took his seat, quivering with mental excitement, old Dr.

of the Southern Church within broader Presbyterian alliances. For a history of his ecclesiastical isolationism, see Lucas, *Robert Lewis Dabney*, 153–60.

149. Johnson, *Life and Letters*, 352.

150. Johnson, *Life and Letters*, 352. Dabney believed that his reputation as a "terrible" man was unfair and unearned, and he seemed unable to recognize that a few warm personal relationships with those who were his social, ecclesiastical, or theological bedfellows could not obviate the negative reputation he earned through his polemical writings and caustic public speeches. See Dabney, unpublished autobiography, 103.

151. Johnson, *Life and Letters*, 546–47.

> Wilson sidled up and whispered, "Dr. Dabney, you have saved the Southern Church." Some of the men who had spoken on the wrong side that evening rose to retract and to thank Dr. Dabney for "the light" he had thrown on the subject.[152]

Under Dabney's leadership, the Assembly rejected the Northern Church's olive branch. Twelve years later, however, the Southern Church ignored Dabney's counsel, which offered the same passionate opposition, and established fraternal relations with the Northern Church. Dabney again confessed fear for his church, writing: "She seemed to me bent on committing suicide."[153] The Southern Church, however, ventured no further than fraternal relations, and the Northern and Southern Churches did not reunite until 1983.[154]

Last Years at Union Seminary

Two parallel trends developed during the 1870s that led Dabney to the difficult decision to leave Union Seminary in 1883, which Dabney referred to as "one of the strangest and saddest revolutions of my troubled life."[155] First, his health, which was never strong, declined. From 1858 Dabney had served as co-pastor of College Church,[156] sharing the ministry with his brother-in-law, B. M. Smith, who served as Professor of Oriental Literature at the seminary.[157] The church prospered, and Dabney continued to shepherd it until 1874, when he resigned because of "a spell of bronchitis."[158] Noting, "I was now 54 years old," he stated: "[I] felt it my duty to husband my remaining strength for the service of the Sem[inary], which had the first claim on me."[159] In reality, Dabney was bedridden from April to August of 1873,[160] suffering a "complete and total breakdown in health."[161] He endured increasingly severe bouts of respiratory and bladder infections, as well as

152. Johnson, *Life and Letters*, 354.

153. Dabney, unpublished autobiography, 105.

154. Hart and Muether, *Seeking*, 243.

155. Dabney, unpublished autobiography, 91. For more information on Dabney's decision to leave Union Seminary, see 91–103.

156. Johnson, *Life and Letters*, 162.

157. Moore and Scherer, *Centennial*, 34.

158. Dabney, unpublished autobiography, 23.

159. Dabney, unpublished autobiography, 44.

160. Dabney, unpublished autobiography, 44.

161. Lucas, *Robert Lewis Dabney*, 199.

malarial fevers, and his physician exhorted him to move to a drier climate in order to avoid an untimely death.[162]

Second, Dabney's influence at Union Seminary and in the Southern Church waned. Dabney never reconciled himself to postbellum Virginia, and he resisted all "Yankee" influences,[163] distrusting those whom he believed had compromised their principles by reconciling with the New South.[164] He feared the loss of a distinctive Southern Christianity and culture,[165] and increasingly became "an anachronism"[166] to Southerners who desired to move on from the war. The General Assembly of 1882, which initiated fraternal relations with the Northern Church over Dabney's objections, testified to the loss of his authority, and Dabney understood that "his time as a Southern Presbyterian leader had passed."[167] New South sympathizers controlled the seminary's Board of Trustees, and while Dabney insisted, "My acceptance with my own pupils was warm, generous, yea, glowing," he also acknowledged at that he was losing "weight and influence" with the board.[168] As Dabney defended his decision to leave the seminary, astonishingly he claimed:

> *In all my life I have never had a personal application or a reconciliation to seek or to grant with a brother minister, elder or colleague in a faculty or with a neighbor*. Yet I shall die with the reputation of being a hot, resentful and imperious man! Well, there is to be a more correct judgment hereafter. Thank God.[169]

162. Dabney, unpublished autobiography, 91.

163. Dabney's strident manner contributed to his isolation. Frank Lewis recorded the opinion of Dabney's peer, Richard McIlwaine, who called Dabney's postbellum antagonism toward the North "bad blood and yankee phobia and war recollections and illogical reasonings and mental phantasmagorias." Lewis, "Robert Lewis Dabney," 232.

164. The phrase "New South" came to refer to the new economic, political, and social realities that emerged in the South after the Civil War. While New South proponents believed that adaptation to the new normal represented progress, Dabney felt that it represented a betrayal of principle. See Groce, "New South Critique."

165. In June of 1882 Dabney gave the commencement address at Hampden-Sydney College, serving as a last-minute replacement for a cancelled speaker. The address, later published as "The New South," lamented the loss of the antebellum South, and encouraged graduates to pursue the principles of that era in order to preserve the Southern way of life. For a history of this speech, see Johnson, *Life and Letters*, 400–01. See also Dabney, "New South," 1–24.

166. Overy, "Apostle," 320.

167. Lucas, *Robert Lewis Dabney*, 159.

168. Dabney, unpublished autobiography, 96.

169. Dabney, unpublished autobiography, 103 [emphasis original].

When Dabney tendered his resignation, the board—much to his chagrin—accepted it without protest.[170]

Final Labors

To Texas

In the fall of 1883 Dabney moved to Austin, Texas, assuming the Chair of Moral and Mental Philosophy at the newly formed University of Texas. While in Austin he joined with R. K. Smoot to found the Austin Theological Seminary, in which he taught systematic theology.[171] Dabney's sight, however, began to fail and "[a]fter 1889, he was absolutely sightless."[172] He continued to decline physically,[173] and changes at the university toward a secular model of education led to Dabney's ouster from the faculty in 1895. His intellectual labors continued unabated.

Closing Years

In 1886 Dabney had travelled to Baltimore to consult an eye doctor. While there, he preached at Franklin Square Presbyterian Church. F. P. Ramsay, a student at Johns Hopkins University, attended the church that day but arrived late, unaware that Dabney was preaching. He remembered:

> I was quite late, and was disappointed at seeing a stranger in the pulpit . . . There was no introduction of the stranger after my entrance, and there was no one near me to tell me his name. His appearance did not much impress me . . . His subject was "The Vicarious Atonement." The method was to state and refute the false or incomplete theories of the atonement, and then to establish the true theory. The discourse lasted an hour or more. I was soon listening with profound interest . . . When he had been speaking perhaps half an hour, stating with the clearness of light false theories, and crushing them to powder under resistless

170. Johnson, *Life and Letters*, 439.

171. Currie, *Austin*, 1–8.

172. Johnson, *Life and Letters*, 486.

173. In February of 1890 Dabney suffered a life-threatening illness, and rumors spread that he had died. Newspapers published memorials and Mrs. Dabney received letters of condolence. In reference to one particularly complimentary memorial, Johnson recorded: "When Dr. Dabney heard this estimate . . . read to him, he said, 'There should have been more of censure and less of praise.'" Johnson, *Life and Letters*, 481.

> logic, I came to the conclusion that he must be Dr. Dabney. I had never seen him or his picture, but had heard his students talk of his teaching, and was familiar with his writings; and I saw in the giant reasoner, aflame with scorn of error and of subterfuge, yet bowing with meekness at the cross, one so like our great Dabney, that Dabney it must be. And so it turned out to be.[174]

Neither age nor faltering sight diminished the power with which Dabney preached.

In the summer of 1897, Dabney served as a delegate to the General Assembly, which convened in Charlotte, North Carolina. The organizing committee of the assembly solicited a series of papers, one of which Dabney authored, to commemorate the 250th Anniversary of the Westminster Assembly. Of the North Carolina assembly that summer, S. A. King wrote:

> There had been no such gathering of noted men since the Assembly at Louisville in 1870. Among those brought together on this memorable occasion . . . Dr. Dabney was easily the most prominent and the most honored. Many who were there had been his students; he was the Gamaliel at whose feet they had sat. To all he was the Moses who had been the leader in "times that tried men's souls."[175]

King continued, writing: "The most notable feature of that Assembly was the celebration of the two hundred and fiftieth anniversary of the Westminster Assembly," and he recalled that Dabney "had been assigned the subject of 'The Doctrinal Contents of the Confession.'"[176] Due to Dabney's blindness, another minister read Dabney's paper, and the paper "was listened to with most profound attention. It was a masterly setting forth of the doctrinal contents of the Confession," and "[w]hile this was one of Dr. Dabney's latest public services to the church, it was one of his greatest."[177]

Later that fall, Dabney presented a series of lectures[178] at Davidson College and Columbia Seminary that spanned several weeks. Dabney's former student, J. B. Shearer, lauded the lectures, writing that Dabney's "mental vision is as bright and keen as ever," and "his power of expression and of acute analysis, his logical force and ability to argue his thesis

174. Ramsay, March 9, 1901 letter to Charles W. Dabney.

175. Johnson, *Life and Letters*, 513.

176. Johnson, *Life and Letters*, 514. See Dabney, "Doctrinal Contents," 119–42.

177. Johnson, *Life and Letters*, 514.

178. Dabney's lectures were later published as Dabney, *Christ Our Penal Substitute.*

to an incontrovertible conclusion, abide with him as in the days of yore."[179] Shearer continued his glowing review, writing:

> It is an intellectual delight, and, at the same time, a severe exercise of one's reasoning faculties to follow him as with steady force and in absolute confidence, he states the false postulate of his opponents, and then proceeds to annihilate them."[180]

T. D. Witherspoon, who served as Professor of Homiletics and Pastoral Theology at Louisville Seminary in Kentucky, offered a more sober analysis, stating: "There was no hesitation of speech, no confusion of thought, no inaccuracy of method to suggest any decline of mental power. It is gratifying to be able to record that as a teacher his natural strength is not abated."[181] Although Dabney was physically feeble and completely blind, his lectures, which he delivered by memory, evidently challenged the most able hearers present.

Death and Memorials

On Monday, January 3, 1898, Dabney rose and worked as usual. That evening he suffered chest pain, and at ten minutes before eleven he died.[182] He was 77 years old. News of his death brought forth not only expressions of sympathy to his wife and children, but also testimonials to the man, his life, and his work, many of which focused on the profundity of Dabney's intellect. His lifelong friend, Moses Hoge, praised Dabney, writing: "Some are endowed with such genius, and their natural capacities have been so strengthened and illumined by vast and varied learning, that they are compelled to occupy conspicuous positions."[183] Another minister acclaimed: "Dr. Dabney's mental powers remained to the last unimpaired. There was no touch of decadence to be seen or felt in the working of the glorious machinery."[184] That machinery had indeed displayed mastery of broad philosophical principles as well as fine theological distinctions, and Shearer aptly recognized: "He combined great strength and power with the keenest and most delicate analysis. It is not often that the same hand can wield the sledge hammer and handle the scalpel."[185] Dabney's intellect was so ad-

179. Johnson, *Life and Letters*, 520.
180. Johnson, *Life and Letters*, 520.
181. Witherspoon, "Dr. Dabney's Work."
182. Johnson, *Life and Letters*, 524.
183. Hoge, "Regnant," 26.
184. Marye, "Light," 31.
185. Shearer, "Scholar," 18.

mired that his former student, S. Taylor Martin, abandoned any semblance of objectivity, effusing: "The versatility of Dr. Dabney's genius was one of his most striking characteristics. Had he occupied Calvin's position, he might have done Calvin's work. Had he been substituted for John Knox, he could have performed the part of Knox."[186] While these evaluations may represent hagiography more than sober analysis, they nevertheless contain a kernel of truth that testifies to Dabney's genius.

It was not, however, merely the power of Dabney's intellect that his friends remembered. They also recalled the aggressive and often caustic manner in which he employed it in the public defense of his convictions—conservative, biblical, Old School convictions—and the concomitant refutation of all that he defined as error. Benjamin Morgan Palmer, who along with James Henley Thornwell and Dabney, comprised part of a triumvirate of notable Southern Presbyterian theologians,[187] acknowledged that Dabney possessed "a massive intellect capable of searching into the foundations of truth, and with an intellectual as well as a moral indignation against every form of falsehood."[188] This indignation often prompted Dabney to initiate immediate and overwhelming action. J. H. Rice described Dabney's polemical writings as a form of hunting, stating: "Dabney never waited for evil to mass its forces; he fell on it with savage fury in its camp—tracked the beast to its lair and there laid hold with the dauntless courage of his kind."[189] Noting, "He did nothing by halves,"[190] Shearer likened Dabney's writings to hand-to-hand combat, recalling:

> He found the weak spot in a system of errors, and hurled his missile with the same precision and power as when David overthrew Goliath . . . He decapitated error with its own sword, and exposed the bleeding trophy so relentlessly that some people thought him cruel.[191]

186. Martin, "Tribute," 40.

187. "No church on this continent has been more favored of heaven in having at its very organization three such men as Thornwell, Palmer and Dabney—each fitted by splendid genius, profound scholarship and consecration to the noblest ends, to give direction to its future life and to enrich it for all time by their published contributions to theological science." Hoge, "Regnant," 28.

188. Palmer, "Warrior," 20.

189. Rice, "Lover," 33.

190. Shearer, "Scholar," 19.

191. Shearer, "Scholar," 18.

Even Johnson acknowledged that Dabney seemed to be "at war with much in his age,"[192] while Rice may have summarized it best, dubbing Dabney "a born gladiator,"[193] not seeming to realize that few descriptors could less befit a servant of Christ than to be called gladiatorial.

Dabney's place within the Southern Church, for good and ill, looms large. His friend, Moses Hoge, acknowledged that Dabney bequeathed no ordinary contribution to the church, writing:

> [I]t had been the privilege of the man whose loss we mourn today to be distinguished, first as an able and impressive expounder of the Word in the pulpit; second, as one of the strongest of writers on philosophic, secular, and theological themes; and, third, as one of the most successful teachers in a seminary devoted to the training of young men for the Gospel ministry; that it was his rare lot not only to win distinction in each but to combine and nobly employ all three of these great instrumentalities for wide and permanent usefulness.[194]

Dabney also bequeathed to his family, friends, and followers the racial segregation of the Southern Church and a policy of Southern isolation from and bitterness toward Northern Christians. His legacy was far more mixed than Hoge was able to acknowledge. Nevertheless, Dabney authored the only systematic theology,[195] the only moral philosophy,[196] and the only homiletics textbook[197] produced in the Southern Church in the nineteenth century. His contribution was immense. Dabney's erstwhile student, G. B. Strickler,[198] who held Dabney's former chair as Professor of Systematic, Polemic, and Pastoral Theology at Union Seminary,[199] wrote of his late beloved mentor:

> [A]s the result of thirty years' teaching in the seminary and of the contributions he has made to our religious and ethical and theological literature, he has left a deeper impression for good

192. Johnson, *Life and Letters*, 568.

193. Rice, "Lover," 33. William Groce concurred, writing: "Dabney was particularly suited to intellectual combat." Groce, "New South Critique," 17.

194. Hoge, "Regnant," 26.

195. Dabney, *Lectures in Systematic Theology*.

196. Dabney published two significant philosophic texts in the latter quarter of the nineteenth century: Dabney, *Sensualistic Philosophy*, and Dabney, *Practical Philosophy*.

197. Dabney, *Sacred Rhetoric*.

198. Moore and Scherer, *Centennial*, 85.

199. Moore and Scherer, *Centennial*, 34.

> on our Southern ministry and Southern Church than any other man who has ever been connected with our denomination.[200]

Not unlike Hoge and other friends, Strickler failed to mention Dabney's more unseemly contributions.

Remembrances poured in for years after Dabney's death, and many recalled the power of his pulpit ministry. P. P. Flournoy claimed for Dabney's preaching a place of preeminence, writing:

> There may have been others with oratorical gifts which he lacked, who were, *for the average audience*, more popular preachers; but as a preacher for preachers and educated thinkers of all professions, I think there can be no question that he stood without an equal.[201]

Another friend concurred, citing with approbation the opinion of W. T. Hall, who believed that while other men displayed more eloquence in the pulpit, "[F]or blasting rocks, I would take Dr. Dabney."[202]

Burial

Robert Lewis Dabney is buried in Hampden-Sydney, Virginia, in a small cemetery plot adjacent to the seminary classrooms in which he once labored. Adorning his tombstone is the following inscription:

> In unshaken loyalty of devotion to his friends, his country, and his religion, firm in misfortune, ever active in earnest endeavor, he labored all his life for what he loved with a faith in good causes, that was ever one with his faith in God.

Reflecting on their father's legacy, Samuel Dabney wrote to his brother, Charles, in 1904, acknowledging that Robert Dabney had indeed been a complex man who engendered both deep admiration and deep opposition. Whatever the world may have believed about his father, Samuel Dabney concluded simply: "He was what he was. Let the Heathen rage."[203]

200. Strickler, "Our Loss," 24.
201. Cited in Johnson, *Life and Letters*, 539 [emphasis original].
202. Marye, "Light," 31.
203. Cited in Overy, "Apostle," 323.

Conclusion

Summary

Robert Lewis Dabney was a powerful preacher, a defender of the Old South, a brilliant theologian, and a tireless advocate for the independence of the Southern Church. His life testified to his devotion to duty, theological and social conservatism, and strict adherence to unchanging principles. He also harbored an ugly, unrepentant racism, bitterness of spirit, and lifelong a lack of charity toward any person or group of people whom he believed unworthy to receive it. He bequeathed a legacy of church-condoned racial segregation to the American South, the consequences of which reverberate to the present. He won both admirers and enemies, and left an indelible mark—for good and ill—on the Southern Church and on American Presbyterianism. His historical and homiletical significance make him a worthy figure for continuing research.

Preview of Chapter 2

Chapter 2 interacts with prior Dabney biographers and researchers, specifically engaging those who have canvassed Dabney's homiletic and preaching ministry. After describing the research materials employed in this paper and outlining the parameters of the research, chapter 2 briefly analyzes prior thematic evaluations of Dabney's preaching while also engaging Lawrence Calvin Trotter, whose research into Dabney's extemporaneous didacticism extended beyond mere thematic evaluation. By so doing, it exposes the lack of attention given to Dabney's classroom pedagogy and his distinct structure for expository sermons, while also describing Trotter's interpretation of Dabney's homiletical legacy. Chapter 2 closes by offering an alternate interpretation of Dabney's legacy, and states the thesis of this work.

2

Thesis

Introduction

A Largely Neglected Figure

Thirty years ago Douglas Kelly argued: "Robert Lewis Dabney was perhaps the greatest, and certainly the most prolific, Southern Presbyterian theologian of nineteenth-century America,"[1] noting that Dabney displayed "a wider and deeper cultural, social, and political interest than any other theologian of nineteenth-century America."[2] Nevertheless, fifteen years later David Coffin claimed that despite Dabney's literary output, his enduring shaping influence upon the Southern Church, and his continuing ecclesiastical, theological, and social significance within American Presbyterianism, Dabney had remained a "largely neglected figure."[3]

While the intervening years have witnessed a resurgence of interest in Dabney, including needed engagement with his work as a homiletical theorist and preacher,[4] a full analysis of Dabney's expository preaching theory, expository classroom pedagogy, and personal practice of expository preaching remains wanting. This paper exposes the outlines of and contributes to the work of filling that historical and homiletical lacuna.

1. Kelly, "Robert Lewis Dabney," 37.

2. Kelly, "Robert Lewis Dabney," 53.

3. Coffin, "Reflections," 3.

4. The most thorough treatment of Dabney's homiletic to date is Trotter, "Blasting Rocks." Trotter later revised "Blasting Rocks" for publication. His unpublished manuscript is entitled *Always Prepared: Robert Lewis Dabney, the Preacher*. It is used by permission of the author.

The Plan of This Chapter

This chapter interacts with authors who have analyzed Robert Dabney as a homiletician or preacher. Engaging prior thematic evaluations of Dabney's preaching, it highlights the extent to which these evaluations have neglected his expository theory and pedagogy, revealing also a lack of attention to Dabney's distinct structure for expository sermons. It then describes and critiques Lawrence Trotter's analysis of Dabney's homiletic. Trotter suggested that Dabney exercised a relatively small homiletical impact upon the students whom he trained, and chapter 6 of this paper defends an alternate interpretation of Dabney's legacy. This chapter closes by stating the thesis of this work.

Research Materials

Primary Sources

The Robert Lewis Dabney Collection at Union Presbyterian Theological Seminary in Richmond, Virginia houses Dabney's extant sermon manuscripts,[5] a selection of personal correspondence, and other miscellany. Chapter 4 of this paper describes and utilizes Dabney's sermon collection at length, explaining the different varieties of manuscripts within Dabney's collection and their significance and use. The Albert and Shirley Small Special Collections Library at the University of Virginia in Charlottesville, Virginia likewise houses a Dabney collection featuring personal correspondence as well as Dabney's unpublished autobiography, which he prepared in 1895.[6] Five volumes of Dabney's *Discussions* preserve articles that Dabney contributed to Presbyterian newspapers and magazines, including a handful of articles that address various aspects of preaching.[7] Dabney also

5. Although Dabney's manuscript collection contains roughly 470 sermons, the exact number of sermons is subject to debate. See chapter 4, note 11 for further discussion. For the most complete list of Dabney's sermons housed at Union Seminary, see Coffin, "Reflections," Appendix 1 and Appendix 5.

6. See Coffin, "Reflections," 411–14 for a full list of Dabney papers and collections. The collections at Union Seminary and the University of Virginia proved the most germane to the present research.

7. C. R. Vaughan collected material for four volumes of Dabney's *Discussions* between 1890 and 1897. J. H. Varner, of Sprinkle Publications in Harrisonburg, Virginia, issued a fifth volume in 1999. These volumes boast 177 entries, which comprise 3216 pages of text. Despite their breadth, the volumes do not exhaust Dabney's literary output. Dabney admitted: "During my ministry I have published almost countless articles, essays and criticism in newspapers, magazines and reviews." Dabney, unpublished

authored several books, the most germane of which to the present work is his *Sacred Rhetoric*,[8] which captures the substance and specific features of his expository homiletic theory. Dabney's nineteenth-century peers locate the place of his expository homiletic within a broader nineteenth-century American homiletical context,[9] while Dabney's eldest son, Charles, published a memorial volume to his father that features tributes to Dabney from his Southern Presbyterian colleagues.[10] Academic catalogues of Union Seminary likewise provide invaluable information about faculty, students, and courses during Dabney's tenure at the seminary.[11]

Secondary Sources

An abundance of secondary sources engage Dabney's life, thinking, social and historical setting, theological and polemical contributions, and continuing significance on a wide variety of historical, theological, ecclesiastical, and social fronts,[12] while a paucity of sources engage his homiletical theory, his role as a teacher of preachers, and his personal practice of expository preaching.[13] Thomas Cary Johnson and Sean Lucas offer the researcher complementary biographies, the former taking a too-favorable view of Dabney while the latter's work is significantly more critical.[14]

---

autobiography, 51. For the most complete list of Dabney's extant works, see Coffin, "Reflections," Appendix 5.

8. Dabney, *Sacred Rhetoric*.

9. Of particular value are: Broadus, *Preparation and Delivery*; Hoppin, *Office*; Kidder, *Homiletics*; Shedd, *Homiletics*. Each of these pastors taught homiletics at an evangelical seminary, as did Dabney. Each, like Dabney, authored a homiletics text that was intended primarily to train seminary students to preach, and each work was published at roughly the same time that Dabney published *Sacred Rhetoric*.

10. Dabney, *Memorium*.

11. The most important of these to the present research was Moore and Scherer, *Centennial*.

12. Significant to this thesis were: Coffin, "Reflections"; Holifield, *Gentlemen Theologians*; Johnson, *Life and Letters*; Lewis, "Robert Lewis Dabney"; Loveland, *Southern Evangelicals*; Lucas, *Robert Lewis Dabney*; Turner, "Causes Lost and Found."

13. Trotter's work in "Blasting Rocks" and *Always Prepared* represents the only significant examination of Dabney's homiletical theory and practice yet conducted.

14. See Johnson, *Life and Letters*, and Lucas, *Robert Lewis Dabney*.

Parameters of the Research

Summary

The present study explores Dabney's homiletic within a largely American homiletical context, engaging British and other international sources sparingly. It likewise examines written sermon manuscripts over against audiovisual sources, focusing on the content of Dabney's sermons rather than his delivery. Finally, this study primarily analyzes Dabney's expository homiletic in its theory, pedagogy, and practice, rather than attempting a broader analysis of his *Sacred Rhetoric* in its entirety.

An American Context

Scott Gibson noted that the "Victorian era was a period of close cultural relations between Britain and the United States," such that "late nineteenth-century evangelical leaders crisscrossed the ocean . . . building up an elaborate network of relationships."[15] Evangelical theologians and preachers likewise interacted with each other and exchanged ideas, and American homiletical theory benefited from the fruit of British influence.[16]

The colonial context of America's birth guaranteed that early American homiletical theories and practices closely paralleled those in Great Britain. F. R. Webber noted:

> In the days of Colonial America the sermons preached in the New England meetinghouses reflected the thought and homiletical style of the Puritan preachers in England. The Virginia Episcopal preacher of Colonial days differed but superficially from the Anglicans of the same period in London, Manchester and Leeds.[17]

15. Gibson, "Gordon and Guinness," 303. See also Carwardine, *Transatlantic Revivalism*.

16. Testifying to the cross-pollination that occurred between homiletical theorists and practitioners in Great Britain and America is the composition of the twenty-six speakers chosen for the Lyman Beecher Lectureship on Preaching at Yale Divinity School from the inception of the series in 1871 to the close of the nineteenth century. Sixteen hailed from America, while ten came from Great Britain. Interestingly, continental Europeans delivered none of the lectures. A. J. F. Behrends, although born in Holland, moved to the United States when he was four years old, and while George Adam Smith was born in India he was educated in Scotland, serving the Free Church of Scotland as pastor and professor throughout his life and ministry. See Jones, *Royalty of the Pulpit*, 413–19.

17. Webber, *History*, 10–11.

By the time Dabney published *Sacred Rhetoric*, however, American homiletics had also developed unique characteristics that distinguished it from homiletical theories across the Atlantic. Robert Ellison[18] exposed similarities and differences in the respective homiletical theories that commanded influence in Great Britain over against those prevailing in the United States. British and American homileticians united in believing that "[t]he purpose of preaching . . . was not [merely] to bring a congregation to assent to a theological theory or set of propositions, but rather to persuade—indeed, to compel—men and women to embark upon a spiritual course of action."[19] Ellison noted that "[c]lear and specific didacticism" was, for theorists on each side of the Atlantic, "indispensible" to persuasive preaching.[20]

American and British homileticians parted ways, however, in their respective views of the structural components of a sermon. Whereas nearly every mid-to-late nineteenth-century American homiletician inculcated the use of an Introduction, Exposition, Proposition, Argument, and Conclusion in sermon construction,[21] Ellison noted that in Britain "the structural elements of a sermon were ignored or neglected far more than they were emphasized,"[22] and "[t]he only structural component Victorian homileticians insisted on was the application."[23] When, moreover, homileticians addressed the question of whether to employ heads of argument within a sermon, most Americans replied in the affirmative. Not so in Britain. Ellison explained: "Theorists in the Victorian period largely rejected this method" of argument.[24]

18. Ellison, *Victorian*.

19. Ellison, *Victorian*, 19.

20. Ellison, *Victorian*, 19.

21. See chapter 3 for further explanation of this structural pattern.

22. Ellison, *Victorian*, 23. Exemplary of Ellison's observation was British Congregationalist, R. W. Dale. When discussing "The Plan" of the sermon, Dale asserted, "Every sermon stands by itself, in its own grounds, and may be built just as the preacher pleases," and the only structural components Dale directly addressed were the Introduction and Conclusion. Dale, *Nine Lectures*, 138.

23. Ellison, *Victorian*, 24. The same lack of concern for structure also marked the homiletics of continental Europe. Swiss homiletician, Alexandre Vinet, cited only two structural components: Exordium [Introduction] and Peroration [Conclusion], labeling everything in between "Transitions." Vinet, *Homiletics*, xiii. Along with Vinet, Dabney read with appreciation Francois Fenelon and Louis Bautain, both French Catholics, as well as Franz Theremin, a German Protestant. Fenelon and Theremin wrote on the cultivation of eloquence, while Bautain wrote on extempore speech. None addressed sermon structure. See Dabney, *Sacred Rhetoric*, 6. Dabney, however, appears to have been more concerned to defend his church from European higher critical theories than to engage with continental homileticians. See Dabney, "Influence of the German," 444–46.

24. Ellison, *Victorian*, 25.

Much of the analysis of Dabney's expository homiletic that this paper conducts specifically compares and contrasts the structure of a typical American topical sermon over against an alternate structure that Dabney identified for expository sermons. While American homileticians, including Dabney, showed ongoing concern for sermon structure, Ellison explained: "It is style, not structure, that is the overriding concern of many Victorian homileticians."[25] Any attempt to preclude British preachers and theorists in a study of nineteenth-century American homiletics is inadvisable,[26] but recognition of the American context of Dabney's homiletic seems warranted in light of the significant emphasis on sermon structure that was unique to the American setting, and which is integral to the present research.

Written Sermon Manuscripts

Likewise important to the present study is the fact that Robert Dabney left no audio-visual record of his preaching, and therefore his voice, intonations, and mannerisms prove largely inaccessible. Contemporary appraisals of Dabney's preaching, some of which chapter 1 detailed, provide limited second hand access to his pulpit demeanor. Whereas lack of evidence therefore obscures the manner of Dabney's preaching, the matter is more readily accessible.

Dabney's manuscript collection contains a selection of sermons he preached during the Civil War, which he entitled "Army Sermons." David Coffin suggested that Dabney prepared these sermons for publication but they remained unpublished.[27] In his Preface to that collection Dabney wrote:

> [V]ery few of these sermons were preached from written manuscripts . . . But in reducing these oral discourses to writing, no changes have been made, except unimportant verbal ones.

25. Ellison, *Victorian*, 26. In his 1875 Yale Lectures, Irishman John Hall, who had moved to America from Scotland in 1867, noted that his listeners might wonder about sermon construction, but rather than address it directly he recommended that his audience read Richard Whately, Robert Dabney, or James Hoppin. In Hall, *God's Word through Preaching*, 127–28.

26. As a student at Union Seminary, Dabney studied Scottish divine George Campbell for his homiletics text; Trotter, *Always Prepared*, 108; Campbell, *Lectures*. Dabney also read and appreciated Richard Whately, and Trotter ably described Dabney's dependence on and similarity to Whately in his understanding of extemporaneous speech. Trotter, *Always Prepared*, 123. Trotter suggested in fact that much of what comprised nineteenth-century American sacred rhetoric merely applied "classical [rhetorical] categories to biblical preaching." Trotter, *Always Prepared*, 114. See Whately, *Elements of Rhetoric*.

27. Coffin, "Reflections," 327.

> Having been preached *memoriter* from full manuscripts, or from careful briefs, all of which are still in my possession, they were found indelibly impressed upon my memory, as to the whole train of remark. They may now be received as substantially the same which were delivered.[28]

Lawrence Trotter explored at length Dabney's preference for extemporaneous delivery, highlighting Dabney's conviction that thorough preparation and familiarity with the ideas of the sermon must precede and inform the act of preaching.[29] Dabney insisted: "If you are truly masters of your thoughts, you will have no lack of correct words."[30] Trotter ably demonstrated that Dabney practiced "extemporaneous speaking based on extensive prior preparation."[31] Dabney thus left no preparatory stone unturned before ascending the pulpit, leaving only the particular expression of predetermined ideas to the preaching moment. According to Dabney's preface, the only differences between his extant sermon manuscripts and the words he actually preached were thus "unimportant verbal ones."[32] Dabney's testimony, coupled with Trotter's analysis of Dabney's extemporaneous method, offers the researcher a measure of confidence that Dabney's written sermon manuscripts substantially represent what he actually preached from the pulpit.

Expository Homiletic

While Dabney's *Sacred Rhetoric* addressed much more than expository preaching, the current study focuses on comparing and contrasting Dabney's expository homiletic with the topical homiletic that was common to his day. Much of *Sacred Rhetoric* inculcates skill in persuasion while advocating for extemporaneous sermon delivery,[33] and Trotter has capably investigated these rhetorical features of Dabney's thought.[34] This paper therefore evalu-

28. Dabney, Box 6, File 6/3a, "Preface" [emphasis original]. Chapter 4 describes in detail Dabney's manuscript collection. For the purposes of the present chapter, the following information is useful: The Dabney Collection at Union Seminary is comprised of seventeen boxes of material. Each box contains multiple files, and within each file reside multiple documents. The "Preface" cited above is the second document of File 6/3a of Box 6 in the Dabney Collection.

29. Trotter, "Blasting Rocks," 35–87.

30. Dabney, *Sacred Rhetoric*, 337.

31. Trotter, "Blasting Rocks," 22–23.

32. Dabney, Box 6, File 6/3a, "Preface"

33. Dabney devoted six of twenty-four lectures in *Sacred Rhetoric* to argument and persuasion.

34. After describing Dabney's extemporaneous homiletic, Trotter worked lecture

ates Dabney's expository homiletic in particular, emphasizing his distinct structure for expository sermons, while tracing that structure from Dabney's theory to his classroom pedagogy to his personal practice.

In exploring Dabney's broader homiletic, Trotter offered both a survey of Dabney's expository theory[35] and an analysis of Dabney's personal practice. Dabney's classroom pedagogy, however, which bridges his theory and practice, and which holds the key to Dabney's subsequent homiletical influence upon the generation of preachers whom he trained, formed almost no part of Trotter's analysis. This paper therefore compares and contrasts Dabney the expository theorist with Dabney the expository pedagogue with Dabney the expository practitioner, highlighting the structural differences between the ubiquitous nineteenth-century American topical sermon form[36] and Dabney's distinct structure for consecutive expository preaching.

Dabney, the Preacher

Overview

In order to establish the need for research into Dabney's expository homiletic, this chapter analyzes a selection of representative evaluations of Dabney's preaching, demonstrating that prior researchers who have engaged Dabney's sermons have primarily evaluated his preaching thematically, while largely ignoring his work as a homiletical theorist and pedagogue. It then interacts with Lawrence Trotter's rhetorical analysis of Dabney's extemporaneous didacticism, thereby exposing the need for further structural analysis of Dabney's expository homiletic, while also challenging Trotter's suggestion that Dabney exercised a relatively diminutive homiletical influence upon the students whom he trained to preach.

---

by lecture through *Sacred Rhetoric*, focusing on Lectures 12–15 concerning Argument and Lectures 16–17 concerning Persuasion, the former of which Trotter termed "the backbone of Dabney's textbook." Trotter, *Always Prepared*, 57.

35. See Trotter, "Blasting Rocks," chapter 2. Trotter's research evaluated Dabney's expository theory insofar as that theory informed and impacted Dabney's preferred method of sermon delivery. Trotter stated that his "analysis of [Dabney's] homiletic theory" specifically focused on Dabney's "sermon delivery method." Trotter, *Always Prepared*, 33.

36. Chapters 3 and 4 describe and offer examples of this form.

Typical Evaluations

Edward Hallet Carr suggested that "the main work of the historian is not to record but to evaluate."[37] Carr's insight proves itself in the works of Thomas Cary Johnson, David Coffin, and Sean Lucas, each of whom evaluated Dabney's preaching thematically according to his respective research purpose. None addressed Dabney's expository theory or classroom pedagogy. Neither did any attempt a structural evaluation of Dabney's sermons.

Johnson purposed to "to bring out the story of [Dabney's] life largely in his own words, by the use of his letters, and to state the gist of most of his great contentions succinctly and clearly in his own words," stating: "We resolved to do this . . . to give the reader the comfortable feeling of certainty that he had before him the genuine history, and not simply our view of it."[38] Given this goal, Trotter observed that "Johnson referred to Dabney's preaching many times but provided relatively little analysis of it."[39] Broadly emphasizing the didacticism of Dabney's preaching,[40] Johnson wrote: "Thoroughness of investigation and weight of conclusion was characteristic of all his preaching. His sermons were so full of thought that they seemed packed. If this was a fault, it was one that tended to make stable men of those who heard him."[41] While Johnson recalled that Dabney's preaching was well-received,[42] often challenging,[43] and grew increasingly dense as Dabney aged,[44] Johnson seemed driven to champion Dabney's legacy more than to analyze his sermons. He offered no analysis of Dabney's expository theory or serious description of his classroom pedagogy, and the structure of Dabney's sermons did not feature in Johnson's biography.

David Coffin likewise rendered a thematic evaluation of Dabney's preaching, confining himself to analyzing sermons that helped to define Dabney's theology of divine sovereignty in reference to human agency.[45] Dabney believed in the necessity of prevenient grace to empower righteous human behavior, and Coffin wrote: "Such a doctrine, Dabney acknowledges, is 'repugnant to the pride of the human heart,' but it is,

37. Carr, *What Is History?*, 22.

38. Johnson, *Life and Letters*, v.

39. Trotter, *Always Prepared*, 9.

40. Johnson, *Life and Letters*, 110, 197, 318, 552–53.

41. Johnson, *Life and Letters*, 114.

42. Johnson, *Life and Letters*, 99, 106, 162.

43. Johnson, *Life and Letters*, 110, 477.

44. Johnson, *Life and Letters*, 318.

45. Coffin, "Reflections," 62–86.

nonetheless, the teaching of Jesus."[46] Reviewing sections of some twenty sermons, in which Dabney preached on the power and necessity of prayer for ministers,[47] on the importance of cultivating ministerial piety in the service of divine sovereignty,[48] and on the providence of God as distinct from unbelieving fate,[49] Coffin carefully explored how Dabney viewed the relationship between divine and human actions. After analyzing sermons that expose Dabney's view of sin and human inability[50] and the place of missions under the sovereign election of God,[51] Coffin suggested that for Dabney, the "sovereign intervention of God does not destroy man's free agency."[52] Rather, Coffin summarized Dabney's theology, writing: "[T]he doctrine of God's sovereignty in salvation provides the very reason why the Christian's efforts are worthwhile."[53] Not unlike Johnson, Coffin offered no analysis of Dabney's expository theory or classroom pedagogy, and chose not to address Dabney's sermon structure.

In the same way, Sean Lucas provided a largely thematic evaluation of Dabney's preaching. Purposing to depict Robert Dabney as a representative postbellum Southerner,[54] Lucas engaged Dabney's preaching ministry more fully than either Johnson or Coffin, working carefully through seventeen sermons. Lucas suggested that "the majority of Dabney's preaching generally shifted back and forth between passionate and direct evangelistic appeals to unrepentant sinners to come to Christ, and doctrinal sermons on points related to soteriology,"[55] and that much of Dabney's preaching "sought to accomplish a basic twofold goal—to drive sinners from their self-confidence . . . and to point them to the salvation provided in Jesus Christ."[56] While Dabney's pulpit ministry no doubt included these themes, Lucas overstated the extent to which Dabney's fifty-two years of preaching could be reduced to the "back

46. Coffin, "Reflections," 80.

47. Coffin, "Reflections," 66.

48. Coffin, "Reflections," 70.

49. Coffin, "Reflections," 71–74.

50. Coffin, "Reflections," 74–76.

51. Coffin, "Reflections," 78–80.

52. Coffin, "Reflections," 81.

53. Coffin, "Reflections," 86.

54. "[T]his biography argues that Dabney was a representative Southern conservative and provides a window into the postbellum Southern Presbyterian mind." Lucas, *Robert Lewis Dabney*, 17.

55. Lucas, *Robert Lewis Dabney*, 51.

56. Lucas, *Robert Lewis Dabney*, 53.

and forth"[57] appeals and "basic twofold goal"[58] that Lucas identified. Lucas nevertheless rightly observed that "evangelistic preaching was a major part of Dabney's ministerial work,"[59] and Dabney viewed the salvation of the lost as one of the primary goals of pulpit ministry.[60] Arguing that while Dabney's "reputation as a preacher was quite high in the decade before the Civil War,"[61] Lucas recognized that Dabney left relatively few sermons in print, such that "his preaching has been generally ignored."[62] Dabney's preaching ministry has likely also suffered indifference because Dabney's respective legacies as a controversialist, a systematic theologian, and a racist vastly overshadow his remembrance as a preacher or teacher of preachers.

Despite portraying Dabney as a representative postbellum Southerner, Lucas drew from his analysis of Dabney's sermons a seemingly contradictory conclusion, asserting: "[A]fter the war, the style of preaching in the Southern Presbyterian church moved away from doctrinally heavy sermons to a more 'practical style,' rendering Dabney's sermonic approach passé."[63] Dabney, however, cannot both represent postbellum Southern Presbyterianism and represent a passé form of preaching within Southern Presbyterianism at the same time. Lawrence Trotter agreed with Lucas, but also helped to clarify Lucas's probable intent by noting that sermons in the late nineteenth and early twentieth century became more devotional in content and less didactic in presentation.[64] While Dabney's type of doctrinally strident sermons may have therefore faded in popularity, neither Lucas nor Trotter had in view the homiletical structure that undergirded nineteenth-century American preaching. In that structural sense, Dabney's form of topical preaching did not become passé.[65] Preachers continued to employ it. Their social context changed,

57. Lucas, *Robert Lewis Dabney*, 51.

58. Lucas, *Robert Lewis Dabney*, 53.

59. Lucas, *Robert Lewis Dabney*, 55.

60. "The true minister must, of course, have a desire to see souls snatched from hell fire, truth upheld, sin curbed, the happiness of true religion diffused, and the Holy Trinity glorified in the redemption of transgressors. These are the grounds, the motives, of that desire which he feels to preach, if he may rightfully do it." Dabney, "What is a Call," 33.

61. Lucas, *Robert Lewis Dabney*, 62.

62. Lucas, *Robert Lewis Dabney*, 51.

63. Lucas, *Robert Lewis Dabney*, 62.

64. Trotter, "Blasting Rocks," 268–85.

65. Dabney's *Sacred Rhetoric* and Broadus's *Preparation and Delivery* were each published in 1870, and bore such similarities that Charles Hodge reviewed them positively together, writing: "These are both valuable contributions to the great study of Sacred Eloquence." Nevertheless Hodge chided Dabney for his "vehemence of manner," which he felt inappropriate to an introductory textbook, and faulted Broadus for being "ample

their emphases differed, and in some cases their fidelity to biblical orthodoxy waned, but their use of the same topical sermon form that Dabney and his peers employed remained largely consistent.[66]

Significant to the present study, none of these evaluations addressed the structure that Dabney employed in composing his sermons or the extent to which his expository structure differed from the standard topical form that was common to the nineteenth-century American pulpit. Instead, each author bypassed Dabney's expository theory and classroom pedagogy, offering a thematic analysis of Dabney's preaching ministry according to his respective research purpose.

Lawrence Calvin Trotter

Overview

Lawrence Trotter moved beyond mere thematic analysis, engaging Dabney's homiletical theory and personal practice, and traced Dabney's homiletical legacy within Southern Presbyterianism. Focusing on Dabney's rhetorical strategy of extemporaneous delivery in the service of didactic preaching, Trotter chose not to address the features of Dabney's expository pedagogy and offered limited structural evaluation of Dabney's distinct form for expository sermons. The analysis of Trotter's work that follows therefore demonstrates the extent to which the present research is needed. At the same time it highlights Trotter's contention that Dabney exerted a relatively small homiletical impact on the Southern Presbyterian preachers whom he trained. Chapter 6 of this paper challenges that interpretation and defends an alternate understanding of Dabney's legacy.

---

to redundancy" and for desiring too much "to make a book." Hodge, "Notices of Recent Publications," 147–48. Both Broadus and Dabney hailed from Virginia, took the Master of Arts at the University of Virginia, and drew on the same rhetorical tradition. Trotter suggested that "[t]he similarities between Dabney's and Broadus's works are so many that one might profitably have been able to use the work of the other instead of publishing his own." Trotter, *Always Prepared*, 187. *Preparation and Delivery* became the standard seminary homiletics text in America well into the twentieth century. If Broadus's homiletic had not become passé, then neither had Dabney's.

66. Decades after Dabney's *Sacred Rhetoric*, North American homileticians continued to teach a topical sermon structure. See Armitage, *Preaching: Its Ideal*; Fisk, *Manual of Preaching*; Hogg, *Hand-Book*; Kern, *Ministry to the Congregation*; Proudfoot, *Systematic Homiletics*; Hoyt, *Work of Preaching*; Breed, *Preparing to Preach*; Evans, *How to Prepare*.

Dabney's Theory

Trotter's research "focuse[d] on Dabney's sermon delivery method,"[67] seeking "to examine in detail" his "extemporaneous didacticism."[68] Trotter thus primarily investigated Dabney's rhetorical strategy, analyzing his homiletical theory and pedagogy insofar as these shed light on Dabney's practice of extemporaneous delivery. Trotter stated that "the present investigation seeks to focus on *how* [Dabney] preached,"[69] and given that Dabney's classroom pedagogy offers little insight into his personal extemporaneous practice, Trotter chose to describe and evaluate Dabney's homiletical theory, largely to ignore his classroom pedagogy, and to give extended attention to Dabney's personal extemporaneous practice. Stating that the "overriding purpose of this study is to reconstruct Dabney's preaching method,"[70] Trotter's work offered keen rhetorical analysis of Dabney's extemporaneous strategy by "focusing on Dabney's method of delivery in both *theory* and *practice*."[71] Dabney's classroom pedagogy was not the focus of Trotter's research.

As Trotter reviewed Dabney's homiletical theory, he suggested that "[a]lthough a simplification, it is possible to derive many if not all of [Dabney's] ideas from two basic concepts: the preacher as a herald of God's word and preaching as the communion of souls."[72] Trotter understood that Dabney defined preaching as heraldry[73] and eschewed rhetorical flourish in favor of extempore expression.[74] Trotter's chapter-by-chapter analysis of *Sacred Rhetoric* identified Dabney's admiration for expository preaching,[75] highlighted his insistence that ministers preach verse-by-verse sermons through extended sections of Scripture,[76] and chronicled the various benefits that Dabney felt flowed from exposition in course.[77] Dabney urged his students to preach the Scripture in the "dress and connection in which the Holy Spirit has presented them,"[78] faithfully heralding the message of the Scripture, and while Trotter recognized that Dabney's expository theory

67. Trotter, "Blasting Rocks," 1.
68. Trotter, "Blasting Rocks," 9.
69. Trotter, "Blasting Rocks," 22 [emphasis original].
70. Trotter, "Blasting Rocks," 26.
71. Trotter, "Blasting Rocks," 12 [emphasis added].
72. Trotter, "Blasting Rocks," 86.
73. Trotter, *Always Prepared*, 39.
74. Trotter, *Always Prepared*, 38.
75. Trotter, *Always Prepared*, 43, 51.
76. Trotter, *Always Prepared*, 51, 78–79.
77. Trotter, *Always Prepared*, 51.
78. Dabney, *Sacred Rhetoric*, 28.

identified a structure for expository sermons that differed from the topical sermon form that was prevalent to the nineteenth-century American pulpit,[79] it was not Trotter's purpose to define the features of this structure or to trace it from Dabney's theory to his classroom pedagogy. Chapter 3 of this paper provides that structural analysis, defining the distinct sermon structure that Dabney envisioned for expository sermons over against the ubiquitous topical form of his day, while chapter 4 traces and evaluates that structure to and within Dabney's classroom pedagogy.

Dabney's Practice

Trotter's evaluation of Dabney's practice of preaching and public speaking focused on the "ways in which [Dabney] practiced the extemporaneous method that he commended to his students."[80] Reviewing Dabney's preaching career and important speeches, his manuscript collection, and contemporary testimonials to Dabney's pulpit ministry, Trotter carefully reconstructed Dabney's methodology, ably demonstrating the power of his extemporaneous didacticism.[81] That analysis revealed that Dabney preached very few expository sermons, and "[a]lthough Dabney argued powerfully in favor of the ancient practice, he did nothing in his own preaching ministry to restore expository preaching of extended passages to the place it held in the early and Reformation churches."[82] Of Dabney's internal inconsistency, Trotter wrote: "It is truly remarkable that Dabney followed his own advice about expository preaching of extended passages so little in the course of his ministry."[83] Chapter 5 of this paper builds upon Trotter's observation, quantifying and assessing the extent to which Dabney failed to practice his expository theory.

Trotter's rhetorical analysis of Dabney's homiletic invites further structural analysis of Dabney's expository theory, pedagogy, and practice. This paper therefore identifies and defines the distinct sermon structure that Dabney proposed for expository sermons, and evaluates the extent to which Dabney inculcated his expository theory in his classroom pedagogy and exemplified it in his personal practice.

79. Trotter understood the fivefold structure of nineteenth-century topical sermons, and briefly described Dabney's use of this structure. See Trotter, *Always Prepared*, 54–57.

80. Trotter, "Blasting Rocks," 176.

81. Trotter, "Blasting Rocks," 175–238.

82. Trotter, *Always Prepared*, 145.

83. Trotter, *Always Prepared*, 144.

Dabney's Legacy

In addition to analyzing Dabney's extemporaneous homiletic, Trotter also helpfully explored Dabney's homiletical legacy in two ways. First, he examined the extent to which Dabney's *Sacred Rhetoric* and emphasis on extemporaneous delivery continued to exert influence at Union Seminary after Dabney's departure.[84] Second, Trotter explored two collections of Southern Presbyterian sermons[85] in order to determine the extent to which Dabney impacted the generation of Presbyterian preachers that followed him.[86] This paper does not engage the first facet of Trotter's evaluation. The extent to which Union Seminary continued to employ Dabney's *Sacred Rhetoric* after his departure cannot speak to the fidelity with which it was utilized or illumine to the historian the homiletical use that was made of it. Rather, chapter 6 of this paper examines the same sermon collections that Trotter employed, as well as several others, and conducts a different evaluation of those sermons than did Trotter. Whereas Trotter engaged the sermons of students who had personally studied homiletics under Dabney as well as those who studied at Union Seminary after Dabney's departure, this paper examines only the sermons of Dabney's students, specifically locating the extent to which they replicated his distinctive structure for expository sermons, and offered the "true exposition"[87] of the Scripture in their topical messages that Dabney's theory required.

From that perspective, this paper challenges Trotter's interpretation of Dabney's homiletical influence on the preachers whom he trained. Stated briefly, Trotter viewed Dabney as exerting little lasting homiletical impact on his students. He wrote: "While [Dabney] dominated for a time the homiletics at Union, it seems that he never dominated the preaching of the [Southern Church] as a whole."[88] After describing the sermons of Dabney's former students and other Southern Presbyterian preachers, Trotter noted that nearly all "chose brief, isolated texts," that "all assumed that their hearers had great familiarity with Christian teaching," and that "they all moved immediately into the main theme of their sermons" with relatively little exposition of the text.[89] Evaluating these sermons according

84. Trotter, "Blasting Rocks," 239–68, and *Always Prepared*, 197–220.

85. Kerr, *Southern Presbyterian Pulpit*, and Nabers, *Southern Presbyterian Pulpit*.

86. Trotter, "Blasting Rocks," 268–85.

87. Dabney, *Sacred Rhetoric*, 77. Chapter 3 explains the significance of this phrase within Dabney's homiletical theory, while chapters 5 and 6 explore the extent to which Dabney and his students offered true expositions in their topical sermons.

88. Trotter, "Blasting Rocks," 282.

89. Trotter, "Blasting Rocks," 269. Chapter 3 demonstrates that each of these facets contradicts some aspect of Dabney's expository theory.

to "length, treatment of text, type, and directness," Trotter explained that "treatment of text" referred to "the way in which the preacher used the text in the sermon. This factor serves to gauge to what degree the preachers were expository."[90] Conceding that "none of them were expository," Trotter noted that many took "a 'timeless truth' approach" by "extracting from the text"[91] a doctrine or duty, while others were "mostly exegetical,"[92] albeit "less overtly biblical"[93] than Dabney. Trotter therefore lamented that the generation of preachers that followed Dabney more or less rejected "his insistence that all sermons be expository," leading him to conclude that Dabney's homiletic was "in decline"[94] even before his death, and exerted little lasting influence on the Southern Church. Trotter conceded that he "had not found it possible to trace much in the way of direct influence by Dabney on those who are his closest theological heirs."[95] This result confused Trotter, and he acknowledged:

> By 1870 Dabney had everything in place to teach his style of homiletics: a double dose of his theory through his published and spoken lectures, the exercises that he dictated to his students, and frequent opportunities to demonstrate to his students how to preach.[96]

Recognizing, however, that Dabney's students did not preach the expository sermons that Dabney's theory admired, Trotter quipped: "It would seem to take exceptional stubbornness or dullness on the part of the students in order not to be indoctrinated into Dabney's approach to preaching."[97] Trotter therefore concluded that Dabney exercised a relatively diminutive homiletical impact upon the preachers whom he trained, while laying the blame for that result at the feet of Dabney's students.

Fundamental to Trotter's analysis of Dabney's homiletical legacy stands his assumption that Dabney faithfully inculcated in his classroom pedagogy the expository theory that his *Sacred Rhetoric* admired. Trotter's lack of engagement with the extent to which Dabney's classroom pedagogy did or did not equip his students to proclaim expository sermons produced

90. Trotter, "Blasting Rocks," 270.
91. Trotter, "Blasting Rocks," 272.
92. Trotter, "Blasting Rocks," 273.
93. Trotter, "Blasting Rocks," 283.
94. Trotter, "Blasting Rocks," 284.
95. Trotter, "Blasting Rocks," 286.
96. Trotter, *Always Prepared*, 203.
97. Trotter, *Always Prepared*, 203.

a tension in Dabney's legacy that Trotter could not resolve. By defining Dabney's expository theory in chapter 3, analyzing his expository pedagogy in chapter 4, and evaluating his personal practice of expository preaching in chapter 5, this paper traces Dabney's expository homiletic from theory to pedagogy through practice, demonstrating in chapter 6 that contrary to Trotter's interpretation, the lack of expository sermons in the generation of preachers that Dabney trained testifies to Dabney's profound and enduring homiletical influence on his students.

Conclusion

Statement of Thesis

This thesis argues that *while Robert Lewis Dabney crafted a robust expository homiletical theory, his weak expository pedagogy and failure personally to practice expository preaching undermined his theory, and Dabney predominantly equipped and influenced his seminary students to preach the very topical sermons that his expository theory abjured*. Ultimately, Dabney's admiration for expository preaching was empty.

Preview of Chapter 3

Chapter 3 engages Dabney's expository theory as taught in *Sacred Rhetoric* and elsewhere, giving special attention to the structural pattern of the standard nineteenth-century American topical sermon form, contrasting it with Dabney's distinct structure for expository sermons. This evaluation reveals that Dabney's homiletic included a caveat that allowed Dabney and his students to preach topical sermons on clauses or single verses of Scripture, thus circumventing his teaching on the necessity of expository preaching. In spite of this caveat, Dabney crafted a robust expository theory, which furnished a sound theoretical platform from which to equip his students to preach expository sermons.

3

Theory

Introduction

Overview

This paper demonstrates that while Robert Lewis Dabney crafted a robust expository theory, his weak expository pedagogy and failure to practice expository preaching united to undermine his theory. The present chapter employs Dabney's own understanding of the peculiar contributions of his homiletic as a departure point from which to evaluate his expository theory. In offering a self-evaluation in *Sacred Rhetoric*,[1] Dabney suggested:

> If this work has any peculiarities to which value may be attached, they are these: that . . . a theory of preaching is asserted, with all the force which I could command, that honors God's inspired word and limits the preacher most strictly to its exclusive use as the sword of the Spirit.[2]

He concluded: "Nothing is preaching which is not expository of the Scriptures."[3]

1. Dabney, *Sacred Rhetoric*.
2. Dabney, *Sacred Rhetoric*, 7.
3. Dabney, *Sacred Rhetoric*, 7.

The Plan of This Chapter

This chapter explores Robert Dabney's expository theory, examining the extent to which Dabney did or did not commend preaching that is "expository of the Scriptures."[4] That examination demonstrates that while Robert Dabney crafted a robust expository theory, and while he defined a distinct sermon structure for consecutive expository preaching, he also forged a caveat that allowed Dabney and his students to proclaim the very topical sermons that his homiletical theory forbade. This chapter therefore conducts an analysis of Dabney's expository theory that chapter 4 utilizes to determine the extent to which Dabney's classroom pedagogy inculcated his expository theory, and which chapter 5 uses to evaluate Dabney's personal practice of expository preaching. First, this chapter describes how Dabney understood the terms "exposition" and "expository."

Clarifying Terms

The Exposition as a Structural Sermon Component

American homileticians of the late nineteenth century defined *the* Exposition as a formal structural sermon component that followed the Introduction. The Exposition demonstrated that a particular text contained the doctrine or duty upon which the pastor intended to preach.[5] Ebenezer Porter argued that the Exposition "show[s] the hearers that [the text] contains the sentiment which the preacher deduces from it."[6] The Exposition thus established that the text furnished the topic that formed the Argument of the sermon.[7] Henry Ripley, James Hoppin, John Broadus, Robert Dabney, Austin Phelps, and nearly every nineteenth-century American homiletician, agreed.[8] The Exposition was thus a formal structural sermon

4. Dabney, *Sacred Rhetoric*, 7.

5. Nineteenth-century homileticians typically crafted a sermon using five structural components: Introduction, Exposition, Proposition, Argument, and Conclusion.

6. Porter, *Lectures on Homiletics*.

7. Not every topical sermon discussed a doctrine. Some inculcated a duty or imparted wisdom. The distinction drawn here is between sermons that mined from the text a doctrine or duty, proclaiming a biblical subject in a topical form, over against sermons that proclaimed the text itself in the form of a verse-by-verse exposition.

8. See Ripley, *Sacred*, 39; Dabney, *Sacred Rhetoric*, 156; 162–64; Broadus, *Preparation and Delivery*, 250; Hoppin, *Office*, 132–34; Phelps, *Theory*, 139; Hogg, *Hand-Book*, 120; Kern, *Ministry to the Congregation*, 132. A notable exception is W. G. T. Shedd,

component, which grounded the sermon in a biblical text, from which a topical sermon proceeded.

Typifying the practice of Dabney's peers, James Hoppin distinguished the Exposition from the body of the sermon—the Argument—writing: "In every ordinary sermon . . . the explanation has its distinct place, and is applied to the precise matter of defining the text, so that its true subject may be presented."[9] The Exposition was thus preparatory to the body of the sermon, which addressed the "true subject"[10] springing from the text, and Hoppin therefore stated that the Exposition "leads the way to the proposition and argument, but is clearly distinguished from them."[11]

The Exposition therefore followed the Introduction and preceded the Proposition, the latter of which usually identified a doctrinal, ethical, or practical topic, which the Argument unfolded. The preacher employed the Exposition to establish the grammar, terms, and subject of the text as a preparatory step, after which a topical message followed, and the Argument often unfolded apart from further reference to the text. Put succinctly, the Exposition was "only a preliminary."[12]

Exposition as Lines of Evidence

Whereas *the* Exposition indicated a formal component of sermon structure, Dabney and his peers also used the word "exposition" to describe that which took place within the Exposition, namely the work of establishing the topic contained in the text. If, however, contemporary readers conceive of such exposition only in grammatical-historical terms, they will find nineteenth-century homileticians confusing. Dabney and his peers used the term exposition broadly, and within his extant sermons[13] Dabney employed natural theology,

whose homiletic did not directly categorize the Exposition as a structural sermon component, but instead subsumed it under the Introduction. See Shedd, *Homiletics*, 179–83.

9. Hoppin, *Office*, 132. Whether labeled Exposition or Explanation, these terms referred to the same structural component.

10. Hoppin, *Office*, 132.

11. Hoppin, *Office*, 132.

12. Hogg, *Hand-Book*, 120.

13. Chapter 4 describes in detail Dabney's manuscript collection, and discusses the significance of his various types of sermon. For the purposes of the present chapter, the following information is useful: The Dabney Collection at Union Seminary is comprised of seventeen boxes of material. Each box contains multiple files, and within each file reside multiple documents. References to Dabney's sermons in this paper list the box and file number, followed by the Scripture text and the sermon format—Full Text, Skeleton, Brief, or Exercise. Consider the following example: Box 7, File 7/1, Psalm

revealed theology, definitions of terms, intuition, logic, reason, grammar, the analogy of Scripture, and other tools to establish that his text contained the topic that his sermon proclaimed.[14] So far as Dabney was concerned, any and all of these lines of evidence represented exposition, for they established the topic contained in the text, which was the purpose of *the* Exposition.[15] While a verse-by-verse redemptive-historical explanation might best accomplish that goal, it might not. In fact, Dabney often presumed upon the scriptural knowledge of his hearers, foregoing exposition altogether when he felt that the meaning of the text was self-evident.[16]

What, then, did Dabney mean when he suggested that every sermon must be "expository of the Scriptures"?[17] Consider Dabney's insistence that all sermons "should be virtually expository, else they are not true sermons"[18] juxtaposed with what immediately follows: "When the pastor discusses only

139:14 Skeleton. This sermon resides in File 7/1 of Box 7. The text is Psalm 139:14 and Dabney composed the sermon as a Skeleton.

14. See Box 8, File 8/3, Luke 8:18 Skeleton in which Dabney offered exposition by way of interrogatives; Box 8, File 8/3, Luke 9:26 Full Text featured exposition by means of illustration; Box 8, File 8/6, John 15:14 Skeleton presented exposition by way of logical distinction; Box 9, File 9/1, Acts 17:11 Skeleton engaged in exposition by definition and expansion of terms with corroborating Scripture. Dabney argued for careful study of the Scripture from their inspiration, their morality, their antiquity and philosophy, and their ancient and continuing influence, and concluded by asking, "What man of information can be content to be ignorant of such a book?" Box 9, File 9/2, Romans 5:6 & John 6:44 Skeleton offered exposition by way of confessional standards; Box 9, File 9/4, 1 Corinthians 16:22 Full Text featured exposition by means of removing "cavils"; Box 9, File 9/6, Galatians 4:24–26 Brief gave exposition by redemptive–historical theology and context; Box 10, File 10/1, Philippians 2:12–13 Skeleton pursued exposition by negation, explaining what the text is not; Box 10, File 10/3, Hebrews 12:12–13 Skeleton presented exposition by literary context; Box 10, File 10/4, James 5:20 Skeleton offered exposition by analogy of Scripture; Box 10, File 10/4, 1 Peter 1:12 Brief pursued exposition via promise and fulfillment; Box 10, File 10/5, 2 John 10–11 Brief engaged in exposition by refutation of critical scholarship; Box 6, File 6/4, Genesis 2:17 Skeleton offered exposition by way of an explanation of native human faculties, which Dabney viewed through the lens of Scottish Common Sense Realism; Box 6, File 6/7, Psalm 35:6 Skeleton featured exposition by contemporary cultural exegesis; Box 7, File 7/6, Habakkuk 2:15 Skeleton engaged in exposition by way of a chastisement of the Roman Church's idolatry and immorality. Dabney understood all these lines of evidence as fulfilling his broad conception of "exposition."

15. See also Phelps, *Theory*, 149.

16. For example, Dabney's Box 7, File 7/5, Jeremiah 17:9 Skeleton features a note to self, which reads: "No exposition needed." Dabney assumed that his listeners shared a common definition of the word "heart," and that the deceit about which Jeremiah wrote needed no further explanation. Many of Dabney's extant sermon manuscripts likewise feature little to no exposition.

17. Dabney, *Sacred Rhetoric*, 7.

18. Dabney, *Sacred Rhetoric*, 77.

a single sentence or proposition of Scripture, as he will often and legitimately do, it should yet be a true exposition, and evolution of the meaning of God in that sentence, with constant and faithful reference to its context."[19] Insofar as a topical sermon met these criteria, it could, for Dabney, be considered "expository of the Scriptures."[20] John Broadus likewise suggested:

> [W]e draw from the text a certain subject, usually stating it distinctly in the form of a proposition, and then the text has no further part in the sermon, but the subject is divided and treated according to its own nature, just as it would be if not derived from a text.[21]

Exposition bridged text to Argument, after which the text played little role in the sermon. Yet Broadus and Dabney alike believed that such sermons could represent a faithful exposition of the Scripture. This helps the modern reader of Dabney's sermons to understand why Dabney and his nineteenth-century peers more often proclaimed the doctrine or duty of a text in a topical form than the text itself in a verse-by-verse form, while still believing they had faithfully expounded the text.[22] When Dabney asserted that every true sermon must be "expository of the Scriptures,"[23] he meant that the sermon must proclaim a topic that proceeded from and was identified in a text of Scripture.

Agreeing with Dabney, Daniel Kidder asserted: "It is not necessary that the subject of a sermon be strictly identical with the words of a text," suggesting instead that "that the subject [must] be found within the text and be legitimately deducible from it."[24] While Kidder noted the frequent devolution of such sermons into "motto" preaching, in which the text merely offers a platform for the preacher's thoughts, he nevertheless endorsed the practice, writing:

> There is a style of treatment in which a text taken as a motto may be most forcibly employed for instruction, illustration, and encouragement; in which, indeed, both the letter and spirit of

19. Dabney, *Sacred Rhetoric*, 77.

20. Dabney, *Sacred Rhetoric*, 7.

21. Broadus, *Preparation and Delivery*, 289.

22. Hoppin, *Office*, 66–67; 151; Kidder, *Homiletics*, 118–19; Ripley, *Sacred*, 36, 39; Shedd, *Homiletics*, 159–63. Nineteenth-century homileticians largely conceived of preaching as the presentation of a topic contained in the Bible rather than an exposition of the Bible itself.

23. Dabney, *Sacred Rhetoric*, 7.

24. Kidder, *Homiletics*, 118.

> the sacred motto may be so inwrought as to pervade and hallow the whole discourse.[25]

Not unlike Dabney, Kidder felt that topical sermons could represent a true exposition of the text. Dabney employed different words, and offered stronger cautions against misrepresenting Scripture, but he substantially worked within the same broad understanding of exposition that Kidder and other nineteenth-century homileticians used. Frank Bell Lewis summarized this consensus when he wrote that within Dabney's homiletic, "All preaching must be expository, in the broader sense of that term."[26]

Expository Preaching

Over against this broad understanding of exposition, Dabney also wrote in *Sacred Rhetoric* about "expository sermons" and "expository preaching," by which he meant something narrower. Dabney did not offer an explicit definition of expository preaching, but piecing together his understanding presents little difficulty. In an expository sermon, *the Argument is comprised of an extended exposition that unfolds according to the versification of the text.* Dabney wrote: "If the text contains a number of verses of Scripture, the whole of which are to be explained and applied in their connection, the discussion is called an 'expository' sermon."[27] An expository sermon represented "a continuous explication"[28] of the text, presenting "a detailed examination of the verses,"[29] and unfolded "as the phrases or commas of the text stand in the Scriptures."[30] Dabney therefore differentiated between an expository sermon and a sermon that was merely "expository of the Scriptures."[31] While the former offered an extended exposition that unfolded according to the versification of the text, the latter often yielded a sermon more akin to a topical lecture than a verse-by-verse unfolding of a passage of Scripture. Dabney nevertheless believed that either form could offer a "true exposition"[32] of the text.

25. Kidder, *Homiletics*, 119.
26. Lewis, "Robert Lewis Dabney," 93.
27. Dabney, *Sacred Rhetoric*, 76.
28. Dabney, *Sacred Rhetoric*, 164.
29. Dabney, *Sacred Rhetoric*, 166.
30. Dabney, *Sacred Rhetoric*, 218.
31. Dabney, *Sacred Rhetoric*, 7.
32. Dabney, *Sacred Rhetoric*, 77.

Dabney thus wrote of (1) *the* Exposition, which was a formal, structural sermon component, not unlike an Introduction or a Conclusion, of (2) exposition in general, which represented of any and all lines of evidence employed to establish that the biblical text contained the topic about which the preacher intended to preach, and of (3) expository preaching in particular, in which the Argument was comprised of an extended exposition that unfolded according to the versification of the text, and which often continued through a book of Scripture.

Dabney's admiration for expository preaching as a category of sermon distinct from the topical form of his day drives the analysis that follows, and the remainder of this chapter therefore delves into Dabney's *Sacred Rhetoric* and other writings in order to establish the features of his homiletical theory for consecutive expository preaching.

Dabney's Expository Theory

Biblical Foundations

Dabney defined preaching in terms that invited verse-by-verse expository sermons, using Nehemiah 8:5–8 as his biblical template for faithful pulpit ministry.[33] Nehemiah records:

> Ezra opened the book in the sight of all the people, for he was above all the people, and as he opened it all the people stood. And Ezra blessed the LORD, the great God, and all the people answered, "Amen, Amen," lifting up their hands. And they bowed their heads and worshiped the LORD with their faces to the ground. Also . . . the Levites, helped the people to understand the Law, while the people remained in their places. They read from the book, from the Law of God, clearly, and they gave the sense, so that the people understood the reading.[34]

Dabney defined preaching as the act of opening the Bible, making people understand it, and persuading them to respond to it with faith and duty.[35]

Lawrence Trotter has demonstrated that along with Dabney's emphasis upon an extemporaneous method of delivery, much of Dabney's homiletic

33. Dabney, *Sacred Rhetoric*, 23.

34. Unless other wise noted, all Scripture quotations in this paper represent the English Standard Version of the Bible.

35. Of Nehemiah's description Dabney wrote: "We shall seek in vain for a more apt and scriptural definition of the preacher's work than is contained in these words." Dabney, *Sacred Rhetoric*, 23.

hinges upon his understanding of the preacher as herald.[36] Dabney believed that a faithful herald proclaims only the King's message and all of the King's message.[37] Dabney therefore asked the Bible to tell him what preaching is, defining it neither by contemporary practice nor ancient usage, but by biblical warrant. He wrote:

> The nature of the preacher's work is determined by the word employed to describe it by the Holy Ghost. The preacher is a herald; his work is heralding the King's message . . . Now, the herald does not invent his message; he merely transmits and explains it. It is not his to criticise[38] its wisdom or fitness; this belongs to his sovereign alone.[39]

Illustrating this point, Dabney offered the image of a die pressed into hot wax, writing:

> The preacher's task may be correctly explained as that of (instrumentally) forming the image of Christ upon the souls of men. The plastic substance is the human heart. The die which is provided for the workman is the revealed Word; and the impression to be formed is the divine image of knowledge and true holiness. God, who made the soul, and therefore knows it, made the die. He obviously knew best how to shape it, in order to produce the imprint he desired. Now the workman's business is not to criticise, recarve, or erase anything in the die which was committed to him; but simply to press it down faithfully upon the substance to be impressed, observing the conditions of the work assigned him in his instructions. In this view, how plain is it, that preaching should be simply representative of Bible truths, and in Bible proportions! The preacher's business is to take what is given him in the Scriptures, as it is given to him, and to endeavor to imprint it on the souls of men. All else is God's work.[40]

Dabney believed that each generation of preachers must follow the pattern of Nehemiah: open, explain, and press on the consciences of the hearers the claims of the Scripture. Noting that long after Nehemiah, in the

36. Trotter, *Always Prepared*, 78–79. *Always Prepared* is a revision and adaptation of Trotter, "Blasting Rocks." It is used by permission of the author.

37. Dabney, *Sacred Rhetoric*, 36.

38. This paper retains Dabney's original spelling in cases in which his spelling was, for his day, acceptable. Some of his spellings, such as "labour," reflect what today would be considered a British over against an American spelling.

39. Dabney, *Sacred Rhetoric*, 36.

40. Dabney, *Sacred Rhetoric*, 37.

form of Israel's synagogue worship, "[E]xpository preaching prevailed as a regular exercise, following the reading of the Scriptures in the services of the synagogues,"[41] Dabney understood that Jesus also began his ministry with an exposition of Isaiah 61:1–3[42] and that his disciples followed his example. Although differing in structure from Dabney's expository ideal, the sermons recorded in the New Testament demonstrate scriptural fidelity and tend to be comprised of expositions of various passages of Scripture, which interweave to proclaim the gospel and to produce a sense of urgent need for a response.[43] Dabney took this testimony not merely to indicate that preaching must continue as a regular practice in the church, but also that this particular form of preaching—expository heraldry—must likewise continue. He argued:

> Preaching was the chief instrument of the Christian missionary and teacher, of whatever rank. "It pleased God by the foolishness of preaching to save them that believe." And it is very plain from the Acts and Epistles, in both their preceptive and narrative parts, that this continued to be a regular part of the public service of all the Christian assemblies.[44]

From Nehemiah to New Testament synagogue worship to the preaching of the apostles, Dabney identified a pattern of preaching-as-heraldry that was primarily comprised of verse-by-verse exposition of the Scripture, which unfolded the text "in scriptural aspects and proportions."[45]

Church History

In the post-apostolic pastors of the early church, Dabney likewise found evidence of expository preaching, arguing: "The sermons of the primitive pastors were rather expository . . . usually founded on the portions of the Scripture read."[46] The post-apostolic witness represented a continuation of the biblical pattern of preaching, which was, for Dabney, not merely

41. Dabney, *Sacred Rhetoric*, 23.

42. Luke 4:16–21.

43. Paul's sermon in Athens in Acts 17:22–31 offers a notable exception to this pattern.

44. Dabney, *Sacred Rhetoric*, 24.

45. Dabney, *Sacred Rhetoric*, 38. While the majority of Dabney's peers favored a topical sermon form, J. W. Alexander joined Dabney in defining preaching in expository terms. He argued: "The expository method of preaching . . . is the very work for which a ministry was instituted, to interpret the Scriptures." Alexander, *Thoughts*, 229.

46. Dabney, *Sacred Rhetoric*, 24.

descriptive of an ancient biblical practice, but also prescriptive for the current and future church and its preachers.[47] Dabney thus viewed the gradual falling away from this expository form during the early church as a loss, and even as a species of infidelity. Contending that "the state of the pulpit may always be taken as an index of that of the Church," Dabney asserted: "Whenever the pulpit is evangelical,[48] the piety of the people is in some degree healthy."[49] Identifying three stages of preaching, which move from fidelity to infidelity, Dabney argued that each stage produced results in the church ranging from obedience to apostasy. He wrote:

> The first [stage] is that in which scriptural truth is faithfully presented in scriptural garb—that is to say, not only are all the doctrines asserted which truly belong to the revealed system of redemption, but they are presented in that dress and connection in which the Holy Spirit presented them . . . This state of the pulpit marks the golden age of the Church.[50]

For Dabney, a prevalence of expository preaching coincided with the church's "golden age."[51] Over against this, Dabney explained: "The second is the transition stage. In this the doctrines taught are still those of the Scriptures, but their relations are moulded into conformity with the prevalent human dialectics. God's truth is now shorn of part of its power over the soul."[52] By this definition the majority of the church in America in Dabney's day mirrored his second stage, having rejected expository preaching in favor of a topical method that often utilized a verse or clause rent from its context as a source for a topical sermon.[53] James Hoppin corroborated Dabney's insight about this second stage, writing:

47. Dabney, *Sacred Rhetoric*, 24.

48. In defining the term evangelical, Dabney wrote: "We cannot better describe it than in the words of the apostles, when they so frequently speak of their work as 'preaching Christ,' or 'preaching Christ crucified.'" Said succinctly: "I would willingly define evangelical preaching by the term scriptural." Dabney, *Sacred Rhetoric*, 114–15.

49. Dabney, *Sacred Rhetoric*, 27.

50. Dabney, *Sacred Rhetoric*, 27–28.

51. Dabney, *Sacred Rhetoric*, 28.

52. Dabney, *Sacred Rhetoric*, 28.

53. Consider Henry Ripley. In his defense of preaching upon isolated verses or clauses of text, Ripley wrote: "It is a good general rule, that a text should contain a complete sentence; but if a preacher must be bound by this rule, what would be the result? He must never select for a text the clause—A just God and Saviour; nor such as the following, which are perpetually occurring in the Bible—Mighty in the Scriptures:—Having no hope:—Patient in tribulation:—The glorious gospel of the blessed God. Now, though these clauses are not grammatical sentences, yet they so far contain a complete sense, a definite idea, as to suggest a full subject. And who will say that this

> The American sermon . . . is generally built on a logical plan, cast into the form of an argument, with direct and practical lessons drawn from the demonstrated truth; it is synthetic in form, and although generally biblical in tone and aim, yet it is not simply biblical as confining itself to the interpretation of Scripture and the setting forth of the Word of God; it is not satisfied with this, but aims at a philosophical systematization of divine truth.[54]

"A philosophical systematization of divine truth"[55] is an apt descriptor for the work of systematic theology, but also incompatible with Dabney's definition of expository preaching. Dabney therefore noted: "The third stage is then near, in which not only are the methods and explanations conformed to the philosophy of the day, but the doctrines themselves contradict the truth of the Word."[56] By this understanding, Dabney viewed expository preaching as both a barometer of and an elixir for the health of the church.

The reclamation of expository preaching during the Reformation marked, for Dabney, a spiritual victory and a recovery of biblical preaching. He noted: "All the leading Reformers, whether in Germany, Switzerland, England, or Scotland, were constant preachers, and their sermons were prevalently expository."[57] In lecturing on the history of preaching, John Broadus affirmed Dabney's understanding, noting: "Once more, after long centuries . . . preachers, studying the original Greek and Hebrew, were carefully explaining to the people the connected teaching of passage after passage and book after book."[58] Broadus especially commended the Reformer of Geneva, writing:

> Calvin gave the ablest, soundest, clearest expositions of Scripture that had been seen in a thousand years, and most of the other great Reformers worked in the same direction. Such

---

is not sufficient in a text? No one will pretend that such a clause should not be thus employed; or that it must be so connected with the context as not to be an imperfect scrap of the word of God." Ripley, *Sacred*, 36. Ripley so fully conceived of preaching as the proclamation of a topical discourse that he could not imagine a legitimate objection to his use of mere sentence fragments as preaching texts.

54. Hoppin, *Office*, 54.

55. Hoppin, *Office*, 54.

56. Dabney, *Sacred Rhetoric*, 28.

57. Dabney, *Sacred Rhetoric*, 26.

58. Broadus, *Lectures*, 114–15. While noting this historical reality, W. G. T. Shedd justified his preference for topical preaching by citing the pervasive knowledge of the Bible among nineteenth-century Americans, arguing that Sunday schools provided an avenue for exposition in course, thereby freeing the pulpit for more oratorical messages. Shedd, *Homiletics*, 157.

> careful and continued exposition of the Bible, based in the main upon sound exegesis, and pursued with loving zeal, could not fail of great results.[59]

This link between expository preaching and church health was, in Dabney's eyes, no coincidence. He asserted: "We may assume with safety, that the instrumentality to which the spiritual power of that great revolution was mainly due, was the restoration of scriptural preaching."[60] Likewise, the neglect of such preaching could only diminish the vitality of the church. Dabney concluded: "[A] perversion of the pulpit is surely followed by spiritual apostasy in the Church."[61]

Dabney saw himself as speaking into this context of diminishing spiritual vitality,[62] and his emphasis on expository preaching may represent his attempt to correct a perceived drift toward "a perversion of the pulpit."[63] To Dabney's mind, expository preaching preserved not just the doctrinal truth of the text, but also the scriptural context in which that truth lay. He insisted: "Not only must Bible topics form the whole matter of our preaching, but they must be presented in scriptural aspects and proportions,"[64] continuing:

> God, who knew best, has not only set forth such truths, but in such proportions and relations as really suit man's soul under the dealings of the Holy Spirit. There can be no other connections and forms of the truth so suitable as these, for these are they which God has seen fit to give. We may be guilty then of infidelity to our task, though we be not heterodox.[65]

Theoretically, Dabney accorded little room to non-expository preaching, charging the preacher who neglected context with "infidelity."[66]

59. Broadus, *Lectures*, 115–16.

60. Dabney, *Sacred Rhetoric*, 26–27.

61. Dabney, *Sacred Rhetoric*, 27.

62. Dabney, "Phase," 696.

63. Dabney, *Sacred Rhetoric*, 27.

64. Dabney, *Sacred Rhetoric*, 38.

65. Dabney, *Sacred Rhetoric*, 38.

66. John Etter agreed, writing: "A text which is chosen and then soon abandoned, is not a text, but a pretext." Etter, *Preacher*, 167.

On the Text of Scripture

Given his commitment to contextual exposition, we might expect Dabney to speak more strongly in favor of the use of a Scripture text in preaching than many of his peers, and in fact he did. Homileticians of the nineteenth-century engaged in a running debate, asking whether a Scripture text was strictly necessary to a sermon. For Dabney, the question itself was absurd. He argued that "the posture of the preacher is essentially different from that of all other speakers," claiming that "[h]is only work is to expound and apply to the people an authoritative message from God."[67] He explained:

> The whole authority of his addresses to the conscience depends upon the correspondence evinced between his explanations and inferences and the infallible Word. It appears, then, that the use of texts is not an artificial fashion, but a custom dictated by the very nature of the preacher's peculiar mission.[68]

Dabney could not conceive of preaching that was not grounded in or that failed to herald a text of Scripture. Preaching without the Scripture was, for Dabney, not preaching at all.

Dabney also understood that true movement of the will required the "renewal of [the] mind"[69] through the Scripture, for genuine promptings of the conscience originate in the intelligent apprehension of biblical truth.[70] Preachers whose pulpit exhortations manipulated hearers' emotions might prompt short-term action, but the effect must quickly fade. For Dabney, lasting movement of the will could only take place when the conscience intelligently received the word of God. He explained:

> [M]an only feels as he sees, and because he sees with his mind. A moment's consideration of these obvious facts will convince you that there cannot be, in the nature of the case, any other instrument to be used by creatures for inculcating religion and procuring right feeling and action, than that which begins by informing the understanding.[71]

67. Dabney, *Sacred Rhetoric*, 75.

68. Dabney, *Sacred Rhetoric*, 75.

69. Romans 12:2

70. Dabney, *Sacred Rhetoric*, 72.

71. Dabney, *Sacred Rhetoric*, 52–53. James Garretson, in describing Archibald Alexander's instructions to Princeton seminarians, likewise wrote: "Good preaching does not aim directly at the affections; it seeks to enliven the religious affections by informing the mind, thus moving the will." Garretson, *Princeton*, 96.

If a hearer failed intelligently to apprehend the Bible, no lasting movement of the will could occur. Rather, volition always follows understanding. Dabney therefore argued:

> Action is produced only by conviction. The only legitimate weapon of conviction is the truth. The well-ordered, warm, and logical argument is indirectly the best exhortation you can apply. Direct exhortation, which is not founded on argument, is meaningless.[72]

To Dabney's mind, expository preaching offered the best means to connect the Scripture to the sermon, and instruction to exhortation, thereby reaching the will through the renewal of the mind with the word of God.

When discussing the nineteenth-century penchant for preaching topical sermons upon isolated verses or clauses of text, Dabney admitted: "I am not careful to invent a more exact name of this species of discourse upon insulated fragments of Scripture, which should never have had place in the Church at all. We will call them, for convenience, sermons without context."[73] Nevertheless, Dabney conceded that for two reasons he allowed preaching on a single verse or clause of Scripture. The first was that which Dabney called a "capital" text, which he defined as a passage of Scripture that captured a foundational truth such as sin, grace, redemption, or resurrection.[74] The second category was that which Dabney called an "epitome" text, which he defined as an instance in which a single verse interpreted or explained an extended portion of Scripture. The key phrase that illuminates a parable or the summary statement of an extended epistolary argument both fell into this latter category.[75] Dabney emphasized: "I repeat that, unless the single proposition is related to the Word in one of these ways, it is not suitable for a sermon," for "a discussion without scriptural context is not true preaching," and "in the sense above defined, there is no other species of preaching than the expository."[76] The substantive difference, however, between the practice Dabney chided—preaching upon isolated verses—and his own theory of preaching upon capital and epitome texts is difficult to identify.

On the surface, the use of an epitome text offered a measure of built-in contextual safety that the common nineteenth-century topical sermon form lacked. Consider Nathan's rebuke of David in 2 Samuel 12:7. Given

72. Dabney, *Sacred Rhetoric*, 72.
73. Dabney, *Sacred Rhetoric*, 76.
74. Dabney, *Sacred Rhetoric*, 76.
75. Dabney, *Sacred Rhetoric*, 77–78.
76. Dabney, *Sacred Rhetoric*, 78.

that verse seven substantially summarizes the point of the preceding verses, and is largely incomprehensible apart from them, the context prevents the sermon from devolving into the type of preaching Dabney abjured. To preach a true epitome text necessitated exposition of the entire passage in order to ensure that the congregation comprehended the epitome text. Dabney felt comfortable that a sermon based on an epitome text could offer a true exposition of the Scripture while avoiding the pitfalls endemic to the preaching of isolated texts.[77]

More difficult to justify, and more difficult to distinguish from the topical preaching against which Dabney protested, was Dabney's use of capital texts. The structure of the nineteenth-century homiletic invited the practice of abstracting a doctrine or duty from a text of Scripture to proclaim a topical sermon. This structure, coupled with Dabney's own confessional beliefs[78] about the word of God, led him to see in nearly every passage of Scripture a suitable capital text. Unlike the built-in contextual safety required by the use of an epitome text, a capital text offered no such proscription, and without rigorous integrity on the part of the preacher the use of capital texts invited the very "sermons without context"[79] that earned Dabney's strongest disapprobation.

Consecutive Expository Preaching

Despite this caveat in reference to capital and epitome texts, Dabney's theory encouraged his students to preach verse-by-verse expository sermons upon extended sections of Scripture and even whole books of the Bible. Dabney pressed:

77. Dabney believed that an epitome text, when properly employed, represented "a whole discussion" that was "summed up for us by the Holy Spirit himself," and that the true problem of preaching upon isolated texts lay not in the brevity of the text itself, but in the preacher who unfolded from it an argument "of human device" rather than "the argument of the Holy Ghost upon it." Dabney, *Sacred Rhetoric*, 77–78.

78. Dabney's beliefs are summarized in the Westminster Confession of Faith and Catechisms, to which he subscribed throughout the course of his ministry. WCF 1:4 teaches: "The authority of the Holy Scripture, for which it ought to be believed, and obeyed, depends not upon the testimony of any man, or Church; but wholly upon God (who is truth itself) the author thereof: and therefore it is to be received, because it is the Word of God." In the sermon Dabney preached when he assumed the Chair of Ecclesiastical History and Polity at Union Seminary, he testified: "The sacred Scriptures possess plenary inspiration, and are infallible truth in every word." Dabney, "Uses and Results," 5.

79. Dabney, *Sacred Rhetoric*, 76.

> I would urge that the expository method (understood as that which explains extended passages of Scripture in course) be restored to that equal place which it held in the primitive and Reformed Churches; for, first, this is obviously the only natural and efficient way to do that which is the sole legitimate end of preaching, [which is to] convey the whole message of God to the people.[80]

Dabney understood that the church in his generation had largely abandoned expository preaching, and he desired to see it restored. A generation earlier, James Waddel Alexander had lamented the paucity of expository preaching in the American pulpit, excoriating the same faults of the same misuse of fragments of texts that Dabney deplored. Not unlike Dabney, Alexander identified exposition of the Scripture as the legitimate "end of preaching."[81] He found it "remarkable" that the Reformation coincided with "the universal return of evangelical preachers to the expository method," and observed:

> Book after book of the Scriptures was publicly expounded by Luther, and the almost daily sermons of Calvin were, with scarcely any exceptions, founded on passages taken in regular course as he proceeded through the sacred canon. The same is true of the other reformers, particularly in England and Scotland.[82]

Arguing that during and immediately after the Reformation "exposition in regular course was considered a necessary part of ministerial labour," Alexander lamented: "Within our immediate knowledge, there are not a dozen ministers who make the expounding of scripture [*sic*] any part of their stated pulpit exercises."[83] Thirty years later the situation had not changed, and given that Dabney followed Alexander in identifying expository preaching as the strength of both the primitive and Reformation eras, he argued for its restoration to a place of prominence within the church. Dabney insisted that "the scriptural theory of preaching . . . is to unfold to the hearers the counsel of God for their salvation,"[84] and he was convinced that consecutive expository preaching best suited that end.

80. Dabney, *Sacred Rhetoric*, 78–79.
81. Alexander, "Remarks," 36.
82. Alexander, "Remarks," 38.
83. Alexander, "Remarks," 38.
84. Dabney, *Sacred Rhetoric*, 79.

Summary

Robert Dabney admired expository preaching because it represented the biblical, ancient church, and Reformation era practices, because he believed it best promoted the health and vitality of the church, and because he thought it the most efficient way to accomplish the primary end of preaching, which was the expository heraldry of the whole counsel of God.

Expository Advantages

Overview

Dabney also identified certain advantages that flowed from expository preaching, which he believed no other sermon method boasted. An increase in character formation, the development of scriptural and hermeneutical intelligence among the people of God, and an enhancement of the spiritual growth of the preacher all flourished as fruits from the vine of expository preaching. Dabney's convictions about these advantages formed no small part of his expository theory.

Character Formation

Dabney believed that expository preaching best served to form Christian character. Returning to his die image, Dabney asserted that expository sermons pressed the die into the wax evenly, thereby forming the most perfect image of Christ in men and women. He asserted: "To produce a fair transcript, the artisan must press it down equably, and place the whole outline upon the wax. This is accomplished by the exposition in course of the chief parts of the Bible."[85] To the contrary, Dabney suggested:

> Our fragmentary, modern method of preaching without context is as though the servant to whom the die is committed should divide it into small pieces, and then, selecting favorite letters of the legend or features of the carving, should force them into the wax at a high temperature and with extravagant pressure. But the remainder is scarcely brought into the faintest contact with the surface. What can one expect save a cluster of rude, shapeless indentations rather than the symmetrical imprint of the Redeemer's beauteous image on the soul?[86]

85. Dabney, *Sacred Rhetoric*, 79.
86. Dabney, *Sacred Rhetoric*, 79–80.

Dabney thus believed that preachers must pursue expository preaching, for it offered the most profit to God's people. He insisted: "If expository preaching is necessary for the best interests of the people, then the faithful servant of Christ has no option to discard it: he is bound to employ it."[87] To Dabney's mind, expository preaching offered the fittest tool by which a preacher formed the character of Christ in congregants.

Scriptural and Hermeneutical Intelligence

Dabney likewise believed that expository preaching increased the hermeneutical and scriptural intelligence of a congregation. He was convinced that a sermon does not merely impart information, but also demonstrates a hermeneutic by which God's people learn to read the Scripture. Dabney argued:

> The connections of truths among themselves are as essential to the system as the separate propositions. No man understands the system until he comprehends these relations. No, however complete may be the circle of points presented by the faulty, modern mode, their scriptural relations are not taught to the people. Expository preaching is necessary to show them how truth affects truth, and how to connect the parts of their creed.[88]

The type of fragmentary preaching that Dabney rejected not only deprived God's people of the "connection of truths"[89] within the Bible's theology, but also failed to ground the truths of the sermon in the broader context of the Scripture.

Dabney was not alone. Alexander had likewise observed that with reference to the Scripture, a given congregation's "habits of investigation almost always receive their character from the sermons to which they listen,"[90] and Hoppin asserted: "Biblical hermeneutics is the preacher's life-long study. He should have the principles of interpretation clearly established in his mind, so that they may be constantly applied in practice."[91] Austin Phelps agreed, claiming that "popular growth in a knowledge of the Scriptures" comes primarily from "the handling of texts by a skillful preacher."[92]

87. Dabney, *Sacred Rhetoric*, 86.
88. Dabney, *Sacred Rhetoric*, 80–81.
89. Dabney, *Sacred Rhetoric*, 80.
90. Alexander, *Thoughts*, 236.
91. Hoppin, *Office*, 104.
92. Phelps, *Theory*, 56.

Dabney felt that the relative absence of consecutive expository preaching in his generation had exerted a negative impact on the American church, contending: "There is a profusion of preaching and public exercises; yet there is far less scriptural intelligence among our church-goers than among our ruder forefathers."[93] He deduced: "The religious opinions of the Church reflect the narrow, partial and exaggerated traits of the pulpit. The people are not grounded in the Scriptures."[94] As a corrective to this lack, Dabney asserted that consecutive expository preaching fed the biblically ignorant.[95]

On the timeless advantage of expository preaching, Dabney claimed:

> Good expository preaching is always permanently attractive, and always most important to those whom it is most important to attract. It meets the great appetite of the human mind—the desire to know; it instructs. No man who has any intelligent sensibility toward sacred things can fail to make the reflection that, if the Bible is our authoritative rule of faith, then it is a matter of transcendent, of infinite concern to him to get the right meaning of that book . . . Hence, he who proposes to open the meaning of the Scriptures meets the most serious desire of their religious nature. If this work is done successfully, without undo pedantry and prolixity, but with a plain and honest mastery of the task, which is obvious to the good sense of the hearer, if his judgment is convinced that the preacher has indeed given him the clue of correct understanding, nothing can be so attractive to him. He feels that this is precisely what he needed.[96]

Dabney thus believed that expository preaching best helps congregants to know the Bible. A biblical hermeneutic requires raw materials to construct, and the raw material is comprised of basic knowledge of the Scripture,[97] without which any Christian's hermeneutic must be warped, akin to the piecemeal die of Dabney's illustration. He thus claimed: "Good expository preaching . . . presents divine truth in those aspects and relations in which it was placed by that God who knew what was in man."[98]

Recall that Dabney felt that preachers too often "detach a cardinal truth from its context," and in so doing, the preacher "discard[s] the argument by which the Holy Ghost has seen fit to sustain it," instead "recasting the

93. Dabney, *Sacred Rhetoric*, 81.
94. Dabney, *Sacred Rhetoric*, 81.
95. Dabney, *Sacred Rhetoric*, 80–81.
96. Dabney, *Sacred Rhetoric*, 87.
97. Dabney, *Sacred Rhetoric*, 37.
98. Dabney, *Sacred Rhetoric*, 88–89.

elements of proof in forms dialectical or theological, according to the rules of our human science. The effects always disappoint us."[99] To the contrary, Dabney trusted that expository preaching increased the scriptural knowledge of hearers and equipped them with a sound hermeneutic by which to read the Scriptures profitably for themselves. Dabney therefore opined: "God's sermons will tell upon them as men's sermons never do."[100]

The Growth of the Preacher

In addition to forming the character of hearers and increasing their scriptural and hermeneutical intelligence, Dabney also argued that expository sermons grow the minister like no other form of preaching. He suggested:

> The improvement of the pastor in biblical knowledge is closely connected with that of his people. He must profit in the Scriptures for their advantage. He who does not preach many expository sermons will seldom become an able and learned interpreter . . . He will find himself compelled to study mainly those things which will prepare him for the next Sabbath's sermon. If this is to be a discussion on a single proposition without context, his inquiries may lead him to theological text-books, to literary sources, to human dialectics. These are the helps which furnish him the artificial division and topics which he seeks. But he will be diverted from direct study of the Word, which should be his chief labor. If, on the other hand, his message is expository, his studies must be of that kind. Thus he will become mighty in the Scriptures.[101]

Simply put, Dabney saw no substitute for the profitable effects that consecutive expository preaching produced in the faithful minister.

Those effects mattered to Dabney. His was an age of the professionalization of the ministry,[102] and Dabney expected his students fully to absorb the Scripture and its theology, which was their particular field of study, possessing "a real mastery of the theology of redemption."[103] Increasing industrialization,

99. Dabney, *Sacred Rhetoric*, 89. This description is strikingly similar to the practice of preaching upon "capital" texts that Dabney endorsed. Although he chided those who "detach a cardinal truth from its context," it is unclear how Dabney felt that his teaching on capital texts avoided this very practice.

100. Dabney, *Sacred Rhetoric*, 89.

101. Dabney, *Sacred Rhetoric*, 81–82.

102. Sean Lucas offered a helpful discussion of the professionalization of the ministry during the nineteenth century. See Lucas, "Hold Fast," 69–81.

103. Dabney, *Sacred Rhetoric*, 264.

rapid growth in various departments of science, and specialization in education meant that a local pastor might not, for the first time in Protestant history, boast more formal education than the members of the congregation.[104] Nevertheless, Dabney insisted that the pastor demonstrate erudition within those departments of study that belonged to an educated clergy, urging:

> In your own department, that of evangelical history and doctrine, you are sacredly bound to display such competency, such maturity of opinion, such faithful and honest research, as will make every fair-minded hearer respect your theological *dicta*.[105]

Dabney therefore instructed his students to master the Scripture, admonishing them:

> You need not pretend to talk agriculture, physics, politics, belles-lettres, fine arts, with the experts in the various branches of knowledge; but you may honestly avow, when they are the subject of conversation, that you have not judged it your business to master them, and may keep your mouth closed. Such an attitude is always respectable. But when the votaries of these arts and sciences approach the theology of redemption, show them that there you are master of them all. To do this, you need only constant and faithful study of your own department, and this, I repeat, it is your clear duty to bestow.[106]

In order to accomplish this lofty ideal, the minister must, as Alexander stated, "heroically . . . determine to be ignorant of many things in which men take pride."[107] Stated positively, Dabney believed that the practice of expository preaching cultivated theological mastery in a minister.[108] Nothing put the minister in close contact with the Bible more consistently than consecutive expository preaching. Hoppin concurred, arguing:

> True expository preaching is most profitable of all to the preacher himself, because it enriches his scriptural knowledge, and leads him deeper into the word of God. It gives him broader views of revealed truth, it teaches him to read the sacred writings in a

104. Lucas argued: "[A]s Dabney dealt with various public issues in the postbellum era, he constantly was trumped by a 'new' professionalism in which Dabney's 'amateur' knowledge of various topics was challenged by the specialized and expert knowledge of his opponents." Lucas, "Hold Fast," 69–70.

105. Dabney, *Sacred Rhetoric*, 265 [emphasis original].

106. Dabney, *Sacred Rhetoric*, 265–66.

107. Alexander, *Thoughts*, 132.

108. Dabney, *Sacred Rhetoric*, 81.

> connected way, and it follows out an inspired train of thought or argument sometimes through a whole book.[109]

Dabney therefore contended that expository preaching, above every other sermon form, grows the preacher, and he argued that no preacher was free to disregard it.

Summary of Advantages

Dabney argued that expository preaching formed the character of Christ in hearers, increased the scriptural and hermeneutical intelligence of congregants, and grew the preacher in mastery of the Bible and its theology, and that it accomplished these benefits better than any other method of preaching. Dabney's theory therefore exhorted his students to pursue it.

Expository Objections

Overview

Nevertheless, expository preaching had fallen into virtual disuse during Dabney's lifetime,[110] and Dabney acknowledged that expository preaching was challenging. Among the supposed objections to it, Dabney listed first that expository preaching is difficult.[111] Second, expository sermons lack the unity afforded by topical messages.[112] And finally, expository sermons limit the creative scope of the preacher.[113] Dabney refuted each objection in turn.

Expository Preaching Is Difficult

Regarding the difficulty of expository preaching, Dabney conceded:

> It is not easy . . . to conceive correctly the precise scope of the Holy Ghost in the passage; to state this perspicuously to the common reason; to evince the correspondence of your statements with the very mind of the Spirit by a plain, homely, exegetical logic without pedantry, which shall be clear and convincing to

109. Hoppin, *Office*, 162.
110. Alexander, "Remarks," 34.
111. Dabney, *Sacred Rhetoric*, 90.
112. Dabney, *Sacred Rhetoric*, 90–92.
113. Dabney, *Sacred Rhetoric*, 38–39.

> common sense; to apply the truth to heart and conscience; to select the most appropriate and useful inferences; to preserve throughout the "analogy of the faith," and to superfuse the whole with evangelical warmth,—this is not easy.[114]

For Dabney, such difficulty offered no legitimate excuse, for "if it be well done, it will prove 'the power of God and the wisdom of God unto salvation.'"[115] The prospect of the salvation of the lost was, to Dabney, sufficient motive for the minister to pursue expository preaching despite any and all difficulty. Dabney viewed vigorous pursuit of the lost through preaching as part and parcel with a call to the ministry. Asking, "What, then, is a call to the gospel ministry?" Dabney answered: "*It is an expression of the divine will that a man should preach the gospel*."[116] Dabney defined a call to ministry as a call to preach the gospel to the world for salvation.[117]

As he discussed the necessity of ministerial education, and his conviction that all theological studies must augment and enable the call to preach,[118] Dabney asserted that the difficulty of expository preaching, so far from offering an excuse to the indolent, demanded of the faithful preacher extra labor. Dabney insisted: "It is each minister's duty to love God, not with a part, but with all of his heart; and to serve him, not only as well as some weaker brother is doing, but with the fullest effectiveness possible for him."[119] To this conviction Dabney appended the analogy of a laborer in the service of a beloved master, writing:

> He may be gifted by nature with a giant frame, so that with a dull and inferior axe he cuts more wood for the master in the day that another with his natural feebleness who has the keenest axe. By "putting to more strength," he may even cut the average day's task. But if, by grinding his axe thoroughly, he is able to cut even two days' task in one, if he loves the master he will grind it. And even if his day is advanced toward the middle of the forenoon, if he finds that an hour devoted even then to a thorough grinding, will result in a larger heap of wood well cut by nightfall, he will stop at that late hour to grind.[120]

114. Dabney, *Sacred Rhetoric*, 90.

115. Dabney, *Sacred Rhetoric*, 90.

116. Dabney, "What Is a Call," 27 [emphasis original].

117. "The appropriate mission of the minister is to preach the gospel for the salvation of souls." Dabney, *Sacred Rhetoric*, 41.

118. Dabney, *Sacred Rhetoric*, 19–20.

119. Dabney, "Thoroughly," 659–60.

120. Dabney, "Thoroughly," 660.

Dabney believed that the minister who refrained from preaching expository sermons because such preaching is difficult was a lazy servant, unwilling to put forth the highest effort for the Lord.

Expository Sermons Lack Unity

Dabney recognized that preachers and homileticians of the nineteenth-century likewise devalued expository preaching because they felt it stunted the rhetorical unity the preacher of topical sermons could achieve. He noted: "By some, an objection is raised against expository preaching, that it is less consistent with the purposes of oratory, because of its lack of unity."[121] Dabney was not unsympathetic. He understood the value of unity, listing it among the "Cardinal Requisites" of a sermon.[122] For Dabney it was a matter of emphasis. Textual fidelity came first and furnished the proper means by which to secure rhetorical unity. Dabney understood the importance of choosing a proper preaching unit, writing: "[I]f the text is discreetly chosen so as to contain one main subject, and if the discourse is faithful to the text, this is itself a sufficient guarantee that unity will not be fatally wounded."[123] The text, when properly chosen, unifies the sermon.

Not everyone agreed. Representative of the tendency to exalt rhetorical unity over textual fidelity was fellow Old School[124] Presbyterian, W. G. T. Shedd, who asserted: "The sermon must preserve an oratorical character."[125] Shedd continued, expressing sentiments with which Dabney could not agree:

> [The preacher] must aim to pervade [the sermon] with but one leading idea, to embody it in but one doctrine, and to make it teach but one lesson. In constructing an expository sermon . . . the preacher should make the same endeavor; and although he must in this instance be less successful, he may facilitate his aim, by selecting for exposition only such passages of Scripture as have but one general drift, and convey but one general sentiment.[126]

121. Dabney, *Sacred Rhetoric*, 60.

122. Dabney, *Sacred Rhetoric*, 105.

123. Dabney, *Sacred Rhetoric*, 106.

124. In 1837 American Presbyterians divided into Old and New School branches, the former pursuing doctrinal purity according to the Westminster Standards, while the latter embraced doctrinal latitude, including a more open stance toward revivals. See Hart and Muether, *Seeking*, 121–27.

125. Shedd, *Homiletics*, 146. Shedd did not explain why "oratorical character" was a "must," but instead assumed that a sermon ought to represent a form of religious oratory, subject to the canons of classical rhetoric.

126. Shedd, *Homiletics*, 147.

Shedd was convinced that an expository sermon "must . . . be less successful"[127] in offering a unified message because he believed that a given preaching text could have more than "one general drift."[128] Dabney, however, believed that if the preacher's text contained more than one leading idea, then the preacher had improperly divided the text. If it contained less than the biblical author's full idea, either by omission or truncation of verses, then it was likewise not a proper preaching text.[129] To suggest that an expository sermon necessarily precluded unity was, for Dabney, to deny that the Scripture is comprised of readily identifiable thought units.[130] Dabney repudiated this suggestion, writing: "Now this obligation [unity] is founded on the assumption, which is untrue, that the Scriptures themselves lack rhetorical unity. They readily divide themselves into sections, each of which contains some one dominant scope."[131] Dabney therefore questioned:

> Why may not the "workman rightly dividing the word of truth" select one of these parts, bounded by its natural limits, as the text of his discourse? Then, inasmuch as the passage has its own unity, his exposition will be the more truly rhetorical as it is the more faithful.[132]

Offering practical counsel, Dabney suggested: "An important point remains—the fixing of the *termini* of the passage to be treated in the next sermon," and "the chief consideration to guide him here will be the unity of the topic. He will terminate his exposition for the occasion, where he finds such a natural change of subject as introduces independent matter."[133] Dabney's counsel exposed the false assumption that expository preaching necessarily lacked unity by affirming that the Scripture "has its own unity."[134]

Dabney contended furthermore that sermons preached upon fragments of texts and clauses of verses deformed the unity that already existed within properly chosen preaching texts. He wrote: "No passage of the Scripture is suitable for a text which does not contain a distinct and important point."[135] He rejected the practice, common from the Puritans to his own day, of preaching on each clause of a verse independently, rather

127. Shedd, *Homiletics*, 147.
128. Shedd, *Homiletics*, 147.
129. Dabney, *Sacred Rhetoric*, 93–94.
130. Dabney, *Sacred Rhetoric*, 90–91.
131. Dabney, *Sacred Rhetoric*, 90–91.
132. Dabney, *Sacred Rhetoric*, 91.
133. Dabney, *Sacred Rhetoric*, 93–94 [emphasis original].
134. Dabney, *Sacred Rhetoric*, 91.
135. Dabney, *Sacred Rhetoric*, 100.

than following the author's thought units in the text.[136] Dabney understood that not every phrase of Scripture contains a full idea, nor should a clause be preached apart from its context. He chided:

> That conceit of some of the Puritan divines, which caused them to compose a separate sermon on each verse of a book of Scripture or of a Psalm was therefore but a serious trifling. Under an appearance of great reverence and value for the Scripture, it really misrepresented and perverted its fair meaning. The Holy Spirit did not mean a sermon in every sentence he uttered: it is incorrect for us to represent him so.[137]

Preach the text, as the text divides itself. Dabney believed that if preachers followed this advice, their expository sermons would not lack unity.

Dabney was not, moreover, convinced that a sermon was most powerful, most beneficial, or most effective when clothed in rhetorical polish. He asked:

> Is it proved that all the pastor's instructions needs be rhetorical? True, the regular sermon is a sacred oration, and I define the oration as a discourse always converging to a practical end. But may not the pastor have public teaching functions, which are homiletical rather than rhetorical?[138]

Dabney may not have been aware that his objection to the rhetorical nature of the sermons of his day sprang from the fact that he defined oratory somewhat differently than his peers. Whereas his peers tended to define a good oration in terms of its unity,[139] Dabney tended to define it in terms of its practical end,[140] writing: "The one ulterior end of preaching is the holiness

136. A. J. F. Behrends observed that Puritan preaching "converts the Bible into a storehouse of texts, without any regard to the linguistic peculiarities of the writer, the people whom he addressed, and the end which he had in view." Behrends, *Philosophy*, 112.

137. Dabney, *Sacred Rhetoric*, 100. Sydney Ahlstom suggested: "Puritanism in the broadest sense is a perennial tendency." In describing the nature and fruit of that tendency, Ahlstrom asserted that Puritanism represented "a 'precisionistic' effort to apply God's law to every aspect of the world's affairs, private and public, personal and institutional." Ahlstrom, *Theology*, 24–26.

138. Dabney, *Sacred Rhetoric*, 92. A tension between the sermon as oration and the sermon as exposition runs unresolved though Dabney's homiletic.

139. Broadus, *Preparation and Delivery*, 304, and Shedd, *Homiletics*, 146.

140. This is a matter of emphasis rather than dichotomy. Shedd, whose preference for topical preaching infused with oratorical polish differed from Dabney, nevertheless argued: "[The sermon] should be a discourse that exhibits singleness of aim, a converging process towards an outward practical end." Shedd, *Homiletics*, 146.

of the hearers."[141] In other words, Dabney defined effective oratory by its product, while his peers often defined it by its polish. Assuming that the polish of the sermon produced greater results than a less unified discourse, most nineteenth-century homileticians argued that unity was indispensable to effective preaching.[142] Dabney, while agreeing that unity contributed toward power,[143] believed that the teaching function of the sermon stood preeminent. That which was didactic, whether oratorically polished or not, constituted the driving mandate of the sermon.[144] If rhetorical unity increased didactic power, which Dabney believed it did,[145] then such unity offered a useful tool in the service of didactic instruction. But Dabney theoretically would not abide subordinating the didactic to the merely oratorical, or tampering with the parameters of the biblical author's thought unit in order artificially to produce a unified sermon.[146]

Dabney therefore indicted preachers who proclaimed topical sermons from fragments of Scripture, insisting that such messages failed accurately to make known the mind of the Holy Spirit. He stated:

> The reason which requires this completeness in the text is, that otherwise our presentation of the truth is fragmentary, and therefore incorrect. The objection to this requirement is not valid. The objectors claim that, if his discussion is faithful to the meaning of inspiration as far as it goes, this is enough, though it is fragmentary. I reply that our expository theory of the sermon leads us to a different conclusion: the preacher has no other task than to unfold the mind of the Spirit.[147]

According to Dabney, the mind of the Holy Spirit is not fragmentary. Rather, he believed that the Spirit is logical and that the Spirit produced clearly defined units of thought within Scripture. Dabney felt that artificial fragmentation of such thought units necessarily resulted in the proclamation of

141. Dabney, *Sacred Rhetoric*, 238.

142. Broadus, *Preparation and Delivery*, 275, 304; Hoppin, *Office*, 66; Shedd, *Homiletics*, 129–30.

143. Dabney, *Sacred Rhetoric*, 108–14.

144. Dabney, *Sacred Rhetoric*, 234.

145. Dabney wrote: "Unity is necessary to every work of art—to the oration, the drama, the poem, the painting, the architectural structure, the statue. There is no canon of rhetoric more universally admitted as this, which demands unity in discourse." Dabney, *Sacred Rhetoric*, 108.

146. Dabney, *Sacred Rhetoric*, 108–09.

147. Dabney, *Sacred Rhetoric*, 101.

that which is not the "mind of the Spirit."[148] Such preaching was, for Dabney, an infidelity[149] to the minister's task, while expository sermons, rightly prepared and proclaimed, mirrored the unity of the Scripture itself.

Expository Preaching Limits the Preacher

Some nineteenth-century homileticians felt that expository sermons restricted the freedom of the preacher in range of subjects and in the preacher's ability to shape messages rhetorically.[150] Decrying this sentiment, Dabney asked: "What is the true nature of that spirit in the minister which thinks it necessary to take a more ample range in preaching than simply showing the people what the Bible means?"[151] He answered:

> Now what else is all this but unbelief? Or else unbelief combined with ignorance of those treasures of heavenly wisdom which the word of God contains. God puts his sword in the minister's hands, and tells him that with this he shall conquer. He distrusts it, and endeavors to add something more trenchant. God tells him, "take this die and press it on the human soul; the result shall be the lovely image of God." He insists on re-carving it before he will apply it. God says, in his infinite wisdom, "these are the truths which are quick and powerful, and sharper than any two-edged sword, piercing even to the dividing asunder of soul and spirit, and the joints and marrow, and which are discerners of the thoughts and intents of the heart." "No," says the unbelieving servant, "they are dull; I can devise truths more piercing." This is the spirit of infidelity, and such preaching breeds infidelity.[152]

Dabney thus felt that when a preacher valued anything more highly than Scripture, whether the canons of rhetoric or the personal freedom of the

148. Dabney, *Sacred Rhetoric*, 101.

149. Dabney, *Sacred Rhetoric*, 38–40.

150. John Broadus noted that "some able and devout preachers, disliking expository and even textual preaching, and wishing that every sermon should be a philosophical discussion or an elaborate discourse upon a definite topic, incline to regard the custom of always taking a text as an inconvenient restriction." Broadus, *Preparation and Delivery*, 41. Broadus was not describing the attitude of faithless ministers, but instead explained that some "devout" preachers considered the text a restriction. This tends to reinforce the observation that nineteenth-century homileticians sought to proclaim biblical truth, but often failed to connect that truth to the Scripture from which it proceeded.

151. Dabney, "Gospel," 598.

152. Dabney, "Gospel," 598–99.

pastor to shape the message, preaching suffered. Topical sermons tended, in the name of rhetorical unity, to shear biblical truths from their contexts, and while congregants learned the truths of the Bible, they did not learn the Bible itself. Dabney saw that by rending text from context many preachers had "dissected, or sublimated, or evaporated, truths which they should have embodied in the warm proportions of life, as though they would try to feed the sheep with an analysis of grass instead of the grass itself."[153] He concluded: "If the business of the preacher is simply to make the people see and feel what is in the word of God, preaching should usually be what is popularly known as 'expository.'"[154]

Dabney understood, moreover, that to preach expository sermons was to preach through books of the Bible. Over time, such preaching put a congregation in contact with the "whole counsel of God"[155] in a way that a steady diet of topical sermons could not. He advised:

> In most cases, it is no fair exposition of the divine meaning to single out a single proposition from its connection, and fix the whole attention on it, to the exclusion of those truths which God has placed beside it. The Scriptures are a whole . . . passages of Scripture must be unfolded in their connection. Yea, whole books and epistles must be so applied to the Christian soul.[156]

Arguing that expository preaching constituted no real restriction of preachers, save for restricting them to proclaiming the Scriptures in their context, Dabney contended that expository messages were more suited to offer the congregation the full counsel of God than were topical sermons.

Conclusion

Summary

Robert Dabney believed that his *Sacred Rhetoric* offered "a theory of preaching . . . that honors God's inspired word" such that "nothing is preaching which is not expository of the Scriptures."[157] This chapter has examined that self-assessment, demonstrating that Dabney's *Sacred Rhetoric* crafted a robust expository theory by grounding expository preaching in the example

153. Dabney, "Gospel," 600.

154. Dabney, "Gospel," 600.

155. Acts 20:28.

156. Dabney, "Gospel," 600–601.

157. Dabney, *Sacred Rhetoric*, 7.

of Nehemiah 8, commending the ancient and Reformation practice, chronicling its benefits, refuting objections against it, and castigating as unfaithful all ministers who rejected it in favor of a steady diet of rhetorically polished topical messages. Dabney offered a distinct structure for expository sermons, in which the Argument is comprised of an extended exposition that unfolds according to the versification of the text. Nevertheless, by means of his caveat regarding capital and epitome texts, Dabney offered himself and his students the freedom to preach topical sermons based upon isolated fragments of text, which was the prevailing sermon form of his day.

Preview of Chapter 4

Chapter 4 describes and evaluates Dabney's expository pedagogy, that is, the classroom method by which he equipped his students to preach, demonstrating that while Dabney crafted a robust expository theory, his weak expository pedagogy undermined his theory. Dabney's pedagogy failed to equip his students to preach the expository sermons he admired, instead predominately equipping them with the topical sermon structure that was common to his day, thereby teaching them to proclaim the very "sermons without context"[158] that his expository theory castigated.

158. Dabney, *Sacred Rhetoric*, 76.

4

Pedagogy

Introduction

Overview

The preceding chapter has demonstrated that Robert Dabney crafted a robust expository theory. Dabney grounded his admiration for continuous expository preaching in the pattern of Nehemiah 8, and argued that expository sermons represent the biblical, ancient church, and Reformation era practices. Despite his caveat regarding capital and epitome texts,[1] which offered Dabney and his students the freedom to proclaim topical sermons on isolated verses of Scripture, Dabney's expository theory identified a distinct structure for expository sermons and encouraged preachers to unfold books of the Bible according to the versification of the text. In so doing, Dabney denigrated the practice of preaching topical sermons upon clauses of text that was endemic to his day, pejoratively terming such messages "sermons without context."[2]

The Plan of This Chapter

The present chapter describes and evaluates Dabney's expository pedagogy, that is, the classroom method by which he equipped his students to preach.[3]

1. See chapter 3 for Dabney's use of these terms.

2. Dabney, *Sacred Rhetoric*, 76.

3. "The course of Sacred Rhetoric is taught to the MIDDLE CLASS, by weekly lectures, and frequent exercises on the Construction and Expositions of Sermons." *Annual*

After describing Dabney's manuscript collection and explaining the homiletical model Dabney learned as a seminarian, this chapter assesses a category of Dabney's sermon manuscripts that he entitled "Exercises," which Dabney composed as replicable sermon templates for his students, by which he trained them to preach. This assessment demonstrates that Dabney's classroom expository pedagogy was far weaker than his robust expository theory. Rather than equipping his students to preach expository sermons through books of the Bible, Dabney instead predominantly equipped them with the topical model that was common to nineteenth-century American preaching, thereby undermining his robust expository theory.

Dabney's Expository Pedagogy

Dabney's Manuscript Collection

Robert Dabney's extant sermons reside in William Smith Morton Library at Union Presbyterian Theological Seminary in Richmond, Virginia. Every Dabney researcher owes a debt of gratitude to David Coffin, who organized Dabney's sermons into files and created a finding aid that allows the researcher to locate sermons by chronology of first preaching or Scripture text.[4] Lawrence Trotter expanded on Coffin's work, creating an index that allows the researcher to compare sermons based upon the original and subsequent preaching occasions.[5] Dabney's manuscript collection is worth describing at length.

Dabney's sermons took a variety of forms. Many are "Full Text" manuscripts, which Dabney designated numerically, and which he formatted as small, hand-written booklets comprised of twenty or more pages of script.[6] Others, which Dabney entitled "Skeletons," are shorter booklets. Rather than taking the form of a word-for-word manuscript, a Skeleton includes fully written sentences coupled with terse statements, clauses, notes to self, bullet

Catalogue, 11 [emphasis original]. William Sweetser noted that in addition to lectures "students were expected to learn by doing," and seminarians often preached "at the Wednesday night service." Sweetser, *Copious Fountain*, 136.

4. Coffin, "Reflections." See Appendix 1 and Appendix 5. Coffin's finding aid is available at the Union Seminary library.

5. Trotter, "Blasting Rocks". The author owes a debt of gratitude to Lawrence Trotter for the use of his sermon index, which has been an invaluable tool in the present research.

6. Whereas Coffin and Trotter refer to these sermons as "Numbers," this paper terms them "Full Texts." Trotter noted that the numbers are incomplete. Some are missing, and duplicate numbers exist. Designating them by their Full Text format rather than their number offers a measure of clarity to the researcher and reader alike.

points, and other devises, which together produce something more than an outline but less than a Full Text. Other sermons, which Dabney entitled "Briefs,"[7] almost exclusively offer summary statements, bullets, and notes to self.[8] Dabney left other sermons unnumbered and unlabeled altogether.[9] The final sermon variety, the "Exercise," is similar to a Brief, but in an Exercise Dabney clearly designated each structural component of the sermon, such that the structure of the sermon stands visible to the reader.

Trotter noted that Dabney's sermon collection[10] "includes 41 briefs, 62 exercises, 133 'numbers,' 178 skeletons, and 49 with no designation," while also recognizing that "Dabney's labeling system was imperfect, because there are duplicate labels for different sermons. The collection also appears to be incomplete, because there are many missing numerals."[11] Trotter observed,

7. Dabney described a Brief as "the plan of an extempore sermon," in which "all important ideas are briefly stated in their intended order, but not in the language which is to be employed in preaching." Dabney, *Sacred Rhetoric*, 342.

8. Dabney also entitled some manuscripts "Outlines." These are clearly Briefs that carry an alternate designation. This paper follows Coffin, "Reflections," 438n12, and Trotter in treating them as Briefs. Trotter, *Always Prepared*, 136. *Always Prepared* is a revision of Trotter's "Blasting Rocks." It is used by permission of the author.

9. Complicating the designation of and distinction between Dabney's various sermon forms is the fact that Dabney changed the nomenclature "from 'skeletons' to 'briefs' in 1865." Trotter, *Always Prepared*, 137. Trotter suggested that this "conclusion [is] almost certainly confirmed by the fact that the last numbered skeleton is 195, and earliest brief is 196," although "the briefs were less homogenous than the skeletons." Trotter, *Always Prepared*, 140.

10. The Dabney Collection at Union Seminary is comprised of seventeen boxes of material. Each box contains multiple files, and within each file reside multiple documents. References to Dabney's sermons in this paper list the box and file number, followed by the Scripture text and the sermon format—Full Text, Skeleton, Brief, or Exercise. Consider the following example: Box 7, File 7/1, Psalm 139:14 Skeleton. This sermon resides in File 7/1 of Box 7. The text is Psalm 139:14 and Dabney composed the sermon as a Skeleton. Dabney's sermon manuscripts begin in Box 6, File 6/3a and continue through Box 10, File 10/6.

11. Trotter, *Always Prepared*, 136. Trotter's list does not account for several "hidden" sermons, which, though present in Dabney's collection, are absent from Coffin's finding aid. Box 10, File 10/1, Colossians 2:10 Full Text contains an extra Outline on Colossians 2:9–10. Box 6, File 6/4, Exodus 20:12 Full Text contains a single sheet Outline for a sermon on Leviticus 19:32. Box 6, File 6/7, Psalm 66:18 Outline is not listed in the finding aid. Two sermons in the manuscript collection are not in Dabney's hand: Box 9, File 9/4, 1 Corinthians 9:24–27 Expository Exercise and Box 10, File 10/4, 1 Peter 1:16 Full Text. Another sermon is clearly a discarded draft, which Dabney likely never preached: Box 7, File 7/6, Hosea 6:1. This partial Skeleton ends mid-sentence just after the statement of the second head of the Argument, and no date or place of preaching appears on the back of the manuscript. The exact number of manuscripts in Dabney's collection therefore depends upon which of these the individual researcher chooses to include, and how the researcher chooses to classify them.

for instance, that only one hundred ninety-six sermons remain from Dabney's six years as pastor at Tinkling Spring.[12] This is a significant fact. If Dabney had only preached forty weeks per year, one service per week, he would nevertheless have preached two hundred forty sermons while pastor of Tinkling Spring. More likely, however, Dabney preached more than forty weeks per year, conducting morning and evening services each week, as was the Reformed custom. This pattern required that Dabney preach two different sermons each Sunday. Given, then, that Dabney would likely have preached no less than five hundred separate sermons while pastoring Tinkling Spring, the number of extant sermons from his tenure there is small.[13]

Dabney's collection reveals change over time. Trotter observed:

> The first 248 manuscripts are all "numbers" and skeletons, and they cover the first twelve years of Dabney's preaching ministry, from August of 1845 to June of 1857. That period covered one of his years as a seminarian, his year as missionary to Louisa County, his six years at Tinkling Spring, and his first four years as professor at Union Seminary.[14]

This pattern held until Dabney began to teach homiletics at Union. Trotter wrote: "Beginning in July of 1857, there is an abrupt shift with the first appearance of the first exercise," and "[a]fter that date, most of the manuscripts were either skeletons or exercises, and the 'numbers' were few."[15] It appears also that as Dabney grew in experience, he took less into the pulpit,[16] and wrote out sermons in full only for special occasions.

Helpful to the researcher is the fact that Dabney recorded the original and each successive preaching occasion on the back of each sermon manuscript. Following Coffin, Trotter related that no sermon manuscripts exist from Dabney's years in Texas, and that none of Dabney's extant sermons contain preaching dates from his time there.[17] Trotter offered:

12. Trotter, *Always Prepared*, 143. See Coffin, "Reflections," Appendix 1.

13. In his farewell sermon to the congregation at Tinkling Spring, Dabney claimed: "In this congregation I have preached 375 times," which may indicate that Dabney was frequently absent from the pulpit or that he underestimated the number of sermons he had preached there. The number Dabney claimed seems small, but even if Dabney is correct, then the 196 extant Tinkling Spring sermons represent just 53% of those that he claimed to have preached. See Box 7, File 7/5, Jeremiah 3:15 Full Text.

14. Trotter, *Always Prepared*, 140.

15. Trotter, *Always Prepared*, 140.

16. "Dabney tended to shorten the length of his sermon manuscripts as he matured." Trotter, *Always Prepared*, 140. See also Lucas, *Robert Lewis Dabney*, 51.

17. Coffin stated: "The collection represents RLD's preaching from May 1845 . . . until May of 1883, when his move to the University of Texas apparently provided the

"The simplest explanation for these omissions is that he did not take his sermon manuscripts with him to Texas, and that any sermons he wrote while in Texas have been lost."[18] Even without Dabney's Texas sermons, his manuscript collection records some fifteen hundred separate preaching occasions, and "Dabney preached 35 sermons more than 10 times each, accounting for 554 occasions," and thus "8% of the sermon manuscripts account for 35% of the preachments."[19] While incomplete, Dabney's extant sermon collection is more than adequate to establish the outlines of his expository pedagogy, and to provide the researcher with a clear picture of the manner in which Dabney sought to equip his students to preach the expository sermons his theory admired.

Dabney as Seminarian

Samuel Wilson taught preaching at Union Seminary while Dabney was a student,[20] and Dabney's student preaching demonstrates that he learned to employ a topical sermon form, based upon isolated texts of Scripture, in order to craft sermons utilizing the structural components of Introduction, Exposition, Proposition, Argument, and Conclusion. One of Dabney's earliest extant sermons, which he read to staff and students at Union Seminary in March of 1845 on Psalm 119:18, demonstrates this pattern.[21]

The Psalmist prayed: "Open my eyes, that I may behold wondrous things out of your law." Dabney composed his sermon as a Full Text, and as was his habit when writing his sermons in full, he did not label the

occasion to donate his papers to the library." Coffin, "Reflections," 438. Nevertheless, Dabney's collection contains at least one sermon that records a preaching occasion in Texas: Box 6, File 6/5, Deuteronomy 32:13–15 Skeleton. The last recorded preaching states: "Baptist Church, Austin, November 27, 1884."

18. Trotter, *Always Prepared*, 143.

19. Trotter, *Always Prepared*, 142. Dabney traveled as a home missionary before pastoring Tinkling Spring, and again during his early years at Union Seminary in a fundraising capacity. He marched with the Confederate Army on various occasions during the Civil War, and often spent summers away from Hampden-Sydney. His manuscripts therefore record a wide variety of places at which Dabney preached. These included private homes and open fields as well as proper church buildings.

20. Moore and Scherer, *Centennial*, 34. See also Trotter, *Always Prepared*, 198.

21. Box 7, File 7/1, Psalm 119:18 Full Text. Dabney recorded on the manuscript that he *read* this sermon while at Union and *preached* it thereafter, which may indicate the pattern of instruction at Union Seminary, or may indicate Dabney's dissatisfaction with the result of reading a sermon. In his personal practice and in his instruction as a professor, Dabney advocated well-prepared, extemporaneous discourse. He wrote: "Reading a manuscript to the people can never, with any justice, be termed preaching." Dabney, *Sacred Rhetoric*, 328.

structural components. The structure does not, however, lie far below the surface. Dabney's Introduction functioned as Exposition as Dabney noted that the Psalmist prayed for "mental illumination." After discoursing on this truth at length, Dabney exhorted his hearers: "You must be convinced like [the Psalmist] that your eyes are really closed." Dabney's unstated Proposition purported to prove "in what this spiritual blindness consists," and his subsequent Argument unfolded under two heads: 1. It does not consist of natural lack of mental ability to comprehend, but 2. It is due instead to sinful, dull hearts. After proving these heads, Dabney's Conclusion encouraged his listeners to pray just as the Psalmist himself had prayed.

The first sermon that Dabney preached to a local congregation followed the same pattern.[22] Delivered in July of 1845 on a clause of John 6:44, in which Jesus taught, "No one can come to me unless the Father who sent me draws him," Dabney's sermon featured an Introduction that led to Exposition comprised of clarification of terms and the analogy of Scripture. His Proposition defended the necessity of coming to God through Christ alone, which his Argument sustained at length. His Conclusion suggested that the proper way to seek the salvation of others was to bring them to Christ in the Scripture with prayer for the Holy Spirit to work.

The same pattern marked a sermon on 1 Timothy 6:12, which Dabney preached in January of 1846 in the seminary chapel.[23] The Scripture admonishes: "Fight the good fight of the faith. Take hold of the eternal life to which you were called and about which you made the good confession in the presence of many witnesses." Dabney's Introduction again functioned as Exposition, in which Dabney reviewed the literary and historical context of the text. His Proposition engaged the question: What does it mean to fight the good fight? and his Argument unfolded under four heads: 1. "The Christian life resembles a contest," in which the Christian fights against the

22. Box 8, File 8/5, John 6:44 Full Text. Dabney recorded his feelings about his first experience preaching in a letter to his mother dated July 8, 1845: "The congregation was small, pretty select and pretty critical, the very worst sort of a place to preach in you ever saw; and, besides, they only regard the preaching of the seminarians as a sort of imitation of the reality, and look on with no other feeling than curiosity to see how complete the mimicry will be. I kept the attention of my congregation pretty well; only two leant on their elbows for a few minutes, which I think was very well for so hot, sleepy a day. I found preaching tired me, both body and voice, much more than I expected. The bodily labor is not any great thing, but the strain of mind is so great that when the excitement passes away the preacher feels like a drunken man sobering . . . I am convinced by my first trial that I can never read sermons to my people in any comfort. *Extempore* preaching is the thing for me . . . It is much more important that sinners should be excited to listen to the truth than that I should have the reputation of a pretty writer." Cited in Johnson, *Life and Letters*, 87 [emphasis original].

23. Box 10, File 10/2, 1 Timothy 6:12 Full Text.

opposition of men and the Devil. 2. Dabney asked his congregation if they were fighting. 3. He admonished them to put on the armor of God, and asked 4. How must the battle be fought?[24] His Conclusion offered exhortations to the congregation to fight the good fight.

These early sermons demonstrate a clear pattern: Dabney's own seminary training inculcated in him the ubiquitous homiletical model of his day, which consisted of a topical sermon, usually proclaimed from a single verse or clause of Scripture, developed according to five immutable structural components: Introduction, Exposition, Proposition, Argument, and Conclusion. Whether Dabney labeled these components or clothed them under the body of the message, they appear regularly from Dabney's earliest extant sermons.

Dabney as Instructor of Sacred Rhetoric

Dabney assumed responsibility for teaching homiletics at Union Seminary during the 1855–56 school year.[25] Trotter observed that Dabney "used his exercises for instructional purposes," for they provided "an easily transferrable and visibly simple format to show his students how to construct a sermon."[26] Thus "[t]he instructional purposes of his exercises also explain why they suddenly appear in July of 1857, one year after he began teaching homiletics at Union."[27] Trotter helpfully noted that Dabney's Exercises[28] are dated between July 1857 and March 1883, which closely parallels the span of time during which Dabney taught homiletics.[29] Dabney appears to have created his Exercises specifically to provide a replicable template

24. At some later date Dabney noted on his manuscript: "Should be the second head of the discourse." Dabney sometimes rewrote or renumbered portions of sermons, making changes before preaching them again. A large section of the present sermon Dabney later crossed out.

25. In 1854, one year after arriving at Union Seminary, Dabney began to support Samuel Wilson as Wilson's health declined. Initially helping Wilson only with his theology classes, in 1855 Dabney assumed responsibility for homiletics as well. *Centennial Catalogue*, 34, and Trotter, *Always Prepared*, 199.

26. Trotter, *Always Prepared*, 202.

27. Trotter, *Always Prepared*, 202–03.

28. One Exercise is not in Dabney's hand. At least one sermon is probably an Exercise without being labeled such. For the sake of consistency, this chapter employs the sixty-one Exercises that Dabney labeled Exercises, which are written in his hand.

29. Trotter, *Always Prepared*, 137.

for his students, from which they learned to preach.[30] As Trotter described these Exercises, he wrote:

> [Dabney's] exercises are sermon outlines with clearly designated parts, usually including introduction, exposition, proposition, discussion (or argument), and conclusion. All the parts are simple, except for the discussion section in which Dabney outlined his points and sub-points and included many related Scripture references. The exercises use some complete sentences, some short phrases, and Dabney's cryptic instructions to himself.[31]

Important to the current discussion is Trotter's passing observation, which this chapter substantiates and quantifies, that Dabney's Exercises almost uniformly carried forward a topical sermon form, featuring the five structural components that Dabney had learned during his own seminary education.

The Exercises

Introduction to Dabney's Exercises

Dabney produced several unlabeled Exercises. These represent his standard topical sermon format. Nevertheless, Dabney labeled the majority of his Exercises with various descriptors: Doctrinal, Didactic, Practical, Narrative, other hybrid forms, and germane to the present chapter, Expository.[32] Twenty-eight out of the sixty-one Exercises in Dabney's manuscript collection feature at least one sermon of another format—a Full Text, Skeleton, or Brief—which was composed on the identical or nearly identical verse(s) as a given Exercise. These non-Exercise companion sermons offer the researcher a window into the manner in which Dabney fleshed out the bare structure an Exercise exposed. Conversely, an Exercise reveals visibly the structural components of a fleshed out sermon. Dabney preached several of his Exercises in a lecture room of the seminary, in the chapel, or at College Church. These represented locations in which his students learned by Dabney's example how to reduce a Full Text to an Exercise or to expand

30. Box 11, File 11/6 is labeled "Class Notes by R. L. Dabney's Students." Trotter observed that these notes contain several "verbatim copies of Dabney's exercises," which his students created as they learned to preach. Trotter, *Always Prepared*, 201.

31. Trotter, *Always Prepared*, 138.

32. Dabney also designated funeral, baccalaureate, fast and prayer, education, missionary, and presbytery sermons, as well as several sermons that were specifically composed for antebellum slave audiences. Rather than indicating alternate varieties of sermon, these designations describe differing occasions for preaching.

an Exercise into a fully fleshed out sermon. These companion sermons therefore offer a clear picture of the type of preaching Dabney inculcated in his students by means of his Exercises.

Of the twenty-eight Exercises that feature one or multiple companion sermons, the composition of the Exercise postdates the composition of the companion sermon in all but four instances. Three Exercises reverse this order: Dabney composed the Exercise first and a companion sermon later fleshed out the Exercise. One Exercise offers no date by which to make a comparison.[33] In the vast majority of cases, Dabney's Exercises reduced previously written Full Text or Skeleton sermons to an Exercise, thereby making the structural components of the sermon visible to his students.

While the overwhelming majority of Dabney's non-Exercise sermons are not labeled—they bear no indication of being Doctrinal, Didactic, Practical, Expository, etc.—the majority (fifty-one of sixty-one) of his Exercises bear such labels. Though the companion sermons from which he most often produced his Exercises carry no label, the Exercises he produced from them do. This indicates that Dabney may have had in mind a stated purpose or an implied designator for many of his Full Texts, Skeletons, and Briefs that he did not specify on the manuscript itself.

The analysis of Dabney's Exercises that follows demonstrates that rather than describing a different sermon structure, Dabney's labels describe different purposes toward which he pressed the same sermonic form.[34] A Doctrinal sermon did not differ in structure from a Practical sermon. It differed only in the purpose Dabney intended that sermon to accomplish in his hearers.

Plan of Evaluation

In order accurately to evaluate Dabney's expository classroom pedagogy through his Expository Exercises, this paper first describes the features of a standard, unlabeled Dabney Exercise, evaluating it over against his variously labeled Exercises, ultimately comparing and contrasting these with his Expository Exercises. This comparison demonstrates that while Dabney crafted a robust expository theory, his classroom pedagogy did

33. Two Exercises boast two companion sermons each. In both cases, one of the companion sermons chronologically precedes and one chronologically follows the composition of the Exercise.

34. Dabney's Expository Exercises, when implementing his expository ideal, do manifest a different structure than his unlabeled and otherwise labeled Exercises. This structure, and its place in Dabney's pedagogy, is explored more fully later in this chapter.

little practically to equip his students to proclaim the expository sermons that his theory admired. Instead, he predominantly equipped them with the same topical sermon form that he himself had learned, and which was common to his day.

Unlabeled Exercises

Dabney's sermon collection includes nine unlabeled Exercises, which demonstrate the standard sermon template with which he equipped his students. Each of these sermons manifests the five structural components that comprised most nineteenth-century American preaching: Introduction, Exposition, Proposition, Argument, and Conclusion, clearly designated for the student to see. Two Exercises omit the designation Argument,[35] but still include that portion of the sermon under clearly enumerated heads. Another omits the designation Conclusion,[36] but still concludes. The presence of these designators offered Dabney's students a visible, repeatable structure, and he therefore rarely omitted them from his Exercises.

A closer look at one unlabeled Exercise, based on 2 Corinthians 13:5,[37] preached in 1860 at Hampden-Sydney College and again in the seminary Lecture Room in 1881, suffices to demonstrate the standard template with which Dabney equipped his students. This particular Exercise is instructive because Dabney preached a Full Text on the same verse in 1851,[38] and his 1860 Exercise is a reduced form of the longer text. Whereas the Full Text unfolded both what to do and how to accomplish it, the Exercise unfolded only the former. In an 1863 Skeleton that addressed the latter Dabney wrote that the "same text was used by me to enforce [the] precept, i.e. 'Do it.' Showing importance. Sermon of today [is a] practical sequel, showing '*How to do it.*'"[39] In other words, his 1851 sermon was too long. Dabney therefore divided the two heads of Argument from that sermon into two different sermons, creating the 1860 Exercise out of the first head, while the 1863 Skeleton expounded the second head. The Full Text helps to reveal how Dabney fleshed out the structural components that appear in his later Exercise.

35. Box 8, File 8/1, Matthew 5:43–44 Exercise, and Box 9, File 9/4, 1 Corinthians 16:2 Exercise.

36. Box 8, File 8/1, Matthew 10:29–30 Exercise.

37. Box 9, File 9/5, 2 Corinthians 13:5 Exercise.

38. Box 9, File 9/5, 2 Corinthians 13:5 Full Text.

39. Box 9, File 9/5, 2 Corinthians 13:5 Skeleton. All emphasized words and phrases from Dabney's sermons are original to Dabney unless otherwise noted.

While the paragraph from 2 Corinthians 13 from which Dabney's text originates includes verses five through nine, Dabney preached verse five only. The Scripture commands: "Examine yourselves, to see whether you are in the faith. Test yourselves. Or do you not realize this about yourselves, that Jesus Christ is in you?—unless indeed you fail to meet the test!" In reality, Dabney's sermon addressed only the first half of verse five, and he focused on the command, "Examine yourselves, to see whether you are in the faith."

By way of Introduction, Dabney referenced the admonition of the pagan philosophers, who insisted: "Know thyself." He suggested that a distinctively Christian self-evaluation stands as a Christian duty. Dabney's Exposition offered context for his text, teaching that Paul was responding to claims against his apostolic *bona fides*. Paul's command to the Corinthians to test themselves purposed to verify their own salvation, which would at the same time prove the veracity of Paul's teaching and his genuine apostleship. Dabney then suggested: "The duty urged on special grounds," namely, self-evaluation in order to prove Paul's apostolic credentials, "may legitimately be urged on gen[eral] grounds." By means of this segue, Dabney moved from the original audience to his contemporary hearers, arguing that his Proposition would "enforce the duty of self-examination, whether we are true Christians."

In his 1851 Full Text, the first head of Argument unfolded under six points, which Dabney reduced to five and re-ordered in his 1860 Exercise. In the latter version, Dabney presented the following motives for self-examination: 1. Without self-knowledge, we cannot know our duty. 2. Without self-knowledge, we cannot grow in grace, and other Christian graces are hampered. 3. Self-examination is necessary because our hearts are liable to deceive us, and the difficulty of searching our hearts is significant. 4. The importance of self-examination is seen in the punishments of those who are mistaken about their standing before God. 5. Self-examination adds to Christian enjoyment. The Conclusion to Dabney's Exercise lifted up Christ in his sufferings as an exemplar of self-examination, whereas his 1851 Full Text lacked this example. Mirroring the Full Text, however, Dabney exhorted his hearers to conduct their self-examination according to the Scripture and with continual prayer for the guidance and aid of the Holy Spirit.

This topical sermon form, utilizing five structural components, based upon a small segment of Scripture, undergirds each of Dabney's nine unlabeled Exercises. This form represents the classroom pedagogy Dabney had received, and which he primarily passed on to his students. Seven of the nine unlabeled Exercises employ a single verse or clause of Scripture.

The other two employ two verses. None cover what might be considered a proper preaching unit.

Doctrinal Exercises

Dabney's sermon collection features seventeen Doctrinal Exercises. A careful examination of these Exercises demonstrates that these sermons did not differ in structure from Dabney's standard sermon template. They contained the same five structural components, and differed only in the purpose Dabney hoped to accomplish through them. In the case of his Doctrinal Exercises, Dabney purposed them to inculcate in his hearers a particular belief. In such sermons, Dabney offered no practical exhortations or duties. Belief in the truth that Dabney preached comprised the only application.[40]

Dabney achieved this end imperfectly. Several of his Doctrinal Exercises manifest very little difference from his standard, unlabeled Exercises. Consider Dabney's Doctrinal Exercise on John 15:5,[41] in which Jesus says: "I am the vine; you are the branches. Whoever abides in me and I in him, he it is that bears much fruit, for apart from me you can do nothing." After a brief Introduction and Exposition, Dabney's Proposition purported to prove that the only good works that are truly good are those accomplished in and by union with Christ. His Argument unfolded under three heads and culminated in a Conclusion, in which Dabney exhorted sinners to "fall on a Saviour's arms," while urging Christians toward gratitude, a life lived near the throne of grace, and the exercise of care in not grieving the Holy Spirit. These directions to believers comprise practical applications, and do not appear in the Skeleton Dabney preached on this same text thirteen years earlier.[42] His Skeleton was more strictly doctrinal, explaining his theology of union with Christ by faith. His Exercise, though labeled Doctrinal, was more or less indistinguishable from a standard, unlabeled sermon.

Similarly, Dabney's Doctrinal Exercise on Acts 4:12[43] was not strictly Doctrinal, but concluded instead with true applications from the text. His Full Text[44] sermon on this verse, preached fourteen years prior to the

40. Dabney stated: "Doctrinal preaching is that which aims to instruct the people methodically in the truths of the Gospel," and its "object is neither the pleasure of taste nor the immediate movement of the will, but the exact ascertainment of truth by the understanding." Dabney, *Sacred Rhetoric*, 51.

41. Box 8, File 8/6, John 15:5 Doctrinal Exercise.

42. Box 8, File 8/6, John 15:5 Skeleton.

43. Box 9, File 9/3, Acts 4:12 Doctrinal Exercise.

44. Box 9, File 9/1, Acts 4:12 Full Text.

composition of the Exercise, made this clear. Peter declared: "And there is salvation in no one else, for there is no other name under heaven given among men by which we must be saved." After a brief Introduction with limited Exposition, Dabney's Proposition asserted that there is no salvation outside of Christ. An Argument under three heads followed, which culminated with Dabney meeting various objections to the exclusivity of the gospel. He ultimately purposed to show that no salvation exists outside of Christ, which he demonstrated ably, but his sermon was not content to inculcate that truth. Dabney's Conclusion suggested that the world's heathen gather at the foot of cross, waiting for the world's Christians to tell them about Christ. His application was thus implied rather than stated explicitly, but it stood nonetheless: Christians are duty bound to proclaim Christ, lest the lost of the world remain lost.

Other Doctrinal Exercises achieved Dabney's purpose beautifully, strictly confining the sermon to the inculcation of a particular doctrine. Believing the doctrine comprised the only application.[45] Consider Dabney's Doctrinal Exercise on Romans 3:31,[46] which reads: "Do we then overthrow the law by this faith? By no means! On the contrary, we uphold the law." Dabney's 1859 Doctrinal Exercise reduced a Full Text that he preached in 1846, just after he graduated from seminary.[47] His Introduction asserted that a person is justified apart from works of the law, after which Dabney met the cavil that salvation by grace produces licentiousness in those who embrace it. Dabney recognized that if this cavil were true, then God stood guilty of authoring a theological system that produced godlessness and impiety. Dabney noted: "The text shows that this objection was as old as the days of Paul."

Elucidating the assumption behind this cavil, namely, that "if works of the law do not justify the doer, then they can have *no use* whatever in religion," Dabney retorted that the free grace of justification, so far from stultifying the desire for good works, offered "far stronger and far nobler [motives] than the selfish purpose of the legalist, who only aims to buy the happiness of God, by his good deeds." Those who offered this cavil proved

45. See Box 8, File 8/3, Luke 7:42 Doctrinal Exercise; Box 9, File 9/4, John 1:1 Doctrinal Exercise; Box 9, File 9/3, Romans 6:23 Doctrinal Exercise; Box 9, File 9/1, Philippians 1:6 Doctrinal Exercise. Dabney's Doctrinal Exercise in Box 7, File 7/6 from Malachi 3:6 is both masterful and disconcerting. Taking only the first clause of a single verse out of context, the sermon stands as a disturbing example of "motto" preaching, but it also offers a masterful explanation of the doctrine of immutability. More fittingly belonging in a classroom than a pulpit, it nevertheless testifies to Dabney's gifts as a teacher of theology.

46. Box 9, File 9/2, Romans 3:31 Doctrinal Exercise.

47. Box 9, File 9/2, Romans 3:31 Full Text.

by it that base self-interest, rather than love for God, motivated their actions. Dabney suggested that God instead seeks good works that flow first "from a sincere, spontaneous regard for his will, and approval of his law, and only secondarily from regard to self." So far from quenching this type of good works, the doctrine of justification by free grace "tends preeminently to produce them."

Moving into his Exposition, Dabney repeated the text, grounding it in the verses that preceded it. He summarized the passage, writing: "The system of justification by faith, so far from tending to the neglect of moral duties, *secures their performance still more effectually*." Dabney noted that Paul addressed substantively the same question in Romans 7, and that he specifically avoided teaching that good works produce justification, instead teaching that justification produces good works. Dabney's Proposition therefore argued: "The doctrine of justification by faith, without the deeds of the law, so far from tending to a neglect of holiness, tends *more effectually* than any other mode of justification, to *produce* it."

In proving this Proposition, Dabney began his Argument by asserting that "our gracious justification through faith is always attended with a crucifixion to sin, and a resurrection to holiness," and thus: "The Scripture doctrine is, that God justifies man freely, without good works; but it is also a part of the doctrine, that he thus justifies him *in order that* he may give him the ability to do good works." Dabney then quoted Ephesians 2:8–10, with an emphasis on verse ten, followed by a quote of Romans 6:6, in which Paul asserted: "We know that our old self was crucified with him in order that the body of sin might be brought to nothing, so that we would no longer be enslaved to sin." Arguing that mortification of sin necessarily flows from salvation, Dabney insisted that "God could not devise a scheme of salvation which should leave the saved sinner in his sin," for any such system would "exhibit the exercise of his benevolence [in saving a person] at the expense of his holiness [in leaving that person in rebellious sin]." Dabney summarized, writing: "It follows therefore, that the great object of the sinner's salvation, is, not so much to save him from the pains of the punishment, as to deliver him from the power of the sin—to form him anew to holiness." He therefore asked: "How can this justification encourage him to the neglect of good works? It is preposterous!"

Seeking to demonstrate that good works form the "*only* sufficient evidence of justification," Dabney buttressed his argument with quotes from John 15, James 2, and 2 Corinthians 5. Declaring that good works are thus "essential to [the justified Christian's] peace of conscience," just as the motive for pursuit of good works must proceed from the gospel, Dabney claimed: "While [justification] is a free gift, it is also given as a reward, and the degree of its glory is measured by the abundance of the good deeds, and the degree of the holiness of each saint." He likewise moved to instill in the unbeliever a dread of sin by revealing its awful cost for Christ, writing: "When the Christian receives the doctrine of justification without works, on account of the imputed righteousness of Christ, he gains a stronger view of the evil of sin," and thus also "of the absolute importance of a holy life." Dabney therefore recognized that the doctrine of justification via free grace "is peculiarly suited to produce holiness of life, because it is peculiarly fitted to beget love and gratitude towards God," for "it binds the soul to God by the strongest possible ties of love and gratitude." No good work recompenses God for salvation, but Dabney asserted that good works must testify to the believer's gratitude, stating: "The believer knows, indeed, that he cannot *repay* God for his goodness; but he can testify his gratitude and devotion."

In his Conclusion, Dabney quoted 2 Timothy 2:19, which declares: "God's firm foundation stands, bearing this seal: 'The Lord knows those who are his,' and, 'Let everyone who names the name of the Lord depart from iniquity.'" Dabney offered the lost the following warning: "Until you believe and are justified, you will find your purposes of reformation all vain. It is only *by* believing that you can become capable of holiness."

Dabney offered almost nothing by way of practical application in this Doctrinal Exercise. He did not exhort his hearers to do anything, for he intended by this Doctrinal message to convince his hearers to believe properly the doctrine of justification apart from works, and to understand the true place of the latter in reference to the former. Dabney's Doctrinal Exercises, when meeting their ideal, purposed to inculcate in his hearers a particular truth, which he enjoined them to believe. Belief comprised the only application. When Dabney felt that that he had sufficiently explained and established the truth in view and had removed all objections to it the sermon ended.

Didactic Exercises

Dabney labeled only two of his Exercises Didactic, which offers the researcher a small sample from which to deduce a pattern.[48] A pattern nevertheless emerges. In the broader sense, all of Dabney's preaching was didactic. The teaching element in his sermons stood preeminent, and his preaching never failed to instruct. Trotter noted that along with his extemporaneous

48. While *Sacred Rhetoric* discusses the respective categories of Doctrinal, Practical, and Narrative sermons, Dabney's lectures do not address Didactic sermons as a separate category, even though Dabney had composed both of his Didactic Exercises prior to the publication of *Sacred Rhetoric*.

methodology, didacticism marked Dabney's preaching,[49] while Thomas Cary Johnson observed that over the course of Dabney's ministry his preaching "was perhaps more severely didactic" with each passing year, especially after the Civil War.[50] Dabney's Didactic Exercises, however, represent more than just broadly instructive preaching. Dabney used his Didactic Exercises to teach Christians and non-Christians alike how to understand the actions, inactions, and providences of God. Constructed as theodicies, Dabney's Didactic Exercises defended the integrity of God's actions or inactions against misunderstandings and cavils.[51]

Consider Habakkuk 1:13, which asks: "You who are of purer eyes than to see evil and cannot look at wrong, why do you idly look at traitors and remain silent when the wicked swallows up the man more righteous than he?" Dabney's 1861 Exercise[52] boasts a companion Outline[53] that bears no date. Both manifest clearly designated structural components and unfold in similar fashion. By way of Introduction, Dabney referenced the "disorder" of Habakkuk 1:14, and the "distress" of Psalm 73:13–14, in which the wicked prosper while the righteous are stricken. With the question of God's providential wisdom hanging in the balance, Dabney's Exposition walked the hearer through verses 6–11. Dabney suggested that the question of verse 12, "Are you not from everlasting, O Lord my God, my Holy One?" questioned not only God's holiness, but also his providence. Stating his Proposition, Dabney determined to explain the "*[r]eason why a holy and almighty God permits wickedness*."

His Argument unfolded under three heads, which were grounded in Dabney's assertion that God's holiness "cannot be impugned." Although no person can explain precisely how God uses evil to do good, Dabney asserted that God nevertheless does just that. Arguing that Christians possess assurance of this truth by faith, Dabney suggested that so far as we can see what God is doing, "we note:" 1. God tolerates sin now as a mercy to his elect. 2. God tolerates sin in order to sanctify his children. 3. God tolerates sin in order to glorify his attributes. Conceding that "a mystery remains,"

49. Trotter, *Always Prepared*, 11.

50. Johnson, *Life and Letters*, 318.

51. Dabney's defense of God from cavils and his desire to prove the rationality of Christian belief represent recurring themes in his ministry, and thus feature in sermons not specifically labeled Didactic. See Box 8, File 8/2, Matthew 25:24–27 Brief, which Dabney entitled, "Insincerity & Wickedness of the Caviler against Christ."

52. Box 7, File 7/6, Habakkuk 1:13 Didactic Exercise.

53. Box 7, File 7/6, Habakkuk 1:13 Outline. Most of Dabney's Outlines represent later compositions, and given that the accompanying Exercise was composed relatively early—in 1861—it is likely that this Outline postdates the Exercise.

but also noting that so far as God has revealed himself, he is good, Dabney moved to his Conclusion, which developed by way of inferences. Writing, "In conclusion, infer," he offered the following points: 1. If there is no afterlife, then God is not just. 2. Sinners are fools. 3. God's people will come through safely in the end.

Dabney's Didactic sermons did not vary structurally from his standard topical form. He employed the same five structural components that are present in his other sermons, but the purpose he sought to accomplish in his listeners differed. While his Doctrinal Exercises sought to inculcate right belief, his Didactic Exercises[54] examined God's providential actions or inactions, and offered theodicies that defended God's integrity against misunderstandings and cavils.

Narrative Exercises

Dabney produced five Narrative Exercises, none of which boasts a companion sermon, and thus the manner in which Dabney fleshed out his Narrative Exercises is uncertain.[55] Structurally, Dabney's Narrative Exercises bear no resemblance to the narrative preaching that stemmed from the New Homiletic[56] movement of the late twentieth century. Only the nomenclature is the same. So far from offering sermons shaped as narratives[57] or containing narrative elements,[58] Dabney's Narrative Exercises employed the same fivefold structure that his unlabeled, Doctrinal, and Didactic Exercises utilized. Properly understood, Dabney's Narrative Exercises crafted biographical sermons, drawn from the life of a biblical character, which offered applications to the contemporary hearer based on that character's life.[59]

54. See also Box 10, File 10/2, 1 Timothy 3:15 Didactic Exercise.

55. Dabney's Box 6, File 6/6, Esther 5:13 Full Text clearly follows his Narrative pattern without carrying the Narrative label, and features practical lessons drawn from the wicked ambition and subsequent demise of Haman.

56. For a critical history and evaluation of the New Homiletic, see Gibson, "Critique," 476–81, and Gibson, "Defining," 19–28.

57. Lowry, *Homiletical Plot*.

58. Craddock, *Without Authority*.

59. Dabney argued that the "peculiarity" of the narrative sermon is that "by employing the parables, biographies, and histories of the Scriptures, it teaches in the concrete," and Dabney recognized that "more than half of the revealed Scriptures is narrative or biography. God, who knows what is in man, has evidently judged this a suitable way to instruct him." Dabney, *Sacred Rhetoric*, 65.

Consider Dabney's Narrative Exercise on Luke 22:54–62,[60] in which he reviewed the history of Peter's threefold denial of Jesus. The Scripture records:

> Then they seized him and led him away, bringing him into the high priest's house, and Peter was following at a distance. And when they had kindled a fire in the middle of the courtyard and sat down together, Peter sat down among them. Then a servant girl, seeing him as he sat in the light and looking closely at him, said, "This man also was with him." But he denied it, saying, "Woman, I do not know him." And a little later someone else saw him and said, "You also are one of them." But Peter said, "Man, I am not." And after an interval of about an hour still another insisted, saying, "Certainly this man also was with him, for he too is a Galilean." But Peter said, "Man, I do not know what you are talking about." And immediately, while he was still speaking, the rooster crowed. And the Lord turned and looked at Peter. And Peter remembered the saying of the Lord, how he had said to him, "Before the rooster crows today, you will deny me three times." And he went out and wept bitterly.

Dabney's brief Introduction led to a section entitled Narration,[61] in which Dabney offered Exposition by way of story-telling, recounting the biblical narrative, thereby establishing the context of the passage. His Proposition purported to deal with "the *nature* and *aggravations* of the sins of a *professor* of Christianity," after which his Argument unfolded under four heads, which established the sinfulness of Peter's sin. When Dabney moved to his Conclusion, he offered three lessons drawn from Peter's example: 1. Imitate Peter's repentance—which is not properly a part of the text Dabney preached, for Peter repented in subsequent verses. 2. Don't judge Peter. 3. Hope in the forgiveness of Christ. Life lessons for contemporary Christians drawn from biblical characters—this captures Dabney's purpose for his Narrative Exercises.

The other Narrative Exercises follow accordingly. Each utilized a five-part structure, clearly designated for his students to see. Numbers 22–24 offered lessons from the life of Balaam, 1 Samuel 24 from the life of David, Daniel 3:8–27 from the lives of Shadrach, Meshach, and Abednego, and

60. Box 8, File 8/2, Luke 22:54–62 Narrative Exercise.

61. As far as this author is able to discern, this is the only time this structural component appears in Dabney's sermon collection. What follows manifests no functional difference from that which Dabney normally designated Exposition, and it appears that his word choice describes a form of exposition-as-storytelling unique to this Narrative sermon.

Matthew 27:3–5 from the life and suicide of Judas.[62] In an apt summary of his conviction regarding the value of Narrative preaching, Dabney wrote that the "Bible biography [is] precious, because [the] picture [is] drawn by an *infallible pen-man*."[63] Dabney thus composed his Narrative Exercises as biographical sermons that offered lessons to the hearer based upon the life of a biblical character.

Practical Exercises

Dabney composed twelve Exercises that he labeled Practical. Six boast companion sermons, which flesh out Dabney's intent. Dabney consistently enforced through his preaching those actions and responsibilities he considered to be Christian duties.[64] More than his standard sermons, however, Dabney's Practical Exercises purposed to impress upon his hearers a particular biblical duty, which he exhorted them to pursue.[65] Nevertheless, Dabney's Practical Exercises differ significantly from one another. Some inculcate a duty, others defend the doctrine that requires a particular duty, and still others replicate a standard, unlabeled Dabney sermon.

As an example of the ideal that Dabney had in mind for his Practical Exercises, consider his sermon on Ecclesiastes 12:1,[66] which teaches: "Remember also your Creator in the days of your youth, before the evil days come and the years draw near of which you will say, 'I have no pleasure in them.'" Dabney's Introduction led to a brief Exposition by way of definition of terms, in which he clarified the topic of the text, namely the duty of young men and women early to pursue piety. Moving to his Proposition, by which Dabney taught that each of us must "*[a]ttend to our duties toward God* in the days of our youth," the Argument unfolded three reasons why the young ought to embrace this duty: 1. Because we will all grow old. 2. Only serving God prepares us for the evils of old age. 3. Remember him now. The last of these is not so much a reason as it is the proper response to the reasons previously stated. Dabney's Conclusion pressed upon his hearers the

62. Box 6, File 6/5, Numbers 22–24 Narrative Exercise; Box 6, File 6/5, 1 Samuel 24 Narrative Exercise; Box 7, File 7/6, Daniel 3:8–27 Narrative Exercise; and Box 8, File 8/2, Matthew 27:3–5 Narrative Exercise.

63. Box 8, File 8/2, Matthew 27:3–5 Narrative Exercise.

64. Dabney insisted: "The end, I repeat, of every oration is *to make men do*." Dabney, *Sacred Rhetoric*, 34 [emphasis original].

65. Dabney explained: "By this term [practical] are intended those discourses which discuss the duties of the Christian life toward God and toward man." Dabney, *Sacred Rhetoric*, 56–57.

66. Box 7, File 7/3, Ecclesiastes 12:1 Practical Exercise.

immediacy of the decision the text requires. His intent was clear: impose the duty of early devotion to the Lord, and exhort the young to pursue fervent piety. This same practical pattern unfolds in Practical Exercises on Jeremiah 29:13 and Matthew 3:8.[67]

In an interesting variant, Dabney also used his Practical Exercises to defend the doctrine that undergirded the duty that a given text required. Consider his sermon on Luke 11:41,[68] in which Jesus taught: "[G]ive as alms those things that are within, and behold, everything is clean for you." After a brief Introduction and Exposition, Dabney moved to his Proposition, writing: "The 'grace of giving' is God's appointed way to sanctify earthly good to us." He proved this Proposition under three heads of Argument, which culminated in a Conclusion that asserted that the misuse of wealth has marked every age of temporal prosperity the church has enjoyed. Dabney argued that the text was God's appointed means to remedy this ill, and that Christians must therefore obey it. While the closing exhortation of the sermon thus enforced the practical duty of almsgiving, the bulk of the sermon explained why God requires almsgiving in the first place. In doing so, Dabney highlighted the perpetual sinful tendency in the human heart that necessitated Jesus's command.

Other Exercises do not appear to be Practical at all. Dabney's Practical Exercise on John 16:9,[69] which is a fragment of text in which Jesus says, ". . . concerning sin, because they do not believe in me," unfolds like a standard, topical sermon. Jesus was speaking about the ministry of the Holy Spirit, whom he taught would convict the world of sin and righteousness and judgment. Working from his chosen fragment, which Dabney may have considered something of a capital text, he offered a brief Introduction and minimal Exposition. His Proposition sought to elucidate the nature of true faith, which his Argument sustained by defining true faith over against false faith. In Conclusion, Dabney made two points: 1. No matter how bad your sins seem to you now, they will seem worse when Christ returns. And 2. "Receive Christ now."

While labeled a Practical Exercise, Dabney did not exhort the hearer toward the performance of a Christian duty. Instead he exhorted unbelievers to exercise faith in Christ, while implicitly exhorting Christians to make certain that their faith was grounded in Jesus. While it was therefore doctrinally sound, Dabney's Exercise proclaimed a doctrine that does not appear to be

67. Box 7, File 7/5, Jeremiah 29:13 Practical Exercise; Box 8, File 8/3, Matthew 3:8 Practical Exercise.

68. Box 8, File 8/3, Luke 11:41 Practical Exercise.

69. Box 8, File 8/6, John 16:9 Practical Exercise.

grounded in this text, and his sermon showed little difference from a standard topical message. It enforced no distinctly practical duty.

The same holds true for Dabney's Practical Exercise on Hebrews 3:13,[70] while an Exercise on Luke 14:28[71] inculcated very nearly the opposite of a practical duty. Arguing that the natural person cannot rightly count the cost of discipleship, Dabney exhorted sinners to cry out to Christ to do for them that which they cannot do for themselves. While the helplessness of a sinner to remedy his or her own sins is indeed a biblical theme, it is difficult to discern from this sermon a practical duty that Dabney sought to inculcate in his hearers.

Dabney's Practical Exercises therefore manifest inconsistency and present a diversity of aims, not all of which serve the precise purpose that the Practical label theoretically indicated. Broadly, Dabney purposed his Practical Exercises to impress upon his hearers a biblical duty, although several of these Exercises embody that purpose inconsistently or not at all.

Hybrid Exercises

Dabney composed three Exercises that this paper has categorized as "Hybrid." Dabney's own labels are as follows: A "Practico-Doctrinal" sermon on Psalm 145:16, a "Doctrinal and Practical" sermon on Romans 8:7, and a "Practical-Expository" sermon on 2 Corinthians 6:14—7:1.[72] The first two closely resemble purely Doctrinal Exercises, and it is unclear why Dabney labeled them Practical as well. Each followed Dabney's standard, five-part structure, and each unfolded like a Doctrinal Exercise. The third unfolded much like a standard, unlabeled Exercise.

Dabney's Practico-Doctrinal Exercise on Psalm 145:16,[73] in which the Psalmist declared: "You open your hand; you satisfy the desire of every living thing," closely resembles a Doctrinal message. The Introduction, Exposition, and Proposition hold according to pattern, and after the Argument, Dabney offered the following applications: 1. God's benevolence is splendid. 2. It softens and alarms sinners. 3. God opens his heart to Christ. None of these is, however, a true application. These are indicative statements, not

70. Box 10, File 10/3, Hebrews 3:13 Practical Exercise.

71. Box 8, File 8/4, Luke 14:28 Practical Exercise. Dabney produced two Practical Exercises on Luke 14:28. The other is found in Box 6, File 6/6.

72. Box 8, File 8/5, Psalm 145:16 Practico-Doctrinal Exercise; Box 10, File 10/2, Romans 8:7 Doctrinal and Practical Exercise; Box 9, File 9/5, 2 Corinthians 6:14—7:1 Practical-Expository Exercise.

73. Box 8, File 8/5, Psalm 145:16 Practico-Doctrinal Exercise.

imperative injunctions, and Dabney enforced them as truths not duties. Believing comprised the only application, which reflected Dabney's intent for his purely Doctrinal messages.

Dabney's Doctrinal and Practical Exercise on Romans 8:7[74] followed a similarly Doctrinal vein. The Scripture teaches: "[T]he mind that is set on the flesh is hostile to God, for it does not submit to God's law; indeed, it cannot." Dabney composed a Skeleton on this verse in 1850,[75] and another Exercise in 1875,[76] the latter of which represented a purely Doctrinal Exercise. Both the Skeleton and the Doctrinal Exercise purposed to inculcate the truth that apart from supernatural intervention no person loves God. Dabney's Doctrinal and Practical Exercise followed this purpose, and he made little attempt to enforce a practical Christian duty. Dabney nevertheless labeled this Exercise Doctrinal *and* Practical. Unless further manuscript evidence arises, it is difficult to discern exactly what Dabney purposed when labeling these Exercises Doctrinal/Practical hybrids. Both represent more purely Doctrinal sermons than not.

Dabney's Practical-Expository Exercise on 2 Corinthians 6:14—7:1[77] offers yet another puzzle. His chosen text teaches:

> Do not be unequally yoked with unbelievers. For what partnership has righteousness with lawlessness? Or what fellowship has light with darkness? What accord has Christ with Belial? Or what portion does a believer share with an unbeliever? What agreement has the temple of God with idols? For we are the temple of the living God; as God said,
>
> "I will make my dwelling among them and walk among them,
> and I will be their God,
> and they shall be my people.
> Therefore go out from their midst,
> and be separate from them, says the Lord,
> and touch no unclean thing;
> then I will welcome you,
> and I will be a father to you,
> and you shall be sons and daughters to me,
> says the Lord Almighty."

74. Box 10, File 10/2, Romans 8:7 Doctrinal and Practical Exercise.

75. Box 9, File 9/3, Romans 8:7 Skeleton.

76. Box 9, File 9/3, Romans 8:7 Doctrinal Exercise.

77. Box 9, File 9/5, 2 Corinthians 6:14—7:1 Practical-Expository Exercise.

> Since we have these promises, beloved, let us cleanse ourselves from every defilement of body and spirit, bringing holiness to completion in the fear of God.

Dabney based this Exercise on a Full Text[78] that he wrote in 1869, which helps to flesh out his intent.

In his Introduction, Dabney noted that Christians had exerted a profound cultural impact in the preceding hundred years, but asked: "Has the whole world indeed become spiritually minded?" If it had, then the prohibition the text imposes no longer held. Yet Dabney insisted that the prohibition remained, writing: "The controversy between the church and the world is irreconcilable." After a brief Exposition, in which Dabney explained terms and phrases, he stated his Proposition, arguing that the Scripture "*prohibits to Christians a familiar intimacy with worldly persons.*" His Argument unfolded under the following heads: 1. The world is actively revolting against God. 2. The best that can be said of the world is that "in its more seemly and genteel circles" it "no longer outrages" the Christian sensibility. Rather, unspiritual people see the Christian's gospel convictions as mere "fanaticism." Their goals likewise fundamentally differ from those of believers, while their chief end opposes the Christian's. Moreover, Dabney noted that when Christians do legitimately participate in worldly associations "[t]he practical result is that the godlessness of all its intercourse gains an additional sanction from the conduct of God's own people." He then applied his Proposition to the importance of marrying within the faith, albeit recognizing that religious agreement between husband and wife represented a legitimate implication of the text rather than an explicit command.

Dabney's Conclusion offered the example of Christ, who was a friend to sinners, but whose associations with them always served their good and his mission. Reiterating verses 17–18, Dabney stated: "Here is the alternative choice. You *cannot* have both the world's friendship, and the Christian's adoption," and he called upon his hearers to choose the reward of God over the rewards of worldly friendship.

In the same way that Dabney's purpose for his Doctrinal/Practical hybrid sermons remains unclear, so also this Practical-Expository Exercise most closely resembles his standard, unlabeled topical sermons. Featuring the same five structural components, it unfolded topically rather than offering exposition according to the versification of the text, and it is unclear how Dabney felt that the Practical-Expository label accurately described this Exercise.

78. Box 9, File 9/5, 2 Corinthians 6:14–18 Full Text. Dabney's Full Text terminates at verse 18, and although his Exercise purports to cover 7:1, it too concludes with 6:18.

The Expository Exercises

Overview

The foregoing analysis has revealed that regardless of the label that Dabney applied to a given Exercise, the basic structure of the sermon remained fixed. Each sermon featured an Introduction, Exposition, Proposition, Argument, and Conclusion. In the vast majority of his Exercises, Dabney designated these component parts for his students to see. Dabney's labels—Doctrinal, Didactic, Narrative, Practical, and other hybrids—identified varying purposes that Dabney intended for his sermons, not varying structures by which to compose a sermon. Even when easily identified, Dabney implemented his purposes for these Exercises inconsistently, and in the case of Dabney's hybrid labels, the purpose itself remains elusive.

Topical versus Expository Pedagogy

Of the forty-eight Exercises that are not labeled Expository, thirty-eight are based upon a single verse or a fragment of text, four cover two verses, and six address three or more verses. Of the six Exercises that employ three or more verses, five are Narrative Exercises, which required Dabney to tell the larger story of the biblical character's life in order to draw the lessons the Narrative Exercises purported to apply. The other Exercise in which Dabney used multiple verses was the Practical-Expository sermon referenced above. Dabney's classroom pedagogy, which is captured in his Exercises, thus predominantly imparted to his students a topical sermon form constructed on five immutable structural components. He most often employed capital or epitome texts, and frequently replicated the very form of "fragmentary"[79] preaching that his expository theory abjured.

Dabney labeled just thirteen of his sixty-one extant Exercises "Expository." He therefore devoted only one in five Exercises to equipping his students to preach the very form of sermon that his theory held forth as definitive of true preaching.[80] While Dabney's expository theory contended that consecutive expository preaching ought to form the bulk of the preacher's sermons,[81] fully eighty percent of his classroom pedagogy as revealed in his Exercises equipped his students to preach a type of sermon that Dabney's

79. Dabney, *Sacred Rhetoric*, 79–80.

80. Dabney, *Sacred Rhetoric*, 38. See also Dabney, "Gospel," 600.

81. Dabney, *Sacred Rhetoric*, 79.

theory castigated as "vicious."[82] His classroom pedagogy undermined the heart of his robust expository theory.

Analysis of the Expository Exercises

The present analysis of Dabney's Expository Exercises focuses on the structure of these sermons. Dabney's standard, five-component sermon, in which he limited the Exposition to establishing a topic, is incompatible with his own definition of expository preaching. So far from merely serving as a structural component within a larger sermon, in expository preaching exposition is the main thing to be done. In an expository sermon, *the Argument comprises an extended exposition that unfolds according to the versification of the text.*

From that structural perspective, Dabney's Expository Exercises divide roughly into three categories: First, Dabney composed Expository Exercises that faithfully implemented his expository theory. The second category is comprised of sermons, which, although Dabney labeled Expository, inconsistently carried forward his expository ideal. The third category is comprised of mislabeled Exercises, which although Dabney identified as Expository, show little difference from Dabney's standard topical sermons.

Faithful Expository Exercises

Five of Dabney's Expository Exercises serve to establish the structural difference between his expository sermons and his standard topical pattern. Consider Luke 16:1–12,[83] which recounts Jesus's parable of the shrewd manager. Jesus said:

> There was a rich man who had a manager, and charges were brought to him that this man was wasting his possessions. And he called him and said to him, "What is this that I hear about you? Turn in the account of your management, for you can no longer be manager." And the manager said to himself, "What shall I do, since my master is taking the management away from me? I am not strong enough to dig, and I am ashamed to beg. I have

82. Dabney argued: "It is never proper to employ a text as a mere motto to introduce the sermon. This vicious usage degrades the Bible into a mere collection of literary apophthegms. Nor will the true minister select and mature his subject in his own mind, and then seek a text for it. The sermon should not dictate the choice of a text, but the text should determine the whole character of the sermon." Dabney, *Sacred Rhetoric*, 94.

83. Box 9, File 9/4, Luke 16:1–12 Expository Exercise.

> decided what to do, so that when I am removed from management, people may receive me into their houses." So, summoning his master's debtors one by one, he said to the first, "How much do you owe my master?" He said, "A hundred measures of oil." He said to him, "Take your bill, and sit down quickly and write fifty." Then he said to another, "And how much do you owe?" He said, "A hundred measures of wheat." He said to him, "Take your bill, and write eighty." The master commended the dishonest manager for his shrewdness. For the sons of this world are more shrewd in dealing with their own generation than the sons of light. And I tell you, make friends for yourselves by means of unrighteous wealth, so that when it fails they may receive you into the eternal dwellings.
>
> One who is faithful in a very little is also faithful in much, and one who is dishonest in a very little is also dishonest in much. If then you have not been faithful in the unrighteous wealth, who will entrust to you the true riches? And if you have not been faithful in that which is another's, who will give you that which is your own?

Dabney's Introduction led to his Exposition, in which he wrote: "Must be interwoven with Discussion." Following his Proposition, an unlabeled section, most likely the "Discussion" just mentioned, progressed in five heads that *unfolded according to the versification of the text*. These led to a designated Conclusion.

Dabney's sermon on Matthew 3:7–12[84] is similar. John the Baptist was ministering in the desert and Matthew records:

> When he saw many of the Pharisees and Sadducees coming to his baptism, he said to them, "You brood of vipers! Who warned you to flee from the wrath to come? Bear fruit in keeping with repentance. And do not presume to say to yourselves, 'We have Abraham as our father,' for I tell you, God is able from these stones to raise up children for Abraham. Even now the axe is laid to the root of the trees. Every tree therefore that does not bear good fruit is cut down and thrown into the fire.
>
> "I baptize you with water for repentance, but he who is coming after me is mightier than I, whose sandals I am not worthy to carry. He will baptize you with the Holy Spirit and fire. His winnowing fork is in his hand, and he will clear his threshing floor and gather his wheat into the barn, but the chaff he will burn with unquenchable fire."

84. Box 7, File 7/6, Matthew 3:7–12 Expository Exercise.

Dabney's Introduction led to a Proposition, after which he began to expound the text. There is no designated Exposition. Dabney's Argument offered five heads, which *unfolded according to the versification of the text*. Each head represented a verse. His Conclusion offered three brief inferences.

Likewise, an Expository Exercise on Matthew 20:1–16[85] began with a designated Introduction, in which Dabney reminded himself: "Paint the Oriental custom here employed for [the] parable." In that parable, Jesus taught:

> For the kingdom of heaven is like a master of a house who went out early in the morning to hire laborers for his vineyard. After agreeing with the laborers for a denarius a day, he sent them into his vineyard. And going out about the third hour he saw others standing idle in the marketplace, and to them he said, "You go into the vineyard too, and whatever is right I will give you." So they went. Going out again about the sixth hour and the ninth hour, he did the same. And about the eleventh hour he went out and found others standing. And he said to them, "Why do you stand here idle all day?" They said to him, "Because no one has hired us." He said to them, "You go into the vineyard too." And when evening came, the owner of the vineyard said to his foreman, "Call the laborers and pay them their wages, beginning with the last, up to the first." And when those hired about the eleventh hour came, each of them received a denarius. Now when those hired first came, they thought they would receive more, but each of them also received a denarius. And on receiving it they grumbled at the master of the house, saying, "These last worked only one hour, and you have made them equal to us who have borne the burden of the day and the scorching heat." But he replied to one of them, "Friend, I am doing you no wrong. Did you not agree with me for a denarius? Take what belongs to you and go. I choose to give to this last worker as I give to you. Am I not allowed to do what I choose with what belongs to me? Or do you begrudge my generosity?" So the last will be first, and the first last.

Without a formal Proposition, Dabney moved immediately into an extended section of exposition, which *unfolded according to the versification of the text*, leading to a segment of application before closing.

85. Box 8, File 8/2, Matthew 20:1–16 Expository Exercise.

Dabney's message on Acts 5:1–11[86] is almost identical in form to his Matthew 20:1–16 Exercise. Luke recounts the sin of Ananias and Sapphira, writing:

> A man named Ananias, with his wife Sapphira, sold a piece of property, and with his wife's knowledge he kept back for himself some of the proceeds and brought only a part of it and laid it at the apostles' feet. But Peter said, "Ananias, why has Satan filled your heart to lie to the Holy Spirit and to keep back for yourself part of the proceeds of the land? While it remained unsold, did it not remain your own? And after it was sold, was it not at your disposal? Why is it that you have contrived this deed in your heart? You have not lied to man but to God." When Ananias heard these words, he fell down and breathed his last. And great fear came upon all who heard of it. The young men rose and wrapped him up and carried him out and buried him.
>
> After an interval of about three hours his wife came in, not knowing what had happened. And Peter said to her, "Tell me whether you sold the land for so much." And she said, "Yes, for so much." But Peter said to her, "How is it that you have agreed together to test the Spirit of the Lord? Behold, the feet of those who have buried your husband are at the door, and they will carry you out." Immediately she fell down at his feet and breathed her last. When the young men came in they found her dead, and they carried her out and buried her beside her husband. And great fear came upon the whole church and upon all who heard of these things.

Dabney's Introduction led to his Argument under five heads, which *unfolded according to the versification of the text.* He then designated a section of application, which ended with his Conclusion.

Finally, in his 1 Corinthians 13[87] Expository Exercise, Dabney began with a designated Introduction and Exposition. The Scripture teaches:

> If I speak in the tongues of men and of angels, but have not love, I am a noisy gong or a clanging cymbal. And if I have prophetic powers, and understand all mysteries and all knowledge, and if I have all faith, so as to remove mountains, but have not love, I am nothing. If I give away all I have, and if I deliver up my body to be burned, but have not love, I gain nothing.
>
> Love is patient and kind; love does not envy or boast; it is not arrogant or rude. It does not insist on its own way; it is

86. Box 9, File 9/4, Acts 5:1–11 Expository Exercise.

87. Box 9, File 9/4, 1 Corinthians 13 Expository Exercise.

> not irritable or resentful; it does not rejoice at wrongdoing, but rejoices with the truth. Love bears all things, believes all things, hopes all things, endures all things.
>
> Love never ends. As for prophecies, they will pass away; as for tongues, they will cease; as for knowledge, it will pass away. For we know in part and we prophesy in part, but when the perfect comes, the partial will pass away. When I was a child, I spoke like a child, I thought like a child, I reasoned like a child. When I became a man, I gave up childish ways. For now we see in a mirror dimly, but then face to face. Now I know in part; then I shall know fully, even as I have been fully known.
>
> So now faith, hope, and love abide, these three; but the greatest of these is love.

In place of the Argument Dabney designated a section entitled, "For discussion." This discussion progressed under three heads, which *unfolded according to the versification of the text*. His Conclusion asked: "How lovely the Bible ethicks?"

These Expository Exercises demonstrate a clear pattern. They began like a standard topical sermon, offering a clearly designated Introduction. Some also designated an Exposition. The Exposition, however, served a different purpose. In a standard topical sermon, Dabney employed the Exposition to establish the doctrine or duty of the text, which then became the subject of a topical Argument. In his Expository Exercises, however, Dabney used the Exposition to establish literary, theological, canonical, or historical context in order to prepare his hearers for the more thorough verse-by-verse exposition of the Scripture that followed. Sometimes Dabney designated a formal Proposition. Other times he did not. In either case, the crucial structural difference between Dabney's standard topical sermons and his Expository messages was this: in an expository sermon the Argument, whether designated or not, was *comprised of an extended exposition that unfolded according to the versification of the text* rather than proceeding thematically, doctrinally, topically, or as an enforcement of duties. The explanation of the text comprised the body of the sermon in Dabney's Expository messages, and unfolded according to the versification of the text.

A fuller examination of Dabney's Expository Exercise on Philippians 4:4–7,[88] which he composed in 1857, along with a companion Full Text[89] from 1861, readily confirms and fleshes out this pattern. The Scripture teaches:

88. Box 8, File 8/2, Philippians 4:4–7 Expository Exercise.

89. Box 6, File 6/3a, Philippians 4:4–7 Full Text.

> Rejoice in the Lord always; again I will say, rejoice. Let your reasonableness be known to everyone. The Lord is at hand; do not be anxious about anything, but in everything by prayer and supplication with thanksgiving let your requests be made known to God. And the peace of God, which surpasses all understanding, will guard your hearts and your minds in Christ Jesus.

Dabney's Introduction asserted: "Religious joy [is] not only a privilege, but a duty." Without a labeled Exposition, Dabney moved immediately to his Argument, which began by comparing Paul's own sufferings and experiences of joy with his command to the believers at Philippi. Dabney argued that "the joy of the Lord is independent of outward circumstances," and because of the great privileges believers possess in Christ, "Nothing can be more inconsistent" for the believer than to exhibit "a murmuring, melancholy spirit." Returning to the text, Dabney quoted verse five, and taught that the joy of the Lord should supersede all "inordinate emotions concerning lower things," while inculcating a self-governing spirit. Given that the "Lord is near," which Dabney took as a reference to the brevity of the believer's life, the Christian ought not to credit the "gains or losses which are soon to be forgotten amidst vaster joys." Dabney then asserted that Christians must cultivate a spirit of joy and moderation, primarily by seeking first the Kingdom. Turning to verse six, which Dabney taught did not forestall normal industry and planning, but instead prohibited "inordinate care for any terrestrial concern," he suggested that every Christian has rebelled against this command. Dabney then addressed the question of whether a Christian could approach the throne of grace with requests small as well as great. He answered that if a Christian failed to approach God for small things, then that Christian "defrauds himself" of the very peace that belongs to those who are in Christ. Stressing that Paul commanded believers to go to God "in everything," Dabney noted that every human care is small to God, assuring his hearers that "all earnest, believing prayer of Christians is surely answered." In consequence, he quoted verse seven, teaching that Paul's promise of peace was no platitude, for the peace in view is "God's own peace; the peace which God himself enjoys, communicated by his own Spirit." Reinforcing this truth with John 14:27, in which Jesus says, "Peace I leave with you; my peace I give to you," Dabney exhorted his hearers to establish their fortitude not in themselves, but in the pledge of God to them by faith.

Noting that the same power that governs the world guards the Christian's soul, Dabney also argued that the same love that died for the believer guards the believer. Thus the peace that faith receives "passes all understanding." Since unbelievers have no peace they cannot fathom it. Believers likewise struggle to comprehend its breadth. Dabney then noted that the word translated "guard" means "to garrison," and encouraged his hearers, insisting that "[s]piritual joy garrisons the heart against corrupt desires." He asserted, moreover, that "[p]eace in believing is the best defense against all erroneous dogmas in religion." Pointing his congregation to Jesus, the source of peace, Dabney's Conclusion asked: "Is not this peace of God worth the pains of gaining it?" Likewise addressing non-Christians, he inquired: "What do *you* think of this peace? Is it not worth having?" Exhorting them to pursue it, he closed with a flourish:

> Bring your spiritual wants to God . . . he will meet them all: Your sins, to be covered with Christ's atonement; your self-will, to be subdued by his Spirit; your darkness, to be illuminated by his light; your weakness of purpose as to all good, to be upheld by his strength; your misery to be enriched by his love.

Dabney's Introduction thus led quickly to an Argument that unfolded the passage according to the versification of the text, offering proofs and applications interspersed with each section of exposition. These led to the Conclusion, in which Dabney challenged both believers and unbelievers with the claims of the text. This sermon clearly embodies Dabney's Expository ideal, in which the Argument is comprised of an extended exposition that unfolds according to the versification of the text.[90]

Inconsistent Expository Exercises

Dabney composed other Expository Exercises that inconsistently implemented the expository ideal described above. While they contain expository elements, they also include structural components that are inconsistent with Dabney's understanding of expository preaching. Consider Dabney's Exercise on 1 Corinthians 3:9–15.[91] The Scripture teaches:

> We are God's fellow workers. You are God's field, God's building. According to the grace of God given to me, like a skilled master builder I laid a foundation, and someone else is building upon it. Let each one take care how he builds upon it. For no one can lay a foundation other than that which is laid, which is Jesus Christ. Now if anyone builds on the foundation

90. For the same pattern, see also Box 10, File 10/3, Hebrews 11:24–27 Expository Exercise.

91. Box 9, File 9/4, 1 Corinthians 3:9–15 Expository Exercise.

> with gold, silver, precious stones, wood, hay, straw— each one's work will become manifest, for the Day will disclose it, because it will be revealed by fire, and the fire will test what sort of work each one has done. If the work that anyone has built on the foundation survives, he will receive a reward. If anyone's work is burned up, he will suffer loss, though he himself will be saved, but only as through fire.

Dabney's Introduction led into a section of Exposition, in which he established the meaning of the text by working through it verse by verse. Foregoing a formal Proposition, he inserted a section entitled, "For discussion." This "discussion" functioned as his Argument, and unfolded under four heads, which sought to apply the text to his hearers. While this Exercise was therefore expository through the Exposition, the bulk of sermon was taken up with applying the text by way of discussion. The Argument, rather than comprising an extended exposition that unfolded according to the versification of the text, instead unfolded as an extended application of the text.

Dabney's Expository Exercise on Matthew 11:28–30[92] provides the clearest example of this inconsistent structural pattern. Jesus taught: "Come to me, all who labor and are heavy laden, and I will give you rest. Take my yoke upon you, and learn from me, for I am gentle and lowly in heart, and you will find rest for your souls. For my yoke is easy, and my burden is light." Dabney's Introduction led to a brief Exposition that provided limited context, leading to a note to self, which urged: "Arg.[ue] Expository." What this meant became clear as Dabney moved to prove his Proposition, which asserted: "*Our rest is to be found in Christ by faith.*" He offered two proofs. 1. "Because the author of [the] invitation is divine," which he supported with verse 28 and several proof texts, and 2. "Because of [the] nature of the *yoke*, and the *master* we receive," which he supported with verses 29 and 30.

To this point, Dabney followed his Expository ideal. But then he asked and began to answer how a person might be said to rest under a yoke. His answer unfolded topically and doctrinally, and failed to follow the versification of the text. His enumerated heads affirmed: 1. All persons are yoked under Christ or Satan. 2. The rest promised is not physical indolence but a peace of soul. 3. The Master under whose yoke we labor is benevolent. 4. By the example of the Master, we learn how to bear the yoke. 5. The yoke is easy and the burden light. If not, then the sinner is trying to bear it in his or her own strength instead of trusting Christ. Love, moreover, "makes all easy." Dabney concluded with three points of application: 1. Using verses 28 and 29, he asserted that "true faith results in [the] immediate assumption of all known

92. Box 8, File 8/2, Matthew 11:28–30 Expository Exercise.

duty." 2. Dabney made sure that his hearers understood the proper order. Strength to bear up is the result of coming to Christ, not the ground of it. 3. "Salvation can only be obtained by an unreserved trust," for even as Dabney explained, no person receives a test-run of the feel of the yoke. Rather, each must trust that Christ's yoke is as it has been advertised.

This Expository Exercise inconsistently implemented the ideal of Dabney's expository theory. The Argument unfolded according to the versification of the text, but only briefly. The bulk of the Argument coupled doctrinal explanations about the nature of resting under a yoke with practical exhortations to come under that yoke. Taken together, these inconsistent Expository Exercises featured extended sections of application, which comprised of the bulk of the Argument, and which might better be labeled Expository-Practical sermons.[93]

Mislabeled Expository Exercises

Dabney also composed several Expository Exercises that are simply mislabeled, and it is difficult to discern how these Exercises differ from his standard topical sermons or why Dabney felt compelled to label them Expository. Consider Dabney's Matthew 25:24–30[94] Expository Exercise. Jesus taught:

> He also who had received the one talent came forward, saying, "Master, I knew you to be a hard man, reaping where you did not sow, and gathering where you scattered no seed, so I was afraid, and I went and hid your talent in the ground. Here, you have what is yours." But his master answered him, "You wicked and slothful servant! You knew that I reap where I have not sown and gather where I scattered no seed? Then you ought to have invested my money with the bankers, and at my coming I should have received what was my own with interest. So take the talent from him and give it to him who has the ten talents. For to everyone who has will more be given, and he will have an abundance. But from the one who has not, even what he has will be taken away. And cast the worthless servant into the outer darkness. In that place there will be weeping and gnashing of teeth."

In his Introduction Dabney asserted that God is absolutely fair, warning: "Let [the] caviler consider carefully if *he* is not deceived by sin; and not God." From that assertion, Dabney argued that Christ's parable addressed all those who possess the attitude of the unbelieving Jews, whom Dabney

93. For the same pattern see Box 7, File 7/4, Isaiah 5:1–7 Expository Exercise.

94. Box 8, File 8/2, Matthew 25:24–30 Expository Exercise.

noted: "Claim to be not hostile, [and] not guilty; but [who were] undecided because of *difficulties*." To which he added: "*Neutrals*: Always have an excuse." He then provided sufficient background to assert: "But [our] topic today is, the *unprofitable Servant*." Dabney worked briefly through the Exposition of the text, leading to the following Proposition: "Pretended difficulties of professed neutrals [are deceitful, and][95] proceed from secret enmity to duty." The remainder of the sermon provided examples of such excuses from purported "neutrals." Followed by Dabney's rebuke, which he presented in the form of a hypothetical interlocutor who questioned Dabney's assertions and suffered his argumentative reply, his Conclusion warned: "Look out! All you do-nothing Christians."

This Expository Exercise utilized a standard topical structure, in which the Exposition established the subject of the text, after which the Argument unfolded topically rather than according to the versification of the text. If anything, this sermon might best be described as Didactic, for Dabney devoted it to defending God against cavilers.

Dabney's Expository Exercise on John 6:28–35[96] is likewise mislabeled. Jesus spoke to the crowds gathered by the Sea of Galilee, and John recorded the interaction:

> They said to him, "What must we do, to be doing the works of God?" Jesus answered them, "This is the work of God, that you believe in him whom he has sent." So they said to him, "Then what sign do you do, that we may see and believe you? What work do you perform? Our fathers ate the manna in the wilderness; as it is written, 'He gave them bread from heaven to eat.'" Jesus then said to them, "Truly, truly, I say to you, it was not Moses who gave you the bread from heaven, but my Father gives you the true bread from heaven. For the bread of God is he who comes down from heaven and gives life to the world." They said to him, "Sir, give us this bread always." Jesus said to them, "I am the bread of life; whoever comes to me shall not hunger, and whoever believes in me shall never thirst."

By way of Introduction, Dabney noted that Jesus had a habit of seizing upon "natural incidents to enforce divine truth." In the present case, Jesus explained his true nature as the Son of God and thus the Bread of Life. Dabney moved immediately into the Exposition, during which he worked through the text, opposing errors, which included his rejection of

95. While this paper has inserted other brackets in Dabney's text in order to clarify his meaning, these brackets are original to Dabney.

96. Box 8, File 8/5, John 6:28–35 Expository Exercise.

the doctrine of the physical presence of Christ in the Lord's Supper. His Proposition followed: "The Christian *life can begin by no act* on [the] sinner's part, but by faith or bel.[ief]." Thereupon unfolded four heads of "Arg. [ument]": 1. "His mission implies the spiritual death of sinners." 2. "God ordains that . . . life shall be derived fr.[om] Chr.[ist] by faith alone." 3. "He who will not *begin by faith* will make no beginning." 4. "Unbelief [is] the chief, because seminal or propagating sin." Each of these heads contained an applicatory statement or question, which weaved argument and application throughout. Dabney's Conclusion asserted: "Honest reform begins at [the] fountain head. Else it is a *sham*."

This Exercise is clearly mislabeled. The sermon unfolded according to Dabney's standard five-part structure, and the Argument proceeded topically rather than following the versification of the text.[97] It does not reflect his expository ideal in any appreciable way.

Summary

Dabney's Expository Exercises reveal both the presence of a structurally different expository sermon form, and also his inconsistent implementation of that form. Seven of thirteen Expository Exercises faithfully embodied his expository ideal. In each of these the Argument was comprised of an extended exposition that unfolded according to the versification of the text. In short, the Argument became an extended exposition. In six Expository Exercises, however, Dabney failed to follow this pattern. Three coupled an extended Exposition with an Argument that unfolded applications, while three were simply mislabeled, and replicated instead Dabney's standard topical sermon form.

The Curious Case of Matthew 3:7–12 and Proverbs 29:18

Dabney's Expository Exercise on Matthew 3:7–12,[98] which this paper cited as an example of a consistent embodiment of his expository theory, also presents a challenge to Dabney's expository pedagogy. Dabney recorded each successive preaching occasion on the back of his sermon manuscripts, and the record of the Matthew 3:7–12 Expository Exercise records the

97. For the same pattern see Box 10, File 10/2, 1 Timothy 3:14–16 Expository Exercise.

98. Box 7, File 7/6, Matthew 3:7–12 Expository Exercise.

following: Dabney first preached this Exercise at Prince Edward Church in January of 1861. The second preaching took place at Tinkling Spring Church in November of 1863. The third occurred at Hampden-Sydney College in October of 1867, while the fifth was delivered in the seminary Lecture Room in February of 1877. A question arises, however, over Dabney's fourth preaching of this Exercise, which took place at "UTS Chapel from Pr. 29:18 on Necessity of Revelation" in October of 1867. From this notation it appears that Dabney, during this fourth preaching occasion, preached an Expository sermon from an alternate text.

That Dabney could preach the same topical sermon from two different texts is not surprising.[99] Desiring to preach on the doctrine of regeneration, a preacher could do so from Ezekiel 36:25–27, John 3:1–8, or 1 Peter 1:22–25. Many texts teach the doctrine of regeneration, and if a preacher desired to proclaim a topic rather than a text, any number of texts might be used profitably, for many texts legitimately speak to any given point of Christian doctrine or duty.

When, however, Dabney recorded that he preached the *substance* of his Expository Exercise on Matthew 3:7–12 from the *text* of Proverbs 29:18, in order to prove the "necessity of revelation," a challenge of a different sort emerges. Expository preaching, by Dabney's own definition, expounds a particular text. No preacher can proclaim an expository sermon from a text other than the text from which it was composed, for an expository message unfolds according to the versification of that particular text. Dabney's theory precluded him from preaching an expository message composed on Matthew 3:7–12 from the text of Proverbs 29:18, yet it appears that he did just that. He employed an expository sermon to preach a doctrinal message in order to prove that it was necessary for God to issue an authoritative revelation to teach fallen people how to be saved.

A comparison between the two texts in question only exacerbates the problem. In Matthew 3:7–12, Matthew records of John the Baptist that:

> When he saw many of the Pharisees and Sadducees coming to his baptism, he said to them, "You brood of vipers! Who warned you to flee from the wrath to come? Bear fruit in keeping with

99. Dabney did this on a number of occasions: Box 6, File 6/6, Psalm 84:11 Skeleton preached from Titus 3; Box 7, File 7/3, Ecclesiastes 1:14 Full Text preached from Psalm 39:6; Box 7, File 7/3, Ecclesiastes 5:5 Full Text preached from Romans 2:9; Box 7, File 7/5, Jeremiah 2:12–13 Skeleton preached from Luke 19:1–10; Box 8, File 8/1, Matthew 5:15 Skeleton preached from 1 Peter 2:11–15; Box 8, File 8/4, Luke 18:7–8 Skeleton preached from Mark 11:24; and Box 8, File 8/6, Acts 2:42 Skeleton preached from Exodus 34:20. Dabney's Box 7, File 7/6, Micah 7:18 Skeleton features a note in which Dabney wrote: "Or better from Psalm 108:4."

> repentance. And do not presume to say to yourselves, 'We have Abraham as our father,' for I tell you, God is able from these stones to raise up children for Abraham. Even now the axe is laid to the root of the trees. Every tree therefore that does not bear good fruit is cut down and thrown into the fire. I baptize you with water for repentance, but he who is coming after me is mightier than I, whose sandals I am not worthy to carry. He will baptize you with the Holy Spirit and fire. His winnowing fork is in his hand, and he will clear his threshing floor and gather his wheat into the barn, but the chaff he will burn with unquenchable fire."

John, as a prophet, offered the very type of divine revelation that Dabney argued is necessary for salvation, but the passage in question does not address the necessity of divine revelation for salvation. It concerns instead Jesus's impending work of dividing the saved from the lost. Alternately, Proverbs 29:18 observed: "Where there is no prophetic vision the people cast off restraint, but blessed is he who keeps the law." Again, the text involves divine revelation through the prophetic mouthpiece, but Proverbs 29 does not address the necessity of revelation for salvation, but rather for the preservation of moral order in society.

Adding to the challenge of interpreting Dabney's thinking at this point is the fact that he had previously composed a Brief on Proverbs 29:18,[100] which he preached in October of 1863 at Union Seminary, fully four years before the odd preaching occasion recorded on the Matthew 3:7–12 manuscript. For reasons that remain unclear, Dabney attempted to press an Expository Exercise from Matthew 3 into service of a topical message on the necessity of revelation from Proverbs 29 when he already possessed a sermon from Proverbs 29 on that very subject. Dabney was neither displeased with nor had he discarded his Proverbs 29 Brief. To the contrary, he preached it again in October of 1868 at a Synod meeting in Harrisonburg, VA, and again in June of 1869 at Petersburg, VA. Preaching at Synod was something of a prestigious opportunity,[101] and it is difficult to imagine that Dabney employed on that occasion a sermon that he felt was inferior. This tends to argue against the possibility that Dabney preached on Proverbs 29 from his Matthew 3 Expository Exercise because he had no better alternative. Dabney's choice to preach the Matthew 3 sermon from Proverbs 29, and later to preach his Proverbs 29 Brief, appears to have been intentional. For reasons that remain

100. Box 7, File 7/3, Proverbs 29:18 Brief. Dabney's Proposition sought to prove: "*A direct and authoritative revelation from God is essential to man's salvation*" [emphasis original].

101. A Presbyterian synod is comprised of the churches of two or more presbyteries, usually in geographic proximity, which work together in matters of regional impact.

clouded, Dabney chose to employ the *substance* of his Expository Exercise on Matthew 3, preached from the *text* of Proverbs 29, to proclaim a topical message on the necessity of revelation. Not only was his choice irreconcilable with his expository theory, but it also contributed to the manner in which Dabney's classroom pedagogy undermined his theory.

Conclusion

Summary

Whereas Dabney's Doctrinal, Didactic, Practical, and other labeled Exercises differed from his standard unlabeled sermons only in the various purposes he intended for his hearers through them, his Expository Exercises offered a different structure. Rather than following the pattern of the five structural components—Introduction, Exposition, Proposition, Argument, and Conclusion—that formed a topical sermon, Dabney's Expository Exercises, when true to their ideal, replaced the Argument with an extended exposition that unfolded according to the versification of the text. This structural pattern, if faithfully imparted to and modeled for Dabney's students, could have equipped them to preach the consecutive expository series that Dabney's Expository theory admired.

The preceding evaluation has, however, revealed that Dabney realized his expository ideal in just seven of his thirteen Expository Exercises. In twenty-eight years of homiletical instruction at Union Seminary, Dabney produced just seven Exercises able to equip his students to pursue the expository preaching he admired. Granted, Dabney's manuscript collection is incomplete, and other Expository Exercises and sermons may have been lost. Nevertheless, in working from those manuscripts that have survived, it is apparent that Dabney's expository pedagogy was far weaker than his robust expository theory, and his classroom pedagogy likely did more to undermine his expository theory than to establish it as a pulpit practice among his students. His seven Expository Exercises that faithfully implemented his expository theory represent just eleven percent of the Exercises he composed, while all Exercises together represent just under thirteen percent of his total manuscript collection. Said differently, these faithful Expository Exercises comprise just one percent of his manuscript collection. His Expository Exercises were simply too few and too inconsistent to prepare his students to preach consecutive expository series, while his non-expository Exercises served pedagogically to undermine his robust expository theory.

Preview of Chapter 5

Chapter 5 of this paper describes Dabney's personal practice of expository preaching, first setting his expository preaching within the context of his broader pulpit ministry by evaluating his topical sermons according to the requirements he set forth in his *Sacred Rhetoric*. That evaluation demonstrates that Dabney exercised varying degrees of fidelity to his own homiletical theory. Second, it evaluates Dabney's non-Exercise Expository sermons, showing that Dabney inconsistently implemented his expository theory. Third, it briefly surveys Dabney's expository series, demonstrating his complete failure to preach the consecutive expository series that his expository theory commended. While Dabney crafted a robust expository theory, his expository pedagogy was weak, and his personal practice of expository preaching was virtually non-existent.

5

Practice

Introduction

Overview

The previous chapter demonstrated that Robert Lewis Dabney's expository pedagogy was weaker than his robust expository theory, and was not only largely inadequate to equip his students to preach the expository sermons he admired, but in fact served to undermine his expository theory. While *Sacred Rhetoric* theoretically commended the practice of continuous verse-by-verse exposition of the Scriptures, Dabney's classroom pedagogy predominantly equipped his students with a topical sermon template that represented the common homiletic of the late nineteenth-century American pulpit.

The Plan of This Chapter

The present chapter is divided into three sections, which explore Dabney's personal practice of expository preaching. The first section sets Dabney's expository practice within the context of his broader pulpit ministry, comparing his standard topical sermons to his homiletical theory. That comparison demonstrates that Dabney's topical sermons offered varying degrees of fidelity to the Scripture and its context. This broader preaching framework also establishes that Dabney's teaching regarding capital and epitome texts[1] became, in his own pulpit practice, the mechanism by

1. See chapter 3 for Dabney's understanding of these terms.

which he consistently preached the very "sermons without context"[2] that his expository theory rejected.

The second section of this chapter analyzes Dabney's non-Exercise[3] Expository sermons, evaluating them according to the pattern employed in the previous chapter: First, Dabney preached Expository sermons that faithfully implemented his expository theory. Second, he preached sermons that he labeled Expository, but which inconsistently implemented his theory. Third, he preached mislabeled sermons, which were not Expository in any demonstrable way. Dabney's Expository sermons, whether faithful to his theory or not, comprised a numerically insignificant percentage of his total preaching ministry, and Dabney demonstrated a lifelong preference for preaching topical sermons based on isolated verses or clauses of Scripture.

The final section of this chapter offers a brief survey of Dabney's Expository series, demonstrating that despite his robust expository theory and his exhortations to his seminary students to preach consecutive expository series, consecutive expository preaching played no part whatsoever in Dabney's own pulpit ministry. This chapter closes by suggesting that despite his theory, Dabney's fundamental stance as a preacher was not that of a herald,[4] but was instead that of a craftsman.

Dabney's Standard Sermon

Introduction

The preceding evaluation of Dabney's Exercises demonstrated that a standard Dabney sermon was comprised of five components: Introduction, Exposition, Proposition, Argument, and Conclusion. Dabney employed minor flexibility with these components, sometimes using the Exposition as an Introduction, at times leaving the Proposition unstated, sometimes intermingling Argument with application, and often penning a true Conclusion, while at times allowing the sermon to terminate with implications, applications, or pointed questions. Within this limited flexibility, Dabney's basic form lent itself to the creation of topical sermons based on single verses or clauses of text, which form the bulk of his extant messages.[5]

2. Dabney, *Sacred Rhetoric*, 76.

3. Chapter 4, page 108 explains the significance of this designation.

4. Dabney, *Sacred Rhetoric*, 36.

5. Including Exercises, Full Texts, Skeletons, and Briefs, Dabney's sermon collection features just twenty-four labeled Expository messages. The rest are topical in design and follow the fivefold structure common to his day.

A "True Exposition"

Recall that Dabney's homiletical theory conceded that a topical sermon could offer a true exposition of the text. Writing that all sermons "should be virtually expository, else they are not true sermons," Dabney argued:

> A prevalent exercise of the pulpit should be the delivery of those explanations of connected passages of Scripture which are called . . . in modern phrase "expository preaching." And when the pastor discusses only a single sentence or proposition of Scripture, as he will often and legitimately do, it should yet be *a true exposition, and evolution of the meaning of God in that sentence, with constant and faithful reference to its context.*[6]

Although granting the legitimacy of preaching upon capital and epitome texts, Dabney reiterated: "A discussion without scriptural context is not true preaching, and . . . in the sense above defined, there is no other species of preaching than the expository."[7] The reader of Dabney's sermons therefore has warrant from Dabney to examine the extent to which his topical messages carry forward the "meaning of God in that sentence," and reveal "constant and faithful reference" to the context of the text, thereby representing a "true exposition"[8] of the Scripture.

The Meaning of God in That Sentence

As an example that represents what Dabney meant by "the meaning of God in that sentence,"[9] consider Dabney's Full Text on John 5:44,[10] in which Jesus asks: "How can you believe, when you receive glory from one another and do not seek the glory that comes from the only God?" Dabney began his

6. Dabney, *Sacred Rhetoric*, 77 [emphasis added].

7. Dabney, *Sacred Rhetoric*, 78.

8. Dabney, *Sacred Rhetoric*, 77.

9. Dabney, *Sacred Rhetoric*, 77. Dabney referred to the text's "meaning" often, but did not define the hermeneutical mechanism by which he purported to arrive at such meaning. He did, however, repudiate the notion that any given passage of Scripture could offer more than one meaning, writing: "Your own good sense should show you that a mode of interpretation cannot be correct, which enables different men to extract the most variant meanings from the same words. It is utterly condemned by what has been established concerning the preacher's mission. He has naught to do save to deliver God's message out of the Scriptures; his only concern is with the intended meaning of the Holy Ghost in the place expounded." Dabney, *Sacred Rhetoric*, 67. For a window into Dabney's hermeneutical world, see Fairbairn, *Hermeneutical Manual*, 79–106.

10. Box 8, File 8/5, John 5:44 Full Text.

Introduction by suggesting that no person is or should be completely unconcerned about reputation, arguing that a person who claims such is either interested in sin or is petulant. By way of Exposition, Dabney noted that the text does not command Christians to set aside a healthy desire for the approval of others, but that it does require Christians to prefer the approbation of God to human praise. Pointing to verses 40 and 42, Dabney suggested: "We naturally desire the love (including the approbat.[ion]) of those whom we love." Dabney nevertheless contended that the men to whom Jesus spoke preferred human approval over God's, writing: "Thus the real, (and insuperable) obstacle to grace was vicious pride and lust of applause from sinners." Reiterating that total neglect of human opinion is not in view in the text, Dabney's Proposition asserted: "The preference of sinners' honour, to that which cometh from God, is utterly inconsistent with true grace."

In unfolding his Argument, Dabney affirmed that desire for human acceptance is legitimate, and taught that God made humans "social beings." Thus "the desire to be beloved is a necessary reflex of love toward any person." He explained, moreover, that the "desire of approbation is a species of confession wh.[ich] the soul makes to itself of the fallibility of its moral judgments. It knows that the scales of conscience are often shaken by self-love or passion." On the right use of this faculty, Dabney offered: "It is *right for us to desire that approbation from our fellows, which it is right for them to give*,"[11] and thus, "It is right for us to desire the honor of our fellow creatures by doing acts of true virtue, or holiness." Nevertheless, he cautioned: "If the obedience had no higher motive than the craving for praise, then it did not truly deserve praise." When this natural desire is corrupted, men and women court human favor as their chief pleasure. Dabney commented: "It is a true idolatry and that of a base idol," for "it sets up self as the chief God, and your fellow sinners as the inferior deities." Dabney asserted that it was therefore impossible for such a person to believe in Christ, because his or her desire for human applause weakened the soul, enthroned pride as the "ruling principle," and repealed God's law in favor of the opinions of sinful men and women. His Conclusion warned: "It takes moral courage to be a Christian." Dabney applied that truth to youths with ambitions of distinction or power, to the "votaries of fashion and style," and to those "who have not moral courage to despise ridicule." In a final note to self, he wrote: "Bring each case to a distinct *issue*; and show *why* the alternative is clear."

Although Dabney provided very little context and largely treated the text as a stand-alone island of thought, he clearly carried forward the

11. All emphasized words and phrases from Dabney's sermons are original to Dabney unless otherwise noted.

"meaning of God in that sentence."[12] Dabney's thought was, in fact, informed by the broader context, such that he rightly proclaimed the meaning of the text, even though he failed to provide that context to his hearers. So long as the sermon carried forward the "meaning of God in that sentence," Dabney counted it a "true exposition."[13]

Constant and Faithful Reference

Along with requiring that a topical sermon carry forward the meaning of the text, Dabney also required that it offer "constant and faithful reference to its context" in order to be considered a "true exposition."[14] He demonstrated the nature of this requirement in a Full Text he preached on Jeremiah 9:23–24,[15] which Dabney composed as a baccalaureate message. The Scripture teaches:

> Thus says the Lord: "Let not the wise man boast in his wisdom, let not the mighty man boast in his might, let not the rich man boast in his riches, but let him who boasts boast in this, that he understands and knows me, that I am the Lord who practices steadfast love, justice, and righteousness in the earth. For in these things I delight, declares the Lord."

By way of Introduction, Dabney asserted that a human being is not an animal of mere instinct. As "a rational and moral being," Dabney taught that "[n]o one's life can be right or well ordered, for which the proper *end* or supreme object is not proposed, and kept steadily in view." After urging his audience to consider that every life must determine a purpose, Dabney read the text, and then described the broad context, writing: "The prophet had been sorrowfully displaying before his countrymen the approaching judgments of God for their national sins." In the face of this, believers ought not boast in human wisdom or strength or wealth. Rather, Dabney taught: "In view of the approaching judgments, let them place their joy, their dependence, their boast, only in this; that they had a saving and transforming knowledge of Jehovah, as the true God; a God of mercy and righteousness." From this Dabney stated his Proposition: "*Man should place his chief dependence, not on any of those things (knowledge, power, wealth) which inspire all the ambition of this world, but on the knowledge and service of God.*"

12. Dabney, *Sacred Rhetoric*, 77.
13. Dabney, *Sacred Rhetoric*, 77.
14. Dabney, *Sacred Rhetoric*, 77.
15. Box 7, File 7/5, Jeremiah 9:23–24 Full Text.

In prosecuting this Proposition, Dabney seized upon the list of boasts, tackling each in turn before turning toward the positive task of understanding and knowing the Lord. He urged that intellectual attainment and wealth be consecrated for the purpose of glorifying God rather than exalting self, while cautioning that power desired often corrupts. He summarized: "*Holiness* is the crowning glory of the divine nature," and referred back to the text to teach that each Christian must pursue holiness.

Having summed up the evils of pursuing wisdom, wealth, and power for their own idolatrous ends, Dabney reminded his hearers that the prophet's words were spoken "in view of approaching retributions," and that none of the former pursuits—wisdom, wealth, or power—could enable "the sinner to evade the angry Providence of God." He thus urged: "We also are approaching a day of judgment, of righteous doom, when we must stand before a strict judge; as guilty offenders." Noting that on that Day no human wisdom or wealth or power would suffice, Dabney returned to the text and suggested that his hearers should "bravely turn your back on *all* that the world counts valuable." In Conclusion, he exhorted the students gathered before him to "seek a wisdom and strength greater than the world's."

While Dabney therefore faithfully explained the context of the passage, he did not so much expound the text as he did refer to it, assuming that its meaning was on the surface and that his hearers shared his understanding. The body of his sermon, which repeatedly referred back to the context, focused on proclaiming the truth that Christians must boast only in the Lord, while Dabney offered specific applications to the students gathered before him. His message therefore offered a fair representation of what Dabney envisioned when he taught that even a sermon on a single verse or a small section of Scripture must offer "constant and faithful reference to its context" in order to be counted a "true exposition."[16]

No "True Exposition"

Despite Dabney's requirement that a true exposition must give the meaning of the biblical author in the text and make faithful reference to its context, Dabney did not always practice his theory. Many of his sermons demonstrate only a loose connection to the text, while others ignore or misrepresent its meaning altogether. This latter group manifests the worst abuses of the age: Dabney used a single verse or clause of text shorn from its context, identified a doctrine or duty in it, abandoned the text, and preached a topical sermon that in some cases defied the plain meaning of

16. Dabney, *Sacred Rhetoric*, 77.

the text. Over against the dictates of his homiletical theory, many of his sermons therefore convey the impression that Dabney had chosen a topic beforehand,[17] employing the text as a mere motto,[18] from which he segued into a pre-determined topical sermon.

Loosely Connected Sermons

As an example of a sermon in which Dabney's message remained connected to the text, but in which that connection was tenuous, consider his Full Text on Acts 16:30–31,[19] in which Luke writes: "Then he brought them out and said, 'Sirs, what must I do to be saved?' And they said, 'Believe in the Lord Jesus, and you will be saved, you and your household.'" The text is drawn from Luke's account of the imprisonment and subsequent miraculous release of Paul and Silas in Philippi. The jailer, terrified, asked Paul and Silas the text's question, and upon hearing their reply, believed in Jesus. Dabney must have considered these two verses an epitome text. They ostensibly stand for and comprise the meaning of the broader story. The way he unfolded and proclaimed the text, however, was only loosely tied to the actual "meaning of God in that sentence."[20]

After reading the text and affirming the singular importance of the question and its answer, Dabney asked: "What is this believing? Of what does it consist, and how may I know that I have done it?" Without Exposition, Dabney moved directly to his Proposition, in which he purposed to show "*the nature of saving faith.*" Specifically addressing unbelievers, Dabney assured them that they would not really understand him, asking:

> Who could explain *vision* satisfactorily to a blind man; or *sound*, to one born deaf? So the natural man, who receiveth not the things of the Spirit, and cannot know them, because they are spiritually discerned, can only gain a clear idea of what faith is, by exercising it.

Dabney thus asserted: "Saving faith is a lesson which none but God can teach," and conceded, "When . . . I attempt to present the subject to your minds, I do it only in the hope, that [the Lord] may give the spiritual vision and direct you to the light."

17. Dabney's theory castigated this practice. Dabney, *Sacred Rhetoric*, 94.
18. Dabney, *Sacred Rhetoric*, 75.
19. Box 9, File 9/1, Acts 16:30–31 Full Text.
20. Dabney, *Sacred Rhetoric*, 77.

Dabney recognized that the word "faith" has many meanings in Scripture. Objectively it can refer to the body of gospel doctrine, to fidelity, or to an "honest, conscientious persuasion of the lawfulness of particular acts." But more often, faith refers to belief, of which Dabney described four species. First is that which Dabney called "historical faith," which is belief in the Bible in much the same way that a person might believe in any other historical document, but "without any effect on the heart or conduct." Second is that which Dabney termed "temporary faith," which describes assent to the truth of the Scripture in such a way that it has some convicting effect on the conscience, but which is born of natural fear rather than regeneration. Third is that which Dabney called "the faith of miracles," which believes that God is with or in the person who performed a miracle, but which does not create in the wonder-watcher living faith in the God who empowered the miracle. Fourth is that which Dabney called "saving or justifying faith," which "receives Christ and infallibly makes all who exercise it partakers of his salvation." Dabney asserted that this final variety is the type of faith in view in Acts 16:30–31. The former three do "not ensure salvation," while the fourth invariably does.

Having explored the kind of faith that Paul commands, Dabney identified the true object of such faith, writing: "The special object embraced by saving faith, is not the whole of revelation, but only that part of it called the Gospel . . . wh.[ich] informs us of the salvation of Jesus Christ." He continued: "When we limit the proper object of saving faith thus, it is not meant that we may willfully reject any part of revelation." Instead, Dabney wrote:

> When we say that Christ alone is the proper object of such faith, we mean that if the sinner has never in his life had an opportunity of learning any part of God's truth, except that which declares Christ's work, still, the belief of this is all-sufficient to save his soul.

Dabney thus argued that faith, when trusting in the Father, trusts in the Son, for the Father sent him. When trusting in the promises of redemption, faith trusts in the Son, for they promise him. When trusting in God's mercy, faith trusts in the Son, for God's mercy is given to men and women only through Jesus Christ.

Noting that true faith requires mental assent, Dabney wrote: "No one . . . exercises saving faith, unless he is fully persuaded of the *truth* of the gospel." But Dabney also taught that true faith is more than mere assent, writing that it is "eminently an *act* of the will." Dabney explained that the Scriptures describe human volition in several ways. It is called trust, looking to Christ, receiving Christ, coming to Christ, feeding on Christ, fleeing to Christ, and obedience to the faith, and Dabney summarized: "Belief is carried out in the actions." He therefore argued that the work of grace must be preceded by a work of the Law, which convicts a person of his or her sin and creates a sense of need for the Savior who is offered. Stating that "[n]o man reaches forth after that which he does not want," Dabney argued that the Law produces conviction of sin and of its consequences.

Describing the Scriptural teaching regarding the kind of faith that saves, Dabney wrote:

> It is a belief and hearty *personal* reception of, and submission to the salvation of Jesus Christ *as it is offered to us by God*, and that flowing from honest and scriptural conviction of sin. He who has saving faith, not only believes, but receives and adopts for himself, by a most voluntary and sincere agreement, the salvation of Christ. He accepts and adopts it on the terms on which God offers it to him, not on some terms of his own devising, and *for the purposes* for which it is offered, not for some imaginary or forbidden purposes which God has not promised to fulfill by it. And he is led to accept it thus, by a sincere conviction that he *is suffering that need*, which Christ offers to satisfy.

This saving faith is followed by "an honest purpose of *obedience,*" for Dabney insisted that God saves Christians from sin for obedience.

Dabney distinguished between the "assurance of faith," which he defined as confidence in the saving work of God in Christ, and "the assurance of hope," which he defined as confidence of personal salvation, suggesting that saving faith necessarily includes the former but not the latter. Admitting that his view contradicted Calvin and other Reformers, Dabney stated that theirs was an over-reaction to Rome, and pointed to Scripture and church history to support his view, noting: "[T]he most eminent bible [*sic*] saints were at times without this assured hope." Dabney thus argued: "He who doubts whether he himself ever truly believed, may be a real Christian; but he who doubts whether Jesus Christ will save those who *have* truly believed, *is not.*" Saving faith must therefore proceed from "the operations of the Holy Ghost on the heart." Dabney's Conclusion returned to the text, exhorting his hearers to ask of God the text's question, and to plead with God for the text's reply to become a reality in their own hearts and lives.

It is important to note that Dabney said nothing in this sermon that is heterodox. His presentation of both the act of believing and of the object on which a person must believe was masterful. Yet there is a real sense in which it appears that Dabney desired to speak on the nature of saving faith, and used Acts 16:30–31 to do so. He provided no context for the history or setting of the text, and whereas Dabney's theological conclusions were orthodox, Luke did not teach in Acts 16 the specific details about saving faith that Dabney proclaimed in his sermon. Luke recorded the miraculous work of God that led to the jailer's salvation. Dabney, however, did not confine himself to the "meaning of God in that sentence,"[21] but moved beyond it in order to offer a theological lecture on saving faith.[22] It is not so much that Dabney was faithless to the text, as it was that he used the Scripture as a platform from which to teach his theology of saving faith.

This pattern is repeated, but with perhaps less attachment to the Scripture, in a Full Text on Colossians 1:12,[23] which is a fragment of sentence which says,". . . giving thanks to the Father, who has qualified you to share in the inheritance of the saints in light." The broader preaching text from which this fragment proceeds includes Colossians 1:9–14, in which the author expresses his desire to see the Colossians grow in knowledge so that they might walk in a manner worthy of their Lord. Dabney's fragment is embedded in a cluster of verses that mingle indicative and imperative statements under the umbrella of a prayer of joy offered for the believers of the Colossian Church. It is difficult to understand how Dabney viewed this fragment either as a capital or epitome text.

In his Introduction, Dabney compared believing sinners to pardoned, but morally wretched criminals. Apart from God making Christians holy, none could be fit for heaven even though forgiven. Dabney's Exposition offered various scriptural references about heaven, after which his Argument sought to address moral, amicable nonbelievers, especially any who believed themselves to be fit for heaven apart from faith in Christ. His unstated Proposition sought to convince these unbelievers that they would not enjoy heaven even if they went there.

In supporting that Proposition, Dabney offered the following points: 1. Unbelievers would not like heaven, for it celebrates the person and practices—God and his worship—that they had shunned while on earth. 2. Unbelievers would miss this present world, for they would leave behind all that they had preferred here over that which is in heaven. 3. Unbelievers, though disliking heaven, would suffer eternity among people who truly enjoyed it. 4. Unbelievers would spend eternity in envy of the happiness of others. 5.

21. Dabney, *Sacred Rhetoric*, 77.

22. See also Box 6, File 6/7, Psalm 85:10 Full Text. This sermon is a well-crafted essay on the penal substitutionary atonement of Christ, and of how its application to the sinner through faith reconciles righteousness and peace such that they "kiss each other." It also has little to do with the text. The sermon offers no Exposition, and Dabney could have chosen any number of texts as his segue to this topic.

23. Box 10, File 10/1, Colossians 1:12 Full Text.

Unbelievers would lack fellowship, for Christian saints made holy would shun their sinful presence. 6. Unbelievers would know that this shunning was just. 7. Unbelievers would be fixed in this situation forever. Dabney thus concluded: "Such a heaven would be only [slightly][24] less dreadful to you than hell." He then cast them upon Christ for the very redemption that they had previously rejected.

This sermon represents a clever imagining of what it might be like for an unbeliever to reside in heaven. It also has little to do with the text. Dabney fixed upon the word "inheritance" and equated it with heaven. Instead of using the text for the purpose for which the biblical author employed it, as an encouragement of and prayer for believers, Dabney used it to show non-Christians the miseries of heaven apart from salvation in Christ. He provided no context, in fact ignoring it, and failed in any appreciable way to carry forward the "meaning of God in that sentence."[25]

The connection between sermon and text is nearly severed altogether in a Skeleton on Exodus 18:21,[26] in which Jethro, Moses's father-in-law, instructed Moses: "Moreover, look for able men from all the people, men who fear God, who are trustworthy and hate a bribe, and place such men over the people as chiefs of thousands, of hundreds, of fifties, and of tens." In the broader context, the administrative duties of judging civil cases and disputes between the people of Israel had overburdened Moses, and his father-in-law's full counsel encouraged him to appoint worthy men to sit as judges so that Moses himself would not falter. The verse Dabney chose failed to meet his criteria for an epitome text, and is difficult to justify as a capital text.

Dabney's Introduction began with a brief overview of various systems of government, noting that the Scripture does not prescribe a system for succession in contemporary civil governments. He then asserted: "In [the] absence of revelat[ion] we must not interpret prov[idence]." Rejecting government by means of hereditary monarchy, Dabney suggested that the text contains principles with which American Christians should enter the voting booth. Thereupon followed a brief Exposition, which set the Mosaic context. Dabney then argued the following points: 1. "We are to choose *able men*." 2. These men must fear God. 3. They must be moral men.

Dabney stated that the text presents the "duty" of principled voting, and that any person who disagreed was sinning. Describing scenes of injustice in American government, Dabney assigned blame, declaring: "*All*

24. While this paper has inserted other brackets in Dabney's text in order to clarify his meaning, these brackets are original to Dabney.

25. Dabney, *Sacred Rhetoric*, 77.

26. Box 6, File 6/4, Exodus 18:21 Skeleton.

this [is] *your fault.*" He then enforced the duty of influencing American political parties to endorse moral, God-fearing candidates, offering the *apologia* that he had not been "meddling," for the "text is in the Bible and the sermon is in the text." He closed by offering thanks for America's national heritage and blessings, and pressed his hearers to embrace corresponding national responsibilities.

The text Dabney used is not properly concerned with elections to civil government posts, nor does it envision representative American democracy. Instead it describes how Moses, as the divinely commissioned prophet, appointed fellow Israelites to exercise judicial functions in the theocratic Kingdom of Israel. Dabney's sermon, which he composed for the American Independence Day holiday, was thus connected to the text only thematically: in both text and sermon stand the necessity in the broadest strokes to secure godly people for positions of leadership. Dabney's sermon came perilously close to making the text say that which it does not. It was far from the "true exposition"[27] of Dabney's theory.

Sermons That Abuse the Text

Along with preaching sermons that were, to varying degrees, only loosely connected to the text, Dabney also preached sermons in which he made the text say that which it simply does not. These sermons represent the worst abuses of the nineteenth-century homiletic, in which the text served as little more than a segue for the preacher's own thoughts or a mere motto for the sermon.

Consider Dabney's Skeleton on Matthew 9:38,[28] which is a fragment in which Jesus says, ". . . therefore pray earnestly to the Lord of the harvest to send out laborers into his harvest." Dabney evidently considered this fragment an epitome text, and began his sermon by asserting that the great means of harvesting is the raising up of preachers. He assumed, without providing exposition to justify his assumption, that the harvesters in Christ's analogy are preachers, whom the Holy Spirit appoints through the prayers of Christians. Without offering a formal Proposition, Dabney moved directly into an Argument that unfolded under three heads: 1. The urgency of prayer. 2. These prayers should be for colleges and schools. 3. These prayers should be accompanied by like conduct. He concluded with an exhortation to young men who were considering entering the Presbyterian ministry.

27. Dabney, *Sacred Rhetoric*, 77.

28. Box 8, File 8/1, Matthew 9:38 Skeleton.

Dabney preached this sermon at Tinkling Spring Church on an appointed day of prayer for colleges. It appears that he had in mind a pre-existing theme—prayer for colleges—and found a text he connected to it. The force of his sermon must lead the casual listener to believe that Jesus, in Matthew 9:28, taught Christians to pray for theological seminaries to produce good preachers who would then become the harvesters whom Jesus mentioned. Dabney's sermon not only allowed lay listeners to absolve themselves of responsibility to labor in the harvest fields, but also encouraged them to believe that this text urged them to offer prayerful support to seminaries and theological colleges. While it is certainly crucial that Christians pray for the fidelity of theological colleges and seminaries, and while such prayer may even represent a legitimate application of this text, the Scripture itself simply does not teach that which Dabney made it teach. He abused the text, using it to proclaim a pre-determined topical sermon on prayer for colleges.

A similar abuse appears in Dabney's sermon on Genesis 4:9,[29] which records: "Then the Lord said to Cain, 'Where is Abel your brother?' He said, 'I do not know; am I my brother's keeper?'" Cain had just murdered his brother and the Lord confronted him. In the words that follow Cain's question, the Lord exposed Cain's guilt and cursed him, but promised to protect him from retribution.

Offering little by way of Introduction, Dabney proceeded directly to ask the question: "*Is there any obligation on us, to promote and protect the virtue and moral character of our brother?*" He replied in the affirmative, offering five proofs: 1. Proved from the nature of virtue, which Dabney defined as "a spontaneous love of the good and hatred of the evil." 2. Proved from Matthew 22:39, in which Jesus taught: "You shall love your neighbor as yourself." 3. Proved from the fact that men and women morally influence other men and women. 4. Proved from the fact that both passive and active deeds of hatred toward our brothers and sisters are culpable. 5. Proved from the great duty that every Christian must seek the salvation of the lost. Dabney then offered his Proposition, declaring: "Our purpose in discussing this principle is to apply it to the subject of temperance reform."

From this point forward, Dabney did not reference the text, but instead began to expound the principle of Christian responsibility to temperance reform. In so doing, he acknowledged: "Drinking moderately of intoxicating drinks is not necessarily *malum per se*," and rebuked the "wicked tampering with exegesis" that suggested that the wine of the Bible was not alcoholic. Affirming that moderate consumption of alcohol is not forbidden in

29. Box 6, File 6/4, Genesis 4:9 Skeleton.

Scripture, Dabney wrote: "I can never consent to drive [the] ploughshare of temp[erance] over [the] ruins of S.S. [sacred Scripture] and excommunicate all who will not say [that] one drop is necessarily a sin." Turning to address scriptural "principles of temperance," he noted the following: 1. "Drunkenness is [a] heinous sin." 2. Our indulgence in alcoholic beverages is to be carefully governed. 3. If our drinking will lead another astray, it is our "positive duty" not to drink. 4. It is "unscriptural to make and sell intoxicating beverages." In proving this assertion, Dabney offered the following reasons: a. Alcohol creates temptation. b. Alcohol compares to seduction. c. Making alcohol creates a nuisance to our neighbors. d. Selling alcohol is the same as selling the means of murder or suicide. e. By appeal to conscience. Anticipating objections to this argument, Dabney wrote a note to self: "Answer defensive pretexts," after which followed arguments that depend more on sociological data than on Scripture.

It is difficult to understand how Cain's murder of his brother affords proper Scriptural grounds for a temperance sermon, or how Dabney felt that he had preached "the meaning of God in that sentence" with "constant and faithful reference to its context."[30] To the contrary, Dabney divorced the text from its context and used it to discuss a pre-determined topic, effectively teaching that the Scripture says or means that which it clearly does not.

The clearest example of textual abuse in Dabney's collection might be his Full Text on Psalm 119:130,[31] in which the Psalmist declares: "The unfolding of your words gives light; it imparts understanding to the simple." After a brief Introduction, Dabney's Exposition asserted that the "light" is "divine knowledge" and "understanding" is wisdom. With these clarifications, he offered the following Proposition: "*Popery is necessarily unfavorable to knowledge and mental improvement.*" His Argument unfolded under four points of proof: 1. Proved by the Roman Church's continued use of Latin. 2. Proved by the Roman Church's restriction of the Bible to her priests. 3. Proved by the Roman Church's rejection of the right to individual interpretation. 4. Proved by the positive changes wrought by the Reformation. Dabney then refuted any who claimed otherwise. His Conclusion suggested that the Roman Catholic Church was incapable of teaching people to think for themselves but that Protestants must teach independent thinking. Ending with a brief word of charity, Dabney exhorted his hearers to "[s]eparate between the system and its followers. The former is the proper subject of reprobation, the latter of charity."

30. Dabney, *Sacred Rhetoric*, 77.

31. Box 7, File 7/1, Psalm 119:130 Full Text.

This sermon simply had nothing to do with the Scripture from which it supposedly was composed. Dabney the theorist had written: "When the pastor discusses only a single sentence or proposition of Scripture, as he will often and legitimately do, it should yet be a true exposition," and thus an "evolution of the meaning of God in that sentence, with constant and faithful reference to its context."[32] Dabney the preacher nevertheless delivered a sermon on the evils of popery from a single verse of Psalm 119, giving neither "constant and faithful reference" to the context, nor "the meaning of God in that sentence."[33] It was an abuse, not only of his homiletical theory, but also of the Scripture itself.

Summary

A standard Dabney sermon most often employed an isolated verse or clause of Scripture. Dabney's caveat regarding capital and epitome texts may explain some of these choices, while other sermons use fragments of text that are hard to justify according to Dabney's homiletical theory. Offering varying levels of theological, historical, or canonical context, Dabney generally employed an Introduction, Exposition, Proposition, a topical Argument, and a Conclusion. Designed to proclaim the doctrine or duty contained in the text rather than the text itself, his topical sermons reveal varying degrees of fidelity to his homiletical theory, which required of a "true exposition" that the preacher offer "constant and faithful reference to its context" and proclaim "the meaning of God in that sentence."[34] Many of Dabney's sermons connected only loosely to his chosen text, while others manifested the worst abuses of the nineteenth-century topical model, using isolated clauses of Scripture to segue into a topical sermon that often proclaimed that which the Scripture did not.

This analysis of Dabney's standard pulpit practice demonstrates that Dabney regularly neglected or contradicted vital components of his own homiletical theory in his topical preaching. From that foundation in Dabney's topical sermons, the following section of this chapter evaluates Dabney's non-Exercise Expository sermons, demonstrating that Dabney's expository sermons implemented his expository theory just as inconsistently as his topical sermons offered a "true exposition"[35] of the text.

32. Dabney, *Sacred Rhetoric*, 77.

33. Dabney, *Sacred Rhetoric*, 77.

34. Dabney, *Sacred Rhetoric*, 77.

35. Dabney, *Sacred Rhetoric*, 77.

Dabney's Expository Practice

Overview

Dabney's manuscript collection contains not only thirteen Expository Exercises, but also eleven non-Exercise Expository sermons. These eleven sermons comprise five Briefs, four Full Texts, one Skeleton, and one unlabeled sermon. Though unlabeled, this sermon was clearly composed in the pattern of a Skeleton. Of these eleven non-Exercise Expository sermons, four boast a companion Exercise that was composed upon the same text.[36] Given that the preceding chapter has already evaluated these sermons in their Exercise form, this chapter focuses on Dabney's seven non-Exercise Expository sermons that offer no companion Exercise.[37] The present evaluation of these sermons demonstrates that only three of Dabney's non-Exercise Expository sermons faithfully implemented his expository theory.

Faithful Expository Sermons

Dabney embodied his expository theory in an Expository sermon on Romans 10:6–10,[38] in which the Scripture teaches:

> But the righteousness based on faith says, "Do not say in your heart, 'Who will ascend into heaven?'" (that is, to bring Christ down) "or 'Who will descend into the abyss?'" (that is, to bring Christ up from the dead). But what does it say? "The word is near you, in your mouth and in your heart" (that is, the word of faith that we proclaim); because, if you confess with your mouth that Jesus is Lord and believe in your heart that God raised him from the dead, you will be saved. For with the heart one believes and is justified, and with the mouth one confesses and is saved.

Dabney's Introduction began with the assertion: "The great end of all the exhortations of the ministry to men is; to flee from the wrath to come—to make their peace with God." Moving to an Exposition that sought to

36. See Box 8, File 8/2, Matthew 11:28–30 Expository Exercise; Box 8, File 8/2, Matthew 25:24–30 Expository Exercise; Box 8, File 8/2, Philippians 4:4–7 Expository Exercise; Box 10, File 10/3, Hebrews 11:24–27 Expository Exercise.

37. Three of these sermons feature in Dabney's "Army Sermons" in Box 6, File 6/3a and 6/3b. All are Full Texts. Two reflect expanded Exercises, while one is a word-for-word repeat of a previously composed Full Text. This Full Text on Romans 10:6–10 was not originally labeled an Expository sermon, but in Dabney's collection of Army Sermons it is labeled Expository. See Box 9, File 9/3 Romans 10:6–9 Full Text.

38. Box 6, File 6/3b, Romans 10:6–10 Full Text.

address misconceptions, Dabney began by noting that Paul quoted from Deuteronomy 30:12–14, offering a note to self: "Recite passage." He then clarified an apparent inconsistency between the frame of reference of Moses's words and the way in which Paul employed them, arguing that Moses commanded the people to turn to "God with all the heart and the soul," which Dabney took as turning in faith toward the work of the promised Redeemer as he was foreshadowed in the Mosaic Law.[39]

Having established this, Dabney moved to the body of the text, and suggested that the sinner needed only to sense his or her sin in order to prepare to believe. He wrote: "There is no righteousness to be brought in by us, no atonement to be invented, no addition to be made to that everlasting righteousness, which Christ brought us, when he descended from the Father, went to the grave, and rose again the 3rd day." Dabney's Argument unfolded under five points, which followed the versification of the text. His first point, employing verses 6 and 7, counseled against viewing salvation as an intellectual awakening, as though redemption consisted merely of "the secrets of heaven, or the mysteries of the world of spirits." Rather, "*All* is [already] revealed, which is to be believed for salvation, and so revealed, that its saving reception requires nothing but a childlike simplicity coupled with humility." Dabney therefore exhorted:

> Lay not in your heart then oh sinner, who shall ascend into heaven, or fathom the abyss, to bring the knowledge of Christ to the soul. All is revealed, all is clear and explicit. No discovery. No laborious wisdom is required of you. All that is needed is a simple and a humble heart, to embrace God's word!

In his second point, which he grounded in verse 8, Dabney taught that faith is "natural and easy, to him who is willing to believe." His third point, which he derived from verse 9, asserted that "Christ's work of redemption" is "the direct object of saving faith," and thus, "To believe in the resurrection is, therefore, to believe in Christ's complete work of redemption. And this is the object of saving faith." In his fourth point, which he grounded in verse 10, and which Dabney called "the centre of the whole subject," he argued: "Saving faith is not a mere *notion* of the understanding; it is and act of the affections and will." In commenting on what it means to believe "with the heart," Dabney asserted: "You must so believe as to act out your belief." Expanding this thought, Dabney taught:

> The S.S. [sacred Scriptures], which aim to give practical, rather than metaphysical views of spiritual exercises, do describe

39. See Westminster Larger Catechism Q&A 34 for Dabney's thought at this point.

> saving faith as embracing two elements, conviction of the understanding, concerning Gospel truth, and the active embracing of it by the will and purposes. The emphatic expression of the text makes this evident. Saving faith is described by almost every term which expresses action.

Dabney then listed some of these terms: trusting, looking, receiving, coming, embracing, fleeing, and laying hold among others. He cautioned: "The truth is, that the real, spiritual and scriptural belief of the essential truths of the gospel, even with the conviction of the understanding, is a work of the renewing Spirit," and thus, "When the Spirit has produced this spiritual apprehension and belief in the understanding, he has done all that is necessary, to secure the actions of faith by the will; for the will follows the understanding." His fifth point returned to verse 9, but was not a point of Argument. Rather it applied his previous exposition[40] as Dabney urged his hearers to believe and confess verbally. His Conclusion exhorted: "Helpless sinner: guilty for thy helplessness, cast thyself upon the Saviour. Away with proud cavils; if thou are impotent, then fall . . . submissive on the Saviour's arms; and he will work in thee and for thee."

Dabney's Argument was therefore comprised of an extended exposition that unfolded according to the versification of the text, which culminated when Dabney called upon his hearers to do that which the texts calls them to do. It was a faithful implementation of his expository theory.

No less faithful was Dabney's Expository Brief from Matthew 19:16–22.[41] Matthew records a conversation between Jesus and a wealthy young man, writing:

> And behold, a man came up to him, saying, "Teacher, what good deed must I do to have eternal life?" And he said to him, "Why do you ask me about what is good? There is only one who is good. If you would enter life, keep the commandments." He said to him, "Which ones?" And Jesus said, "You shall not murder, You shall not commit adultery, You shall not steal, You shall not bear false witness, Honor your father and mother, and, You shall love your neighbor as yourself." The young man said to him, "All these I have kept. What do I still lack?" Jesus said to him, "If you would be perfect, go, sell what you possess and give to the poor, and you will have treasure in heaven; and come, follow

40. Dabney specifically identified verse 9 as his application. His exposition thus moved through verses 6–10, unfolding according to the versification of the text, before Dabney returned to verse 9 for application.

41. Box 8, File 8/2, Matthew 19:16–22 Brief.

> me." When the young man heard this he went away sorrowful, for he had great possessions.

Dabney offered a terse Introduction, in which he noted: "Sinai 'gendereth to bondage,'" adding: "So fell this inquirer." After describing the young man as moral, sincere, and earnest, possessed of a question that was no mere pretext for a trap, Dabney nevertheless noted that "self-righteous pride blinds," and had blinded this young man to his sin. Moving to an extended Exposition, which unfolded according to the versification of the text, and which passed into an extended section of Application, Dabney argued that Christ's words to the young man were no "self-righteous remedy." His Conclusion left his hearers to ponder the necessity of renewal through the Holy Spirit from Titus 3:5. The sermon followed Dabney's expository theory closely, for the Argument was comprised of an extended exposition that unfolded according to the versification of the text.

Dabney's Expository Skeleton on 1 Peter 4:12–15[42] likewise faithfully implemented his theory. The Scripture teaches:

> Beloved, do not be surprised at the fiery trial when it comes upon you to test you, as though something strange were happening to you. But rejoice insofar as you share Christ's sufferings, that you may also rejoice and be glad when his glory is revealed. If you are insulted for the name of Christ, you are blessed, because the Spirit of glory and of God rests upon you. But let none of you suffer as a murderer or a thief or an evildoer or as a meddler.

By way of Introduction, Dabney noted that to be "Forewarned is [to be] forearmed," and that this truth teaches Christians to "act on principle." After reading the text, he noted that prosperity can cause people to forget that the normal lot of Christians is to participate in the sufferings of Christ. Such forgetfulness can lead Christians to astonishment when they face trials. Purposing to unfold the Proposition, "Suffering for consciences' sake is the Believer's *appointed test*," Dabney moved into a section entitled, "Exposit. [ion] and Discussion." He argued against the Roman Catholic teaching that Christian sufferings are atoning, and began to work verse-by-verse through the text. His Exposition, interspersed with application, carried through to the Conclusion of the sermon, in which Dabney offered brief exhortations: "Contest short. Issue sure. Triumph great."

The common thread that binds together these three faithful Expository messages is that in each the Argument is comprised of an extended exposition that unfolds according to the versification of the text. Variation

42. Box 10, File 10/4, 1 Peter 4:12–15 Skeleton.

exists. Dabney's Romans 10:6–10 sermon offered no explicit Proposition and unfolded the text by means of numbered points. His Matthew 19:16–22 sermon offered neither a Proposition nor numbered heads. His 1 Peter 4:12–15 sermon included a formal Proposition, but no points or heads. Each carried forward the crucial structural component of Dabney's expository theory: *the Argument was comprised of an extended exposition that unfolded according to the versification of the text.*

Inconsistent Expository Sermons

Other messages that Dabney labeled Expository included expository elements but inconsistently implemented Dabney's expository theory. Consider his Brief on James 1:21–25,[43] which teaches:

> Therefore put away all filthiness and rampant wickedness and receive with meekness the implanted word, which is able to save your souls.
>
> But be doers of the word, and not hearers only, deceiving yourselves. For if anyone is a hearer of the word and not a doer, he is like a man who looks intently at his natural face in a mirror. For he looks at himself and goes away and at once forgets what he was like. But the one who looks into the perfect law, the law of liberty, and perseveres, being no hearer who forgets but a doer who acts, he will be blessed in his doing.

Dabney's Introduction recounted a story about an outbreak of plague in London and the anxiety it caused. He then imagined a scenario in which a miraculous cure emerged. The recipients of the cure, being healed and grateful, took to the streets to proclaim good news of the cure. Dabney wondered, Would it be heard by the sick, dying, and terrified? Asserting that it would be heard and heard gladly, he lamented that the gospel of Jesus Christ is not similarly heard. Instead, most fail to hear it, and even the healed nit-pick the way in which their heralds tell of the cure. Dabney then read the text, which led directly to his Proposition: "The traits of the profitable hearer."

The Exposition followed, in which Dabney first described how bad hearing takes place. Functionally, this was his first head of his Argument. The second head addressed requirements for good hearing, among which Dabney listed: 1. Meekness. He described the nature of meekness, how meekness grows in the Christian, and possible barriers to becoming meek. 2. Earnestness and heedfulness. 3. Obedience. Dabney noted a challenge

43. Box 10, File 10/4, James 1:21–25 Brief.

that he believed the church faced. If the minister offered too little instruction, the people would "remain practical heathen." If, however, the minister offered too much instruction, the church's teachings would become "*trite by repetitions.*" He concluded with a note to self: "[S]how how, by *doing*, [the] law of habit becomes your friend, instead of your enemy."

Dabney identified a subject from the text—profitable hearing of the Word—and addressed that subject topically. Interestingly, elements from each verse, largely in order, appeared in the sermon. But fundamentally, Dabney's Argument divided the text theologically rather than following the versification of the text, and he offered a topical explanation of bad and good hearing. His message inconsistently embodied his expository theory.

Equally interesting, but also inconsistent, is the Full Text Dabney preached on Psalm 81:10,[44] in which the Lord says: "I am the Lord your God, who brought you up out of the land of Egypt. Open your mouth wide, and I will fill it." Dabney's Introduction addressed those who had been believers for some time, asking: "Have you made that progress in the divine life" that you "confidently expected" by this point in your walk with Christ? He then suggested: "Your actual career has disappointed a bright and glowing promise at the onset," and wondered aloud if that discrepancy was the fault of unrealistic expectations. He replied: "The text answers, *No.*"

In turning to Exposition, Dabney asserted that Asaph followed the history of Israel in order "to illustrate the principles on which [God] acts toward his people," and then claimed: "In the history of Israel then, you have a type of your own spiritual progress from the bondage of sin to the heavenly inheritance." Recounting the promise of the Exodus, God's continual favor, the covenant at Sinai, and the intent of the people to conquer the Promised Land, Dabney asked: "Was it not reasonable to anticipate for such a beginning a triumphant and speedy issue?" He answered that every observer would respond in the affirmative.

After reading the text, Dabney exclaimed: "How lame and impotent was the progress from this auspicious commencement!" Describing the murmuring of Israel at Meribah, their worship of the Golden Calf, and their refusal to conquer Canaan, Dabney noted that even after Israel had entered the land their conquest was partial and their obedience "mixed and imperfect." He then asked, in essence, What happened? Quickly dispatching the notion that God was to blame, Dabney pointed his hearers to verse 11 followed by verse 13, which teach God's slowness to discipline. Dabney then insisted: "Look at the counterpart of this picture in your own spiritual history," declaring: "For you also were wrought deliverances."

44. Box 6, File 6/7, Psalm 81:10 Full Text.

Asking his hearers to recall the moment of their first love to Christ, he declared that they had expected "glorious endowments of spiritual strength," and queried: "[H]ave these hopes been realized?" Answering in the negative, he suggested: "Your life answers but too truly to the history of Israel; a story of blighted promise." He then argued that the reason for both was the same: "'You would not hearken to His voice.'" Dabney affirmed that God had not abandoned his promise, which led to the Proposition: "*God desires the eminent grace of all his people.*"

As he began the Argument, Dabney suggested that too many Christians acted as though the heroes of the faith possessed a special, extraordinary grace that common Christians lack. Decrying this assumption, he insisted:

> It is in opposition to this [attitude], that God urges his people, "open thy mouth wide and I will fill it;" and declares his yearning desire that his people had hearkened unto him, and had walked in his ways, that he might have subdued all their enemies, and fed them with the fatness of their heritage.

His Argument unfolded under three heads: 1. Dabney urged his hearers to consider that there were no chosen few among the chosen. 2. He urged them to remember God's work for them by retelling the gospel. He asked: "What motives prompted your God to all this mighty and gracious work for you?" answering that it could not be with the purpose of receiving from them "a stinted service and halfhearted thanks." 3. Dabney then noted that while "[i]t is never safe for the creature to undertake to speculate concerning the secret purposes of our infinite God," it is in the interest of God's own glory and his plans of redemption to desire the eminent grace of his people. Wondering if the wise master would withhold from his servants the tools necessary to farm his land, Dabney concluded that it could not be God's will to withhold his graces from his people.

Referencing several texts—1 Thessalonians 4:8; John 15:7; John 16:24; James 1:5; Luke 11:13; Deuteronomy 32:29—in which God shows his displeasure with human sin, Dabney addressed the possible rebuttal that since God is sovereign every believer enjoys only the graces God apportions. Dabney suggested that this view misunderstood God's sovereignty and asserted: "*Nothing but the contumacy or waywardness of the recipient*" prevented a Christian from fully employing the available grace of God. He then affirmed that "God foreordains whatsoever comes to pass,"[45] arguing

45. Westminster Shorter Catechism Question 7 asks, "What are the decrees of God?" It answers: "The decrees of God are, his eternal purpose, according to the counsel of his will, whereby, for his own glory, he hath foreordained whatsoever comes to pass."

that divine sovereignty and human responsibility act at the same time. It is thus wicked for any Christian to ascribe his or her low spiritual condition to the sovereignty of God. Referring to verse 10, Dabney exhorted his hearers: "Enlarge thy desires for more liberal measures of grace, and strength, and joy and *God will fill them.*"

In Conclusion, Dabney asserted:

> I have attempted my brethren, to give the S.S. [sacred Scripture's] explanation of this doctrine, because I am persuaded many Christians indolently content themselves with referring their inferior grade of spiritual life to the divine sovereignty. The text teaches us, that this is an abuse of a high and glorious truth. It is an abuse exactly parallel to that of the unbeliever, who should audaciously attempt to justify his rebellion against God, by the same doctrine.

He closed, writing: "It is your duty to aim, not at being a common Christian, but a most eminent Christian."

Dabney apparently felt the need to vindicate God from the cavil that he is responsible for a lack of sanctification in the average Christian, and chose a text that did not truly address it. Dabney offered significant context from Psalm 81 and from Israel's history, but could not pursue exposition according to the versification of the text, for he delimited his preaching text to a single verse. He may have considered this verse the epitome text of the Psalm, but if so then the reader must wonder why Dabney labeled the sermon Expository. The very point of Dabney's teaching on capital and epitome texts was that these represented the only two faithful ways to preach *non*-expository messages.[46] If Psalm 81:10 was an epitome text, then the sermon was not, by Dabney's own definition, an expository sermon. If it was an expository sermon, then Psalm 81:10 could not be an epitome text. Of all the texts that one could employ to vindicate the character of God, or to exhort Christians to pursue piety, this was far from the most satisfactory, and tended toward the very abuse of Scripture that faithful expository preaching theoretically prevents.

Mislabeled Expository Sermons

The reader will recall that the previous chapter identified as mislabeled several of Dabney's Expository Exercises. Two of his non-Exercise Expository

46. Dabney, *Sacred Rhetoric*, 77–78.

messages also falsely bear the appellation Expository. Consider Dabney's Brief on Romans 5:6–11,[47] in which the Scripture teaches:

> For while we were still weak, at the right time Christ died for the ungodly. For one will scarcely die for a righteous person—though perhaps for a good person one would dare even to die—but God shows his love for us in that while we were still sinners, Christ died for us. Since, therefore, we have now been justified by his blood, much more shall we be saved by him from the wrath of God. For if while we were enemies we were reconciled to God by the death of his Son, much more, now that we are reconciled, shall we be saved by his life. More than that, we also rejoice in God through our Lord Jesus Christ, through whom we have now received reconciliation.

Dabney's Introduction began by suggesting that love for God must stand as the prime motivation for a Christian, acknowledging that God does not so much command love as he does evoke it "as spontaneous, by the suitable apprehension of [an] object." Moving into Exposition, Dabney offered a translation and interpretation of several Greek words, all of which led to the following Proposition: "*Divine Love in Redempt.*[ion]." His Argument suggested that his Proposition was illustrated by: 1. Sacrifice, namely Christ's death, and 2. The contrast of the parties involved, namely God's infinity verses human finitude, as well as God's holiness over against human sin. After establishing the outlines of redeeming love, Dabney moved to Application, in which he used verses 9–11 to exhort Christians toward "the duty of Christian devotion," while also encouraging the lost to respond to God's love in Christ with faith.

It is hard to understand how Dabney believed that this message was specifically expository. Aside from the fact that he chose a proper preaching unit rather than an isolated verse, the structure of the sermon is topical, not expository. The Argument does not follow the versification of the text, and the sermon strongly resembles one of Dabney's standard, topical messages in structure and style.

Consider also Dabney's sermon on Mark 9:43–48,[48] in which Jesus teaches:

> If your hand causes you to sin, cut it off. It is better for you to enter life crippled than with two hands to go to hell, to the unquenchable fire. And if your foot causes you to sin, cut it off. It is better for you to enter life lame than with two feet to be thrown

47. Box 9, File 9/2, Romans 5:6–11 Brief.

48. Box 8, File 8/3, Mark 9:43–48 [Unlabeled Skeleton]

> into hell. And if your eye causes you to sin, tear it out. It is better for you to enter the kingdom of God with one eye than with two eyes to be thrown into hell, "where their worm does not die and the fire is not quenched."

Dabney's Introduction began by castigating the Christianity of his age. He chided: "This luxurious Age requires that Christianity shall be *made easy* to it. Soft seats in church; Luscious music—Seductive Rhetoric in Preacher, to 'gild the pill' of Truth," and lamented, "Easy and entertaining illustrations of Lessons, etc., etc.," noting, "If not, men don't feel bound to do their duty at all—So far has it gone!" Turning to Exposition, Dabney asserted: "Christ never courted followers thus." After reading the text he explained: "Members denote sins," and "offend = ensnare." He then wrote that "Excision = crucifixion and denial," which is "a cruel process, to which, yet the reasonable man feels impelled (properly) by a far more fearful alternative: a terrible and endless perdition." Having established the meaning of the words in the text, Dabney stated his Proposition: "Our purpose: To expound simply the surface truths *Christ* here teaches of this *sharp alternative.*"

Dabney noted that people love their sins, but also that sin ultimately imposes a tyranny on the person "of lusts long indulged," comparing such a person to one who long abuses opium, who serves the drug rather than being served by it. Dabney then addressed the truth that Christ does not offer an easy remedy. The malady of sin requires a process "exquisitely painful," a stomach-turning self-surgery. Dabney asked his hearers to contemplate "sawing remorselessly on through flesh and bone," and insisted: "Such [is] the necessity for the mortification of dearest sins."

Asking if Christ expects sinners to do this in their own strength, Dabney replied that only with Christ's grace can a Christian mortify sin. He referenced Matthew 11:28 for comfort during the process of mortification, Philippians 4:13 for strength to engage in mortification, and 2 Corinthians 7:4 as motivation for mortification. Addressing why it must be this way, Dabney argued that Christ framed the issue of mortification of sin harshly because he requires that each Christian learn to hate sin so fiercely that he or she will undertake the brutal spiritual surgery mortification requires. Christians must hope that Christ will carry them through the ordeal, rather than delivering them from it or anesthetizing them to it, and Dabney assured his hearers that aid is promised to those who desire holiness more than sin.

Noting that "*Darling sins are sweets*; and . . . *hell will be bitter*," Dabney taught that while no person consciously trades wholeness in this life for perdition in the next, people do seek a "middle way" by which to avoid the pain of excision or to delay it, pressing it into an indefinite future.

He insisted that his hearers must not do the same, and his Conclusion exhorted: "Be men—Choose the right alternatives. Resolve to crucify the Sin; and Omnipotent Love flies to your aid."

There is little exposition in this Expository sermon. Dabney provided no literary or historical context, and made no attempt other than bare definitions of words to expose the meaning. He assumed instead that the meaning was obvious, and then argued topically, providing a thoughtful theological treatment on the mortification of sin. Offering vivid illustration and exemplification of the alternatives set forth by the text, Dabney pressed his hearers to pursue even painful work in sanctification. His Argument, however, did not proceed according to the versification of the text, and this sermon differs little from a standard topical message.

Summary of Dabney's Expository Sermons

Of the twenty-four sermons that Dabney labeled Expository, including Exercise and non-Exercise sermons, less than a dozen faithfully embody his expository theory. The rest are either inconsistent or are simply mislabeled. Dabney's faithful Expository messages therefore represent approximately two percent of his extant sermons, and just four percent of his total preaching occasions.[49] Given that Dabney's theory defined true preaching as expository preaching,[50] these numbers are difficult to explain.

The final section of this chapter builds upon the preceding evaluation by examining not simply Dabney's individual expository sermons, but also the extent to which he did or did not preach the consecutive expository series that his theory admired, and which he urged his students to pursue.

Dabney's Expository Series

Significance

The present evaluation of Dabney's expository pulpit ministry cannot merely examine individual expository sermons, but must also reveal whether Dabney preached expository series on extended sections of Scripture or books

49. These numbers are necessarily approximations, for they reflect the author's evaluation of Dabney's labeled Expository messages. Nevertheless, even if all of his Expository messages faithfully implemented his theory, both the percentage of such sermons over against his total manuscript collection and the percentage of Expository preaching occasions over against his topical messages would remain quite small.

50. Dabney, *Sacred Rhetoric*, 76–77. See also Dabney, "Gospel," 600.

of the Bible. Dabney's theory called for consecutive expository preaching that presented the truths of Scripture in context. He argued: "A prevalent exercise of the pulpit should be the delivery of those explanations of connected passages of Scripture which are called . . . in modern phrase 'expository preaching.'"[51] He therefore taught:

> The scriptural theory of preaching . . . is to unfold to the hearers the counsel of God for their salvation. To accomplish this it is not enough to dwell with disproportioned fullness on some fragments. A continuous exhibition must be made at least of those important books of Scripture which present the system of redemption, with reference to the remainder for illustration. Let us recur to the just simile of the die impressing its image and superscription on a plastic substance. To produce a fair transcript, the artisan must press it down equably, and place the whole outline upon the wax. This is accomplished by the exposition in course of the chief parts of the Bible.[52]

The student of Dabney's sermon collection ought therefore to find not merely individual examples of expository sermons upon independent texts, but also connected series of expository sermons that cover extended sections of Scripture or whole books of the Bible.

Dabney's Consecutive Expository Record

Robert Dabney *did not preach a single consecutive expository series of any length through any passage or book of Scripture at any point in his fifty-two years of pulpit ministry*. Each of the twenty-four Expository sermons in his manuscript collection represents an independent text of Scripture, and no Expository sermon canonically follows or precedes any other. Each offers a stand-alone message. Dabney consistently preached upon isolated verses or clauses of text. Aside from his Narrative Exercises on Numbers 22–24 and 1 Samuel 24, the only other sermons in which Dabney preached an entire chapter of Scripture were his Expository Exercise on 1 Corinthians 13 and a Full Text on Psalm 23.[53]

Dabney's manuscript collection contains only one series of sermons on a connected passage of Scripture, which he preached on the Ten

51. Dabney, *Sacred Rhetoric*, 77.

52. Dabney, *Sacred Rhetoric*, 79.

53. Box 6, File 6/6, Psalm 23 Full Text.

Commandments at Tinkling Spring Church in 1851.[54] Although covering a seventeen-verse section of Scripture, the series is incomplete, and rather than expounding the text in course via expository messages, Dabney preached each commandment topically. Of the eleven sermons in the series, two covered the First Commandment, one each covered the Second and Third Commandments respectively, two explored the Fourth Commandment, and one dealt with the Fifth Commandment. Two sermons addressed the Eighth Commandment, while one sermon each addressed the Ninth and Tenth Commandments respectively. Dabney did not preach on the Sixth or Seventh Commandments, and while he began the series in February of 1851, preaching the first five sermons consecutively, he then departed from it, resuming it in August of that year. Since no sermons from May of 1851 are extant, it is possible that he preached the Sixth and Seventh Commandments during that time.

His sermons on the Ten Commandments represent the closest Dabney came to preaching an expository series on a passage of Scripture of any length. Of the approximately four hundred seventy sermons in Dabney's manuscript collection, these eleven sermons comprise the sum total of his connected series. Every other sermon stands alone.[55]

Evaluating Dabney's Practice

Though We Be Not Heterodox

Dabney's expository theory described Dabney's expository practice as faithless. Dabney understood that good ministers can preach in bad ways, and he therefore cautioned his students, writing:

> It is the great principle of Protestants that the Bible is for the people. And this implies that God, who knew best, has not only set forth such truths, but in such proportions and relations as really suit man's soul under the dealings of the Holy Spirit. There can be no other connections and forms of the truth so suitable as these, for these are they which God has seen fit to give. We may be guilty then of infidelity to our task, though we be not heterodox.[56]

54. These sermons are located in Box 6, File 6/4.

55. Dabney's manuscript collection is incomplete. It is therefore possible that a series of consecutive expository messages has been lost.

56. Dabney, *Sacred Rhetoric*, 38.

That guilt was, for Dabney, wrapped up in the preacher's failure to proclaim the Bible in its context, for "not only must Bible topics form the whole matter of our preaching, but they must be presented in scriptural aspects and proportions,"[57] which is why Dabney argued that all sermons "should be virtually expository, else they are not true sermons."[58] Dabney was by no means heterodox, but he was, according to his own expository theory, "guilty of infidelity."[59]

Connected expository series, though featuring prominently in Dabney's expository theory, formed no part whatsoever in his personal pulpit ministry. Struggling to explain this dissonance, Lawrence Trotter suggested that expository preaching "was swimming against the prevailing current of the nineteenth century," and that Dabney "apparently felt the need" to preach and teach according to the common "manner of preaching," which "was to preach each week from an isolated text."[60] Recognizing that this hardly justifies Dabney's inconsistency, Trotter noted: "It is truly remarkable that Dabney followed his own advice about expository preaching of extended passages so little in the course of his ministry."[61] He thus acknowledged that "[it] appears that Dabney was content to follow the normal custom of his day by sticking to short, isolated passages."[62]

Trotter nevertheless offered an intriguing explanation for why Dabney preached so few expository messages, specifically during the years in which he was teaching homiletics at Union Seminary. Implying that Dabney's Exercises may stand as evidence that Dabney knowingly limited his own pulpit practice due to his role as a homiletics instructor, Trotter suggested: "The instructional use to which he put [his] exercises also may explain why Dabney did not develop expository series on extended passages during his decades as a professor, because he wanted to give students samplings from many different texts."[63] Trotter's suggestion does not, however, explain Dabney's six years at Tinkling Spring. During his pastorate at Tinkling Spring, Dabney suffered no constrictions upon his pulpit, and was free to preach consecutive expository sermons without obligation to seminary students. That he preached no such series indicates that his

57. Dabney, *Sacred Rhetoric*, 38.

58. Dabney, *Sacred Rhetoric*, 77.

59. Dabney, *Sacred Rhetoric*, 38.

60. Trotter, *Always Prepared*, 52. *Always Prepared* is a revision of Trotter, "Blasting Rocks." It is used by permission of the author.

61. Trotter, *Always Prepared*, 144.

62. Trotter, "Blasting Rocks," 205.

63. Trotter, *Always Prepared*, 202.

practice during his Union Seminary years, so far from representing a self-imposed limitation, continued his previously established preference for topical preaching upon single verses or clauses of text.

Admiration vs. Commitment

Dabney therefore theoretically admired expository preaching, but was not personally committed to practice it. The reader will recall that Dabney offered several fundamental reasons why he admired expository preaching:[64] First, it was the biblical pattern, and Dabney located in Nehemiah 8 his warrant for expository preaching. Continuous exposition was also the ancient and Reformation practice, and Dabney noted an historical corollary between expository preaching and the vitality of the church. Likewise, Dabney believed that continuous exposition best accomplished the fundamental task of preaching, which is heraldry. Finally, Dabney noted a variety of benefits that expository preaching produced both in the preacher and the hearers.

The complete absence of connected expository series in Dabney's pulpit ministry demonstrates, however, that these observations failed to coalesce into a personal commitment. While Dabney noted the pattern of Nehemiah 8, he did not bind himself to it, and while he recognized a relationship between methods of preaching and the vitality of the church, he admired expository preaching as one admires a bygone era, with nostalgia rather than concerted personal action to reclaim the ancient practice. Expository preaching was, for Dabney, biblical, historical, and practically beneficial, but it never owned an exclusive claim on his conscience. Rather, Dabney viewed expository preaching as a legitimate rhetorical strategy rather than a personal hermeneutical commitment. As evidenced by his nearly exclusive use of capital and epitome texts, and even clauses of verses, Dabney admired, but was never personally committed to, continuous expository preaching.

Dabney Was Not Unique

Dabney's peers expressed many of the same admiring sentiments about expository preaching that Dabney offered, but it was Dabney who had defined true preaching as expository preaching, arguing that all sermons "should be virtually expository, else they are not true sermons,"[65] such that

64. See chapter 3 for further explication of these points.

65. Dabney, *Sacred Rhetoric*, 77.

"there is no other species of preaching than the expository."[66] Not unlike Dabney, J. W. Alexander also understood the biblical foundations for expository preaching, writing:

> The expository method of preaching is the most obvious and natural way of conveying to the hearers the import of the sacred volume. It is the very work for which a ministry was instituted, to interpret the Scriptures.[67]

No less than Dabney, Alexander also argued forcefully against the common nineteenth-century practice of preaching upon isolated texts. He contended:

> In the case of any other book, we should be at no loss in what manner to proceed. Suppose a volume of human science to be placed in our hands as the sole manual, text-book, and standard, which we were expected to elucidate to a public assembly: in what way would it be most natural to go to work? Certainly not, we think, to take a sentence here, and a sentence there, and upon these separate portions to frame one or two discourses every week. No interpreter of Aristotle, of Littleton, of Puffendorf, or of Paley, ever dreamed of such a method. Nor was it adopted in the Christian church, until the sermon ceased to be regarded in its true notion, as an explanation of the Scripture, and began to be viewed as a rhetorical entertainment.[68]

Likewise, Wilson Hogg also identified the historical correlation between continuous exposition and church health, and therefore admired expository preaching, writing:

> The value of this method can scarcely be overestimated. It resembles the apostolic manner of preaching the gospel more fully than any other kind of sermonizing does, confining itself more closely and exclusively to the Scriptures, thereby bringing forth the very marrow and richness of Bible truth and doctrine.[69]

John Etter concurred, writing: "It is a noteworthy and historical fact that this mode of preaching always prevailed in the brightest days of the church, and declined with the decline of Christianity."[70] Not unlike Dabney, Etter also

66. Dabney, *Sacred Rhetoric*, 78. Likewise Dabney argued: "If the business of the preacher is simply to make the people see and feel what is in the word of God, preaching should usually be what is popularly known as 'expository.'" Dabney, "Gospel," 600.

67. Alexander, *Thoughts*, 229.

68. Alexander, *Thoughts*, 229.

69. Hogg, *Hand-Book*, 52.

70. Etter, *Preacher*, 283.

noted the correlation between the abandonment of such preaching in favor of more rhetorical forms, the decline of the church during the failing years of the Roman Empire and Middle Ages, and its revival during the Reformation. Etter observed: "When the light of divine truth again began to emerge from its long eclipse by sacerdotal supremacy, at the dawn of the Reformation, there was again a return to the expository mode of preaching."[71]

On the benefit of expository preaching to the preacher himself, James Hoppin argued with even more force than Dabney, writing:

> True expository preaching is most profitable of all to the preacher himself, because it enriches his scriptural knowledge, and leads him deeper into the word of God. It gives him broader views of revealed truth, it teaches him to read the sacred writings in a connected way, and it follows out an inspired train of thought or argument sometimes through a whole book. It prevents him, also from misapplying and misusing individual texts, by taking them out of their right relations.[72]

Regarding the theological and hermeneutical benefits of expository preaching for congregants, Austin Phelps agreed with Dabney's assessment, writing: "It is not a small benefit to a people to have a hundred passages of the Bible expounded every year from the pulpit with the aid of the latest scholarship in exegesis."[73] Such exposition imparts an implicit hermeneutic, which trains a congregation how to read the Scripture for themselves. Phelps therefore continued:

> The popular mind obtains unconsciously its principles of interpretation from the usage of the pulpit. As the one is, so is the other. Clearness in the pulpit is good sense in the pew. Mysticism in the pulpit is nonsense in the pew. The absence of exposition from the pulpit is ignorance of the Bible in the pew.[74]

Hoppin, like Dabney, also noted the collateral benefits of continuous exposition, suggesting:

> Expository preaching also suggests numberless subjects for sermons. It gives an opportunity to remark upon a great many themes on which one would not desire to preach a whole sermon, and it also gives an opportunity sometimes to administer salutary reproof in an indirect way. It is, in fact, the most free

71. Etter, *Preacher*, 283.

72. Hoppin, *Office*, 162–63.

73. Phelps, *Theory*, 55.

74. Phelps, *Theory*, 55.

> and practical method of preaching; it comes home to the heart the quickest. It is, above all, feeding the people with the "bread of life," with real biblical nutriment, with that spiritual food which all souls need, and which this age and every age require. There is also in it less of the exclusively human element than in topical preaching.[75]

On nearly every point at which Dabney admired expository preaching, so did many of his peers. Dabney's admiration for expository preaching was not unique. It was in fact quite common, as was his failure to turn his admiration *for* expository preaching into a career *of* expository preaching.

John Broadus inadvertently offered the clearest postmortem of Dabney's admiring but toothless expository homiletic when he wrote: "[T]reatises of Homiletics, while never failing to urge that this method [expository preaching] has great advantages, seldom furnish the student with any directions for his guidance in attempting it."[76] Expository preaching requires work and training of a different kind than topical preaching. Simply telling students to preach expository sermons, or even preaching such sermons in their hearing, is insufficient to equip them to do so. Broadus therefore argued:

> Men labor for years to acquire the power of producing a good topical sermon. All their rhetorical training, and all their practice, is directed to that end. Then they try the experiment of expository preaching, which requires a different kind of practice, and perhaps even a different method of studying the Scriptures, and wonder that their first attempts prove a comparative failure.[77]

That "comparative failure"[78] defined Dabney's pulpit career. Dabney the seminarian had required more than admiring sentiments in order to become an effective preacher of consecutive expository sermons. Dabney the homiletics instructor could not offer to his students that which he himself did not possess and could not practice.

The Practical Impossibility of Dabney's Caveat

J. W. Alexander was a fellow Virginian, Presbyterian, and advocate of expository preaching. Alexander, however, saw a grave danger in the practice of preaching topically upon fragments of Scripture, which Dabney did not

75. Hoppin, *Office*, 163.
76. Broadus, *Preparation and Delivery*, 302–03.
77. Broadus, *Preparation and Delivery*, 299.
78. Broadus, *Preparation and Delivery*, 299.

fully appreciate. Noting that "a fragment of the word of God . . . may be confirmed and illustrated by parallel or analogous passages," Alexander nevertheless insisted:

> But where no extended exposition is attempted, the preacher is naturally induced to draw upon systematic treatises, philosophical theories, works of mere literature, or his own ingenuity of invention, and fertility of imagination, for such a train of thought as, under the given topic, may claim the praise of novelty.[79]

Alexander understood that there is, practically, no such thing as a true exposition of a single verse. While Dabney had argued that a single verse could offer a "true exposition,"[80] Alexander claimed that any sermon that offered faithful exposition of a single verse was not actually a sermon on a single verse. It necessarily addressed the full context of the passage. Unlike Dabney, Alexander foreclosed upon the notion that a capital or epitome text could offer a true exposition, explaining instead:

> It is true that a man may announce as his text a single verse or clause of a verse, and then offer a full and satisfactory elucidation of the whole context; but, so far as this is done, the sermon is expository, and falls under the kind which we recommend. But this species of discourse is becoming more and more rare . . . In modern sermons, there is, for the most part, nothing which resembles it.[81]

Alexander thus contended that a faithful exposition of a single verse or clause of Scripture in theory amounted to a practical impossibility in an actual pulpit, and he described the result of straying from an expository model in terms that are all-too indicative of Dabney's personal practice:

> A text is taken, usually with a view to some preconceived subject; a proposition is deduced from the text; and this is confirmed or illustrated by a series of statements which would have been precisely the same if any similar verse, in any other part of the record, had been chosen. Here there is no interpretation, for there is no pretence [*sic*] of it. There may be able theological discussion, and we by no means would exclude this, but where a method merely textual or topical prevails, there is an absolute

79. Alexander, *Thoughts*, 235.

80. Dabney, *Sacred Rhetoric*, 77.

81. Alexander, *Thoughts*, 239.

> forsaking of that which we have maintained to be the true notion of preaching.[82]

While Dabney no doubt offered "able theological discussion"[83] in almost every sermon, Alexander's indictment of the topical sermon form prevalent to the nineteenth-century American pulpit only serves to highlight by contrast the fact that Dabney's admiration for expository preaching never crystallized into a personal commitment or homiletical practice.

Summary

Without a hermeneutical conviction undergirding Dabney's admiration of expository preaching, it is not surprising that Dabney followed the path of his training and inclination. His caveat regarding capital and epitome texts became, for Dabney, more than a caveat. It became his constant personal practice over fifty-two years of pulpit ministry. Recall that Lawrence Trotter observed: "Although Dabney argued powerfully in favor of the ancient practice, he did nothing in his own preaching ministry to restore expository preaching of extended passages to the place it held in the early and Reformation churches."[84] To the contrary, the present chapter has demonstrated that Dabney, by virtue of his position of influence in the church, his role as a teacher of preachers, and his personal example, may have done more to prevent the restoration of the ancient practice than he did to restore it.[85]

Evaluating Dabney's Stance

The Purpose of the Text

Dabney's fundamental stance as a preacher in reference to the Scripture may help to explain why his admiration for expository preaching never galvanized into a personal practice. An earlier section of this chapter reviewed Dabney's sermon on Mark 9:43–48, suggesting that while it is labeled Expository it differs little from his standard topical messages. Along with this Expository sermon, Dabney composed a Practical Exercise on Mark

82. Alexander, *Thoughts*, 239.

83. Alexander, *Thoughts*, 239.

84. Trotter, *Always Prepared*, 145.

85. Chapter 6 of this paper defends this claim by analyzing Dabney's homiletical impact on his students.

9:47–48.[86] Together these sermons reveal Dabney's true stance in reference to the text of Scripture.

Dabney did not so much submit his thought to the text as he made various uses of a given text in order to accomplish pre-determined purposes. Dabney's practice of composing sermons of different kinds—Doctrinal, Didactic, Narrative, and Practical—reveals that he purposed certain results through his sermons, which is not in itself unwise. The biblical authors purposed their words to act upon the reader.[87] That Dabney composed both an Expository and a Practical sermon on the same verses, however, reveals that Dabney's purpose in any given sermon was not necessarily representative of the biblical author's purpose. Dabney was comfortable using the same text to accomplish different purposes, forcing the text to serve his pre-determined purpose, rather than submitting himself to the text in order to carry forward the biblical author's purpose.

Submission as a Philosophy

This practice exposes Dabney's stance in reference to Scripture. Haddon Robinson argued: "Expository preaching is at its core more a philosophy than a method,"[88] and that philosophy is comprised of a posture of willing submission to Scripture. Robinson continued, writing: "Whether or not we can be called expositors starts with . . . our honest answer to the question, 'Do you, as a preacher, endeavor to bend your thought to the Scriptures, or do you use the Scriptures to support your thought?'"[89] In theory, Dabney would have agreed with Robinson, for Dabney defined preaching as heraldry, and heraldry is the act of faithfully proclaiming the King's message. Recall that Dabney argued: "The nature of the preacher's work is determined by the word employed to describe it by the Holy Ghost. The preacher is a herald; his work is heralding the King's message," and therefore "the herald does not invent his message; he merely transmits and explains it."[90] Dabney understood that pastors often needed to explain the King's message, or even to translate it for a contemporary audience. He argued that the preacher—though a herald—is still "an intelligent *medium* of communication," for the

86. Box 8, File 8/3, Mark 9:47–48 Practical Exercise.

87. John 20:30–31, for instance, captures the biblical author's purpose in recounting Jesus's "signs." Jeffrey Arthurs therefore urges: "As preachers, we want to say what the text says and do what the text does." Arthurs, *Preaching*, 28.

88. Robinson, *Biblical*, 22.

89. Robinson, *Biblical*, 22.

90. Dabney, *Sacred Rhetoric*, 36.

preacher "has brains as well as a tongue; and he is expected so to deliver and explain his master's mind, that the other party shall receive not only the mechanical sounds, but the true meaning of the message."[91] Nevertheless, Dabney precluded the preacher from altering even the tenor of the text, asserting: "On the other hand, it wholly transcends his office to presume to correct the tenour of the propositions he conveys, by either additions or change."[92] Dabney's practice of employing one and the same text in order to serve alternate purposes, rather than bending his thought to the single purpose of the Scripture, betrays in his practice an infidelity to his theory. As a herald, Dabney regularly stood in the pulpit and altered the King's message, not only in substance, but also in the purpose that the King intended for his word to achieve in those who heard it.

Dabney's Practical Exercise on Mark 9 therefore exposes that his fundamental stance in reference to the Scripture was not that of a herald, but of a craftsman. He viewed the word of God in much the same way that a woodworker might view a piece of mahogany, deciding what purpose a given plank might serve, feeling free to transform it into a chair or a table or a desk. Demonstrating a similar attitude toward the Scripture, Dabney pressed a given text toward the service of a supposedly Expository message, while elsewhere he pressed the same text into the mold of a Practical message. Pursuing different purposes with the same text, Dabney stood over the text as a master craftsman, neglecting or contradicting the divinely inspired purpose of the Scripture in favor of using it to serve his own pre-determined purposes. Above all other theological or practical considerations, this willingness to bend the text to his own design, rather than bending himself to the text, prevented Dabney from developing a truly expository practice. It is therefore not surprising that Dabney's sermon collection reveals a complete absence of consecutive expository preaching.

Conclusion

Summary

While Robert Dabney crafted a robust expository theory, and while his expository pedagogy was weak, his personal practice of expository preaching was functionally non-existent. Less than half of his extant Expository

91. Dabney, *Sacred Rhetoric*, 36–37 [emphasis original].

92. Dabney, *Sacred Rhetoric*, 37. Recently David Helm suggested that expository preaching must carry forward not only the subject matter of the text, but also "the emphasis of a biblical text" into the sermon. Helm, *Expositional*, 13.

messages faithfully implemented his expository theory, and these comprise a numerically insignificant percentage of his total manuscripts and preaching occasions. Dabney did not preach a single expository series of any length during his half-century of pulpit ministry, and his admiration for expository preaching never coalesced into a hermeneutical commitment or personal practice. Despite his theory, Dabney's fundamental stance toward the Scripture was not that of a herald, but rather a craftsman, who often employed God's word for purposes that the biblical author did not intend. Dabney's admiration for expository preaching was ultimately empty.

Preview of Chapter 6

Chapter 6 explores Dabney's homiletical impact upon the generation of preachers whom he trained. In so doing, it first suggests that Dabney possessed the faculty of replicating something of himself in his students. It then attempts to quantify the extent to which Dabney's students were exposed to his preaching ministry, and thus to the indirect pedagogy of his personal example. Finally, it reviews a selection of sermons that Dabney's students preached, demonstrating that they largely absorbed and replicated his topical classroom pedagogy and personal practice rather than his robust expository theory.

Chapter 6 therefore defends a different interpretation of Dabney's legacy than that which Lawrence Trotter offered. So far from exercising a diminutive impact on the preaching practices of his students, Dabney profoundly shaped their preaching to resemble his own, and his students replicated Dabney's classroom pedagogy and personal example over against his robust expository theory.

6

Legacy

Introduction

Overview

Chapters 3–5 have revealed that while Robert Dabney crafted a robust expository theory, his caveat regarding capital and epitome texts furnished Dabney with a mechanism by which to justify topical preaching on single verses or clauses of text. Dabney's classroom pedagogy undermined his expository theory, and Dabney predominately equipped his students with the topical sermon form that was common to his day. Dabney's personal practice of expository preaching was virtually nonexistent and his admiration for continuous exposition never coalesced into a personal or hermeneutical commitment. His topical sermons frequently failed to carry forward "the meaning of God in that sentence" and to make "constant and faithful reference to its context," as Dabney often ignored his own requirement that every sermon must offer a "true exposition"[1] of the Scripture. Despite the claims of his expository theory, Dabney's posture in reference to the text was not that of a herald, but rather a craftsman, and he was comfortable using a text of Scripture for a purpose other than the purpose for which the biblical author employed it.

1. Dabney, *Sacred Rhetoric*, 77.

The Plan of This Chapter

This chapter explores Dabney's homiletical impact upon the generation of preachers he trained, ultimately challenging Lawrence Trotter's claim that Dabney exercised a diminutive influence on the homiletical practices of his students. In order to do so, this chapter first describes Dabney's personal influence upon his students and suggests that Dabney possessed the faculty of recreating something of his own image in the students whom he trained. It then quantifies the extent to which Dabney's students may have experienced the indirect pedagogical influence of his pulpit example. By reviewing a number of sermons that Dabney's former students preached, this chapter demonstrates that his students in fact absorbed Dabney's topical pedagogy and faithfully replicated his pulpit example to the neglect of his expository theory. By so doing, it defends a different interpretation of Dabney's homiletical legacy than Trotter proposed, arguing that the absence of expository sermons among Dabney's students, and the concomitant presence of some of the worst defects of Dabney's topical sermons, testifies to the enduring influence of Dabney's pedagogy and personal example.

Dabney's Personal Influence

Benignant Controversialist

Dabney's public image invited the caricature of a heartless controversialist, and some people assumed he was interpersonally harsh, for his pen and public speeches often thundered against error and falsehood without mercy.[2] Thomas Cary Johnson nevertheless understood that Dabney's severity in intellectual combat sometimes belied a warm heart. Johnson remembered:

> He was remarkably free from base affections. He loved not low things. He delighted in high things. He loved devotedly, and was a good hater, as every good lover must be. He loved passionately the good and hated passionately the evil. His affectional nature was a great fire; it drove him at times almost furiously against what seemed wrong, and in support of what seemed right.[3]

2. Of Dabney's polemical writings, Johnson wrote: "He sees things clearly, and expresses himself accordingly. To the people who cannot see he seems mad with ugly fury. He is really acting under the stress of a stern sense of obligation." Johnson, *Life and Letters*, 549.

3. Johnson, "Sketch," 10. Yet it was exactly Dabney's definitions of right and wrong, and the intensity with which he expressed himself, coupled with his seeming inability to admit that another person could see the matter differently, which created and

Some who knew only Dabney's pen therefore expressed surprise when meeting him in person. In a February 24, 1890 letter to Dabney's wife, A. G. R. Brackett recalled his delight when meeting Dabney for the first time. Brackett wrote:

> Having known him only through his controversial writings, I was prepared to meet a stern and rugged warrior, an austere man, devoid of human sensibility. But when I felt the warm pressure of his hand, looked into his kindly, benignant face, and heard his cordial greeting, I was assured that his heart was as great as his intellect.[4]

Dabney's former student, L. S. Marye, captured this paradox in Dabney's personality when he opined: "His was stalwart strength blended with ineffable sweetness."[5] While Dabney the polemicist attacked errant ideas and practices, exposing falsehood with what seemed a stark lack of charity, Dabney the friend, husband, father, and teacher often displayed surprising warmth. This may help to explain why Dabney did not merely teach his students. He influenced them. They admired him, to a degree sought to emulate him, and desired his approbation.[6]

Self-Replicating Teacher

Throughout his tenure at Union Seminary, Dabney boasted an unrivalled reputation as a teacher. Princeton Seminary sought him,[7] W. G. T. Shedd called him greatest theologian of his generation,[8] and A. A. Hodge required his students to read Dabney's systematic theology.[9] Of Dabney's prowess in the classroom Henry White wrote: "He makes us feel like *ninnies*, and that we have so much to learn in order to become good theologians."[10] Dabney nevertheless combined his classroom instruction with interpersonal

---

sustained the impression that he was interpersonally unpleasant.

4. Johnson, *Life and Letters*, 482.

5. Marye, "Light," 31.

6. Anecdotal observations tend to justify the idea that seminary professors influence their students, and that some teachers achieve hero status in the eyes of their pupils.

7. See Dabney, unpublished autobiography, 25–28; also Johnson, *Life and Letters*, 198.

8. "Dr. W. G. T. Shedd of Union Seminary, New York, in the old days, himself an acute and learned scholar, once said that in his judgment Dr. Dabney was the greatest living theologian." Woods, *Robert Lewis Dabney*, no pagination.

9. Johnson, "Sketch," 9.

10. Johnson, *Life and Letters*, 196 [emphasis original].

warmth. A friend and former pupil wrote: "He scarcely seemed, with all his acumen, to be able to see the faults of a friend and his judgment possibly failed him oftener in speaking or writing of those whom he loved than at any other time."[11] Dabney confessed that he was too soft on his children and too concerned for their happiness,[12] and if student testimonials are any indication, his fatherly tenderness engendered affection from his students as well. P. H. Hoge noted that Dabney "had the faculty of imparting knowledge," and insisted:

> There could never have been any teacher more considerate to ignorance, more patient with dullness, more kindly in correction, and more gentle in reproof, than was this great man. Those who knew him only in the arena of polemical debate could have no conception of the fatherly tenderness of the man, that made his students feel sure of personal sympathy and friendly counsel in every trouble or perplexity.[13]

S. Taylor Martin concurred, writing: "[W]ith all his contempt for truculence and meanness he was a man of profound and tender affection."[14] While Dabney the polemicist could be severe, Dabney the teacher elicited the devotion of his students, combining masterful teaching with fatherly personal affection.[15]

Part of the gravity that drew Dabney's students to him, which created this shaping influence, was his personal piety, which was—at least in the South—unquestioned.[16] Johnson claimed:

> Many men who sat under him, in the early years of his professorial life, have given expression to their conviction that Dr.

11. Sampson, "Teacher," 38.

12. Dabney, unpublished autobiography, 61.

13. Johnson, *Life and Letters*, 480–81.

14. Martin, "Tribute," 41.

15. Published memorials to Dabney necessarily represent a one-sided, favorable view of his character and ministry. It is difficult to imagine that every student Dabney taught would offer such unmitigated praise. These testimonials nevertheless help to explain more sober evaluations of Dabney's impact upon his students. See note 26 for one such evaluation.

16. This invites the question, What is piety? Dabney was a lifelong, unrepentant racist who believed in the racial inferiority of African peoples and their descendants, who fought to continue the enslavement of blacks, and who helped to ensure that racial segregation triumphed in the Southern Church after the Civil War. Nevertheless, "Dabney's piety . . . was unquestioned," and "Dabney was fully committed to Christian piety and particularly to the Old School Presbyterian heritage." Lucas, *Robert Lewis Dabney*, 30.

> Dabney was then the most Godly man they had ever seen. Both the students of his earlier and of his later years unite in saying that he was like the Apostle John on the lovely side of his character. One of them says, 'How he strove to be like his Master, who was meek and lowly in heart.'[17]

Elsewhere Johnson recounted: "His students in his old age at Austin were wont to speak of him as St. John."[18]

Dabney was, however, no flatterer, nor did he win such praise from his students by feigning amiability. B. M. Smith's assessment of Dabney's earnestness is recorded in a letter from the former to the latter dated July 31 1854. Smith wrote: "You are a very sincere man. No one ever accuses you of flattering, and you are not generally in the habit of saying pretty things merely to say them, or to compliment others."[19] Given that Smith was Dabney's brother-in-law, a fellow professor at Union, and later co-pastor of College Church with Dabney, he was well placed to make such an assessment. Given also that Dabney and Smith neither liked nor agreed with each other,[20] Smith's statement tends to reinforce the conclusion that Dabney's influence with his students was neither purchased nor affected. It represented a genuine, reciprocal relationship between teacher and students.

The bonds Dabney forged with his students helped him not only to impart knowledge to the intellect, but also shape to the student. Johnson argued:

> The truth he taught burnt in on the student, made an indelible impression. He had that other rare faculty of the rare and exceptionally great teacher, of seeming to reproduce himself, in a measure, in his pupils . . . He begot in his men something akin to his own vigor and strength, his love of truth and God.[21]

Johnson referred to Dabney's students as "his men,"[22] over whom Dabney exercised power to reproduce something of himself. Dabney stamped "his

17. Johnson, *Life and Letters*, 550.

18. Johnson, "Sketch," 10.

19. Johnson, *Life and Letters*, 147.

20. Sweetser, *Copious Fountain*, 158. Dabney and Smith differed over public education, the New South, and the organization of the seminary, and it appears that they simply did not like one another. Before Dabney gave his "New South" speech at Hampden-Sydney College in 1882, Smith protested by walking out. Lucas, *Robert Lewis Dabney*, 198.

21. Johnson, *Life and Letters*, 554.

22. Throughout Dabney's tenure at Union, the seminary admitted only men.

own vigor and strength"[23] upon students who were training for ministry at Union Seminary. He did not merely teach them. He influenced them. He shaped them.

Dabney's Pulpit Influence

Dabney as Preacher

This shaping influence could only increase the esteem in which Dabney's students held his preaching. Dabney's reputation as a preacher was, throughout his ministry, no less weighty than his status as a teacher.[24] Chapter 1 of this paper quoted F. P. Ramsay in a letter dated March 9, 1901, in which Ramsay recounted his visit to a church in Baltimore. Although Ramsay was unaware that the preacher occupying the pulpit was Dabney, he explained:

> I came to the conclusion that he must be Dr. Dabney. I had never seen him or his picture, but had heard his students talk of his teaching, and was familiar with his writings; and I saw in the giant reasoner, aflame with scorn of error and of subterfuge, yet bowing with meekness at the cross, one so like our great Dabney that Dabney it must be. And so it turned out to be.[25]

Ramsay then offered this significant comment: "Since that day I have understood his great influence upon his pupils."[26] Though never himself Dabney's pupil, Ramsay nevertheless had become acquainted with what was evidently a well-known fact: Robert Dabney profoundly influenced his students. Upon hearing Dabney preach, Ramsay understood why.

Those who had studied under Dabney remembered not only his theology and reasoning in the pulpit, but also his passion. Describing the range of emotion that Dabney exuded when preaching, P. H. Hoge wrote:

> A great preacher he was. In heart-searching power, in terrible denunciation of sin, in grand presentation of great themes, he was unsurpassed, while few could approach him in the melting tenderness with which he presented a Saviour's love.[27]

23. Johnson, *Life and Letters*, 554.

24. "If later testimonials are any indication, Dabney's preaching was memorable." Lucas, *Robert Lewis Dabney*, 50.

25. Ramsay, March 9, 1901 letter.

26. Ramsay, March 9, 1901 letter.

27. Johnson, *Life and Letters*, 481.

Henry White summarized Dabney's pulpit intensity, writing: "Dr. Dabney sometimes used such vehemence that he seemed like a warrior fighting against principalities and powers."[28] During his lifetime and after his death students and acquaintances alike recognized Robert Dabney's power as a preacher.

Dabney's unrivalled teaching and powerful, heart-searching preaching, coupled with his fatherly affection toward his students and deep personal piety, created a dynamic in which Dabney exerted profound shaping influence upon his students, thereby reproducing something of himself in them. By quantifying the extent to which Dabney's students might have been exposed to his preaching ministry it can be demonstrated that the implicit pedagogy of Dabney's pulpit influence reinforced his explicit classroom pedagogy, further undermining his expository theory.

Opportunities for Pulpit Influence

Dabney's students enjoyed ample opportunity to sit under his preaching ministry. Hampden-Sydney, Virginia currently boasts a population of just over fourteen hundred souls. Still today it is remote, located in rural Virginia, and is surrounded by miles of farmland and undeveloped scrub pine forests. During much of Dabney's tenure at Union Seminary, the campus was accessible only by horseback. Hampden-Sydney College, which was and remains an all-male, undergraduate liberal arts institution, Union Theological Seminary, and College Church clustered together on what was then a campus of less than one hundred acres.[29] Students who attended the college or seminary also attended College Church, which from 1858–74 Dabney co-pastored with B. M. Smith. Dabney preached at the church, in the chapels and lecture rooms of the seminary, and at the college. Given Dabney's weight of personal influence, and given the close proximity of the seminary, college, and church—and the isolation of these from any other city or population center—Dabney's students enjoyed ample opportunity to hear him preach, and to learn not merely from his classroom Exercises, but also to absorb the implicit pedagogy of his personal pulpit example.

A cursory examination of Lawrence Trotter's index[30] of Dabney's preaching occasions reveals that during the thirty years of Dabney's tenure at Union Seminary, he preached at the seminary, at Hampden-Sydney

28. White, "Robert Lewis Dabney," 391.

29. In 1898 Union Seminary relocated to Richmond, Virginia.

30. Trotter created an index that allows the researcher to compare Dabney's sermons based upon the original and subsequent preaching occasions.

College, and at College Church on not less than three hundred seventy-nine separate occasions.[31] Given that Dabney's manuscript collection is incomplete, that number is likely higher. Including Full Texts, Skeletons, Briefs, and Exercises, Dabney's manuscript collection features just twenty-four sermons that he labeled Expository, which represent just five percent of his extant sermons. This paper has demonstrated that several of these sermons were expository in name only. Germane to the present evaluation is the fact that ninety-five percent of the messages Dabney preached during his years in Hampden-Sydney were not expository sermons, but instead followed the topical form that was prevalent to his day. Moreover, outside of Dabney's twenty-four Expository messages and five Narrative Exercises, he preached on more than three verses less than a dozen times,[32] whereas on no less than eight occasions he specified on his sermon manuscript that his preaching text included only the first or last clause of a single verse.[33] Dabney overwhelmingly chose to preach on single verses or clauses of Scripture, utilizing a topical sermon form, crafting sermons of varying degrees of fidelity to the text.

The Pedagogical Effects of Preaching

If sitting consistently under the pulpit ministry of a particular preacher imparts an indirect pedagogy, then the pulpit pedagogy under which Dabney's students repetitively sat consisted of a steady diet of topical sermons based most often on single verses or clauses of Scripture. James Hoppin noted not only that a pastor bears a special theological and hermeneutical relation to a congregation, but also that the very nature of that relation can reproduce

31. This number is derived by counting the individual preaching occasions at each of these institutions as recorded on Dabney's sermon manuscripts.

32. Dabney preached two messages on Exodus 20:8–11—the 4th Commandment—and could not take less than four verses without artificially dividing the commandment. Both messages boast a topical structure and argument. Box 6, File 6/4 Exodus 20:8–11 Full Text (#128), and Full Text (#129).

33. Box 6, File 6/6, Psalm 33:5 Full Text; Box 6, File 6/6, Psalm 33:5 Doctrinal Exercise; Box 7, File 7/6, Daniel 4:35 Skeleton; Box 8, File 8/4, Luke 18:14 Outline; Box 9, File 9/1, Acts 24:25 Full Text; Box 9, File 9/1, Acts 24:25 Practical Exercise; Box 10, File 10/6, 1 Corinthians 3:8 Skeleton; and Box 10, File 10/6, Revelation 6:16 Skeleton. These represent sermons in which Dabney specifically noted *on the manuscript* that he was preaching a single clause of a single verse. Dozens of his sermons, although citing a single verse as the text of the sermon, functionally proclaimed a single clause of the cited verse. For one such example, see Box 8, File 8/2, Matthew 22:2–3 Skeleton. While Dabney listed verses 2–3 as his text, his sermon dealt exclusively with Jesus's statement, "They would not come."

within the congregation the hermeneutical deformities the preacher brings into the pulpit. Hoppin contended:

> Men recognize him as a divine messenger; then he will speak to the dying soul of the risen redeemer with words of faith and power; then he will be the means of kindling in dark spirits the immortal hope of Christ. They will awake to his earnest entreaties, and the Holy Spirit will use him as a powerful instrument to apply to their hearts the renewing word. One man is the preordained instrument of the spiritual welfare of another.[34]

If a preacher, who is the "preordained instrument of the spiritual welfare of another," is hermeneutically deficient, then the congregation that looks to that preacher for "the renewing word"[35] will receive that word largely as the preacher presents it. William Taylor therefore admonished seminary students to ground their doctrinal instructions in the text of the Bible, teaching their hearers the Bible in order to teach them its doctrines, and his words paint in stark relief a picture of the poverty of Dabney's preaching. Taylor cautioned: "Biblical intelligence is absolutely essential to doctrinal steadfastness and Christian stability."[36] Such intelligence is not merely comprised of the doctrines and duties of the Bible, but of the Bible itself, and of the growing ability of congregants to read and interpret the Bible profitably for themselves. Dabney theoretically understood that fact and articulated it in *Sacred Rhetoric*, arguing: "A prime object of pastoral teaching is to teach the people how to read the Bible for themselves."[37] His preaching, however, often assumed biblical knowledge among his hearers rather than inculcating it.[38]

While it may sound condescending, more than one preacher can verify from experience that which R. W. Dale questioned: "Have we any reason to believe that even intelligent Christian men and women read the Scriptures intelligently?"[39] Preachers must teach congregants how to read and interpret the Bible, and preaching is the primary public hermeneutical activity by which that teaching takes place. Dabney argued: "It is the preacher's business, in his public discourses, to give his people teaching by example, in the art of interpreting the Word; he should exhibit before them,

34. Hoppin, *Office* , 541.
35. Hoppin, *Office*, 541.
36. Taylor, *Ministry*, 172.
37. Dabney, *Sacred Rhetoric*, 81.
38. See chapter 3, note 16.
39. Dale, *Nine Lectures*, 226.

in actual use, the methods by which the legitimate meaning is evolved."[40] Dabney understood that over the course of years and decades, a congregation learns to read, interpret, and understand the Bible according to the methods that its preacher employs. The manner in which the preacher handles the text in the pulpit eventually reproduces itself in the pews, and the manner in which Dabney handled the text in the pulpit likewise reproduced itself in his seminary students.[41]

So far from being less impressionable and more theologically astute than "regular" Christians, Dabney's seminarians might, if anything, have been more subject to the influence of his example, specifically because of the endearing combination of his teaching and warmth and piety. Union Seminary students who habitually sat under Dabney's pulpit ministry, in which Dabney frequently neglected to make "constant and faithful reference" to the context, in which he often failed to proclaim "the meaning of God in that sentence,"[42] and in which he rarely preached expository sermons, could not have remained unaffected. An examination of several sermons that Dabney's former students preached reveals in fact that Dabney profoundly influenced their preaching practices to resemble his own.

The Sermons of Dabney's Students

Overview

This paper examines several sermons that Dabney's former students preached, demonstrating that they learned and followed his explicit and implicit pedagogy and his personal example rather than his expository theory. Recall that in surveying some of these same sermons, Lawrence Trotter viewed the absence of expository messages among Dabney's former students as indicative of their failure to learn,[43] and Trotter concluded that Dabney exercised a relatively small homiletical influence upon the generation of Southern Presbyterian preachers whom he trained.[44] Understanding, however, that Dabney's direct classroom pedagogy, personal practice, and indirect pulpit pedagogy—coupled with his profound teaching, interpersonal warmth, and undisputed piety—united to undermine his expository theory,

40. Dabney, *Sacred Rhetoric*, 81.

41. The analysis of the sermons of Dabney's students that follows substantiates this claim.

42. Dabney, *Sacred Rhetoric*, 77.

43. Trotter, *Always Prepared*, 203.

44. Chapter 2 describes Trotter's analysis.

this paper defends an alternate interpretation of Dabney's legacy. So far from exercising a diminutive homiletical impact on his students, Dabney profoundly shaped their pulpit practices to resemble his own, and the absence of expository sermons among his students—and the presence of his topical form with many of its attendant defects—testifies instead to his enduring homiletical influence upon the students whom he trained.

What We Should Find

Howard Crosby encouraged preachers to pursue fidelity in their pulpit ministrations, reminding them: "You shall not have lived in vain if it can be written over your grave, 'He made the people understand the Scriptures.'"[45] If Dabney exercised a significant shaping influence upon his students, and if they followed his classroom pedagogy and personal example rather than his expository theory, then we should find that their sermons, like Dabney's, made the people understand the doctrines and duties of the Bible, but not necessarily the Bible itself. We should primarily find topical sermons based on single verses or clauses of text. We should expect that Dabney's caveat regarding capital and epitome texts furnished an avenue by which his students preached sermons that often failed to make "constant and faithful reference" to the context and that inconsistently carried forward "the meaning of God in that sentence."[46] We should not expect to find expository sermons, in which the Argument is comprised of an extended exposition that unfolds according to the versification of the text, for neither Dabney's classroom pedagogy nor his pulpit example equipped his students to preach this form of sermon. We should find that Dabney's students often assumed his posture as a craftsman rather than serving as a herald. In short, if Dabney effectively influenced the preaching practices of his students, we should find that they preached much like he did. That is precisely what we find.

Givens Brown Strickler

"A Most Distinguished Place"

Most of Dabney's students left few if any sermons to posterity, but G. B. Strickler earned acclaim as a preacher and theologian, and several of his

45. Crosby, *Christian*, 190.

46. Dabney, *Sacred Rhetoric*, 77.

sermons have been preserved.[47] He offers something of a bellwether by which to evaluate Dabney's homiletical impact upon his students, for Dabney considered Strickler among his brightest pupils. The two men became friends, and Strickler eventually assumed the Chair of Systematic, Polemic, and Pastoral Theology at Union Seminary, which Dabney had once held.[48] Johnson noted that Strickler had "passed through the Seminary under Dr. Dabney, had won a most distinguished place in his regard, and subsequently an enviable place in the estimation of the whole church."[49] In 1883 Union Seminary nominated Strickler to fill its Chair of Ecclesiastical History and Polity, but his presbytery refused to grant him release. Writing to Strickler on October 8, 1883, Dabney offered him high praise, asserting:

> You have that didactic turn of mind which is so rare, and so hard to find in a high degree, and which is the crowning qualification for eminent usefulness in the Seminary. It exists in few, in combination with mental vigor, learning, prudence and moral character. It is precious and essential in the church's teaching work.[50]

If any of Dabney's students absorbed and reflected his pulpit influence, it was G. B. Strickler.

Strickler's Sermons

Dabney the theorist had insisted that "when the pastor discusses only a single sentence . . . of Scripture, as he will often and legitimately do, it should yet be a true exposition, and evolution of the meaning of God in that sentence, with constant and faithful reference to its context."[51] Chapter 5 nevertheless demonstrated that Dabney frequently failed to offer a true exposition, neglecting the context or altering the meaning of the text, and that his posture in reference to the Scripture was not that of a herald, but instead a craftsman. Given that none of Strickler's fifteen sermons was expository according to the structural form that Dabney proposed in *Sacred Rhetoric*, this paper briefly evaluates the extent to which his sermons offered "constant and faithful reference" to the context and carried forward "the meaning of God in that sentence."[52] Dabney required that every sermon provide

47. Strickler, *Sermons*. See also Strickler, "Consecration," 220–34.
48. Moore et al., *General Catalogue*, 39.
49. Johnson, *Life and Letters*, 138.
50. Johnson, *Life and Letters*, 139.
51. Dabney, *Sacred Rhetoric*, 77.
52. Dabney, *Sacred Rhetoric*, 77.

a "true exposition"[53] of the text, and the present evaluation of Strickler's sermons demonstrates that he largely followed the features Dabney's topical homiletic, manifesting the same inconsistencies toward and violations of Dabney's theory that Dabney's own sermons display.

Of the fifteen sermons this paper evaluated, Strickler composed eight on a single clause of one verse of Scripture,[54] five referenced a single verse,[55] one was comprised of two verses,[56] and one utilized three verses.[57] Of the five sermons in which Strickler listed a single verse, two in fact addressed only a single clause of the verse that he listed,[58] one largely ignored the text altogether,[59] and another strangely suggested that the meaning of the text was unknowable,[60] subsequently employing other texts instead.

Seven of the fifteen sermons offered "faithful reference to the context,"[61] primarily at the beginning of the sermon, but rarely thereafter. Strickler often preferred to make his Introduction by way of establishing the context of his chosen text, but his sermons rarely engaged that context again beyond the Introduction. As an example of this pattern, consider Strickler's sermon, "The Great Salvation," which he preached on Hebrews 2:3, which asks, "How shall we escape if we neglect so great a salvation?"

Strickler's Introduction began by asserting that "[t]he text is closely connected to the preceding chapter."[62] He then walked his listeners carefully through the claims of Hebrews 1, concluding: "Such seems to be the logical setting in which the text is found."[63] Moving directly to his Proposition, he chose to address the greatness of salvation, and argued:

53. Dabney, *Sacred Rhetoric*, 77.

54. Strickler, "Faith," 27–48; Strickler, "Great," 68–86; Strickler, "What Shall I Do," 87–104; Strickler, "Future State," 105–19; Strickler, "Unpardonable," 190–208; Strickler, "Doctrines of Calvinism," 209–35; Strickler, "Take Heed," 236–50; Strickler, "Christ's Willingness to Save," 251–73.

55. Strickler, "Reasonable," 49–67; Strickler, "Condemnation," 120–36; Strickler, "Word," 137–53; Strickler, "Righteous," 172–89; Strickler, "Consecration," 220–34.

56. Strickler, "Divine Origin," 9–26.

57. Strickler, "Heritage," 154–71.

58. Strickler, "Religion Reasonable" and "Righteous Scarcely Saved."

59. Strickler, "Righteous Scarcely Saved."

60. Strickler, "Unpardonable." Strickler devoted much of this sermon to suggesting that no one can know what the unpardonable sin is, choosing instead to preach a selection of other texts in place of his chosen verse.

61. Dabney, *Sacred Rhetoric*, 77.

62. Strickler, "Great," 68.

63. Strickler, "Great," 69.

"[I]t is necessary that we form . . . some conception of its greatness."[64] The remainder of the sermon made no further reference to the context, and the sermon unfolded topically under five heads of Argument, which described various reasons why Christ's salvation is great.

The "Doctrines of Calvinism," which Strickler preached on 1 Timothy 4:13, made no reference to the context whatsoever. The text states: "Till I come, give attendance to reading, to exhortation, to doctrine." Strickler seized upon the word "doctrine," and began his sermon by asserting: "In many minds there is much prejudice against doctrines and especially against doctrinal preaching."[65] He then suggested that certain Calvinistic doctrines suffered particular contempt, and his Proposition intended to "give special attention . . . to those [doctrines] against which most objections are made and that most need . . . to be explained and defended."[66] The remainder of the sermon unfolded an Argument under three heads, topically sustained, which reflected neither the context nor meaning of the text. The text served as a platform for Strickler's doctrinal concerns.

In the same way that Strickler sometimes failed to give "constant and faithful reference" to the context, only five of his fifteen sermons faithfully carried forward the "meaning of God in that sentence,"[67] and two of those addressed that meaning only in their fourth head of Argument.[68] As indicative of Strickler's failure to proclaim the meaning of the text in the sermon, consider his message, "The Righteous Scarcely Saved," which he preached on 1 Peter 4:18. The text asks: "If the righteous is scarcely saved, what will become of the ungodly and the sinner?"

Strickler's Introduction proceeded by way of Exposition, as he asserted: "By the righteous in the text are meant all true Christians."[69] Explaining that all the saints of all ages of redemptive history are in view in the text, Strickler cleared away objections, including what he saw as the error of Christian perfectionism. He likewise explained that the ungodly and the sinner are comprised of "all who have never repented of their sins,"[70] and not simply the exceedingly profane or vicious. Asserting that the phrase "scarcely saved" means "saved only with great difficulty,"[71] Strickler proceeded to

64. Strickler, "Great," 69.
65. Strickler, "Doctrines of Calvinism," 209.
66. Strickler, "Doctrines of Calvinism," 214.
67. Dabney, *Sacred Rhetoric*, 77.
68. Strickler, "Reasonable," and "Condemnation."
69. Strickler, "Righteous Scarcely Saved," 172.
70. Strickler, "Righteous Scarcely Saved," 174.
71. Strickler, "Righteous Scarcely Saved," 175.

his Proposition, by which he intended to demonstrate that "the righteous are saved with great difficulty."[72] The Argument unfolded topically under three heads, and concluded by repeating the question of the text, allowing non-Christians to draw their own conclusions. Strickler thus employed a passage of Scripture that encouraged Christians to bear affliction with faith, trusting God in the midst of persecution, and created from it a doctrinal lecture on the difficulty of salvation, applying it primarily to non-Christians. It is problematic to discern how this sermon accurately carried forward "the meaning of God in that sentence."[73]

Not unlike Dabney, Strickler's sermons manifested varying degrees of fidelity to the text, and Strickler sometimes appeared to use the text to engage his own doctrinal, ethical, or social concerns. In so doing, some of his messages reveal the same abuses of the Scripture that chapter 5 discovered in Dabney's own sermons. Not only did Strickler seize upon the word "doctrine" in 1 Timothy 4:13, preaching a sermon that bore little relation to the text, but he also abused Isaiah 1:18, which teaches: "Come now, and let us reason together, saith the Lord: though your sins be as scarlet, they shall be as white as snow; though they be red like crimson, they shall be as wool." Strickler began his Introduction by stating: "It is so far from being true, as is sometimes asserted, that religion is in any respect contrary to reason, that it invites its calmest and closest scrutiny."[74] His Proposition sought to show the ways in which the biblical religion "does not shrink from the scrutiny of reason,"[75] and the sermon unfolded topically under five heads of Argument. Only in the fourth head did Strickler reference the actual words of the text, and then only to prove his contention that the Christian faith is reasonable. He concluded with an invitation to his hearers to consider the reasonableness of Christianity. Strickler did not mention the context of the text, and failed in any appreciable way to carry forward "the meaning of God in that sentence,"[76] instead using the text for his predetermined apologetic purpose.

Maybe the most striking manner in which Strickler's preaching resembled Dabney's was the stance he took in reference to the Scripture. Although Dabney had identified the fundamental task of the preacher as heraldry,[77] chapter 5 of this paper suggested that Dabney's stance in reference to the text was not that of a herald, but a craftsman. Strickler followed Dabney in this

72. Strickler, "Righteous Scarcely Saved," 176.
73. Dabney, *Sacred Rhetoric*, 77.
74. Strickler, "Reasonable," 49.
75. Strickler, "Reasonable," 49.
76. Dabney, *Sacred Rhetoric*, 77.
77. Dabney, *Sacred Rhetoric*, 36.

stance, and seemed comfortable using a text for a purpose that was clearly different than the purpose for which the biblical author employed it.

Consider "The Word of God," which Strickler preached on Hebrews 4:12. The author to the Hebrews wrote: "For the word of God is living and active, sharper than any two-edged sword, piercing to the division of soul and of spirit, of joints and of marrow, and discerning the thoughts and intentions of the heart." After an Introduction in which Strickler established the context of the passage, he admitted:

> It is not the purpose of this discourse, however, to treat the text in the particular connection in which it is here presented; that is, it is not its purpose to undertake to show how the word of God may be so used as to be an encouragement to labour to enter the rest here mentioned and as a warning of the consequences that will come on those who may come short of it, but it is rather to point out some of the excellencies of God's word, as they are here indicated.[78]

Strickler explicitly stated that while he understood the purpose for which the biblical author wrote Hebrews 4:12, he intended to use the text instead to "point out some of the excellencies of God's word."[79] Not unlike Dabney, Strickler felt comfortable using the Scripture for his own purpose, acting as a craftsman rather than a herald.

Strickler was not, however, a Dabney clone. His sermons reveal independent preferences. For instance, Strickler appeared to lean heavily toward Doctrinal messages, in which the only application was comprised of belief in the truth proclaimed. Strickler rarely used the direct, second person address that Dabney employed, and his sermons tended to offer implications, inferences, and suggestions rather than imperatives. His sermons likewise lacked the soul-searching applications frequently found in Dabney's messages, and Strickler often concluded with gentle questions rather than demanding action from his hearers. Nevertheless, his sermons employed the five-part topical pattern that Dabney's own preaching utilized, and Strickler sometimes chose verses with multiple clauses, creating a head of Argument from each clause, while preaching each clause topically.[80] In short, Strickler's sermons resemble Dabney's sermons, both in structure and in stance, and they demonstrate many of the same inconsistencies and defects that Dabney's manuscript collection reveals.

78. Strickler, "Word," 138.

79. Strickler, "Word," 138.

80. Strickler, "Christian's Heritage," 154–71.

William Sterling Lacy

"As One at Home"

If William Lacy[81] enjoyed a less distinguished ministerial career than Givens Strickler, he nevertheless boasted a more prestigious lineage. The son of Drury Lacy Jr., prominent minister of the First Presbyterian Church of Raleigh, NC, and later President of Davidson College, and the grandson of Drury Lacy, Sr., who from 1789–97 served as President of Hampden-Sydney College,[82] William Lacy had memorized the Westminster Shorter Catechism by the age of six, and graduated Davidson College at seventeen.[83] Immediately thereafter he enrolled in Union Seminary, and "Here he was as one at home."[84] Lacy served as a Confederate soldier and chaplain during the Civil War, and afterward served churches in Virginia and North Carolina.[85]

Lacy's Sermons

Of the thirteen sermons this paper evaluated, Lacy composed nine on a single clause of a verse of Scripture,[86] three utilized one verse,[87] and one sermon covered two verses.[88] None was expository according to Dabney's criteria. Not unlike Strickler, Lacy's sermons manifest varying degrees of fidelity to the text, and likewise mimic some of the worst defects of Dabney's topical pedagogy and practice.

Ten of Lacy's thirteen sermons offered "faithful reference" to the context.[89] Like Strickler, Lacy most often described the context in the Exposition, but rarely referred to it again after the Proposition. Consider "Ambassadors for Christ," which Lacy preached on the first part of 2 Corinthians 5:20,

81. A selection of Lacy's sermons is preserved in *William Sterling Lacy: Memorial, Addresses, Sermons*. See also Lacy, *Sermon Preached at the Buffalo Church*.

82. Smith, "Memorial," 5.

83. Smith, "Memorial," 6.

84. Smith, "Memorial," 7.

85. Moore and Scherer, *Centennial*, 75.

86. Lacy, "Ambassadors," 74–88; Lacy, "In Remembrance of Me," 106–11; Lacy, "Home," 112–24; Lacy, "Attestations," 125–36; Lacy, "What She Could," 149–60; Lacy, "First Duties," 171–78; Lacy, "Is the Young Man Safe?," 179–89; Lacy, "Christian Courage," 190–98; Lacy, *Sermon Preached at the Buffalo Church*.

87. Lacy, "Reward," 63–73; Lacy, "Jesus Loved Martha," 137–48; Lacy, "Choice of Barabbas," 161–70.

88. Lacy, "City," 89–105.

89. Dabney, *Sacred Rhetoric*, 77.

which states: "Therefore, we are ambassadors for Christ, God making his appeal through us." Lacy's Introduction offered a detailed review of Paul's prior relationship with the Corinthians Christians,[90] and walked his listeners through the verses leading up to the text in view.[91] Noting that "[t]his ministry of reconciliation is still committed to us," and that "those who are called to the sacred office of the gospel ministry are still ambassadors for Christ,"[92] Lacy's Proposition purported to prove: "The minister of Jesus Christ is an ambassador."[93] The sermon unfolded under five heads of Argument, topically discussed. The context, although faithfully explained in the Exposition, played no further role in the sermon after the Proposition.

Lacy was not, however, always faithful to the context. In preaching on the text, "Add to your faith, virtue," which is a clause of 2 Peter 1:5, Lacy began his Introduction by addressing the "development of character."[94] Stating that "the natural development of Christian character demands virtue,"[95] Lacy baldly equated virtue with courage and then preached a topical sermon on the "need of Christian courage" and "some reasons and encouragements for its exercise."[96] He made no reference to the context of his chosen Scripture, and it is difficult to discern how his message reflects a "true exposition"[97] of the text.

Whereas Lacy more often than not offered faithful if not constant reference to the context, only three of thirteen sermons accurately carried forward "the meaning of God in that sentence."[98] Several sermons simply abused the text. For example, seizing upon the word "remembrance" in Luke 22:19, Lacy preached a topical sermon under six heads of Argument describing why Christians must remember Jesus.[99] The sermon had little to do with the Lord's Supper. Worse still, Lacy used David's words from 2 Samuel 18:29, in which he asked, "Is the young man Absalom safe?" to address "that season we call youth."[100] Lacy described the respective dangers of disrespect toward parents, of unholy ambition, of evil companions, of

90. Lacy, "Ambassadors," 74.
91. Lacy, "Ambassadors," 75.
92. Lacy, "Ambassadors," 76.
93. Lacy, "Ambassadors," 76.
94. Lacy, "Christian Courage," 190.
95. Lacy, "Christian Courage," 190.
96. Lacy, "Christian Courage," 192.
97. Dabney, *Sacred Rhetoric*, 77.
98. Dabney, *Sacred Rhetoric*, 77.
99. Lacy, "In Remembrance of Me," 106–11.
100. Lacy, "Is the Young Man Safe?," 181.

dalliances with temptation, of making light of duty, and of refusing Christ. His sermon, which purposed to keep young men safe from the temptations of youth, in no way replicated "the meaning of God,"[101] for the text—far from addressing the dangers of youth—describes the usurpative royal ambitions and subsequent death of Absalom.

Maybe Lacy's most blatant abuse of a text came in a sermon on the last clause of 1 Samuel 20:6, in which David says to Jonathan, "[T]here is a yearly sacrifice there for all the clan." In his Introduction Lacy accurately described the context: David's life was in danger and David was replying to Saul through Jonathan in a way that would allow him to ascertain Saul's disposition toward him. Despite this understanding, Lacy equated the yearly sacrifice of the text with a yearly feast, and the yearly feast with the American Thanksgiving holiday. Lacy's Proposition therefore addressed "the happy Christian home,"[102] and his Argument listed several reasons to give thanks to God for the home on Thanksgiving Day. The sermon proclaimed that which the text did not, and it was far from a "true exposition."[103]

Not unlike Strickler, Lacy also adopted Dabney's stance as a craftsman. Preaching on John 11:5, which teaches that "Jesus loved Martha and her sister and Lazarus," Lacy established the context but also conceded that he did not intend to speak on the resurrection of Lazarus. Instead, he wrote:

> [T]urning from this whole panorama of splendor, let us look on yonder spot, irradiated by the light of this wondrous miracle—a part, and accessory only of the scene, yet full of beauty, peace and comfort. Let us consider not the great event itself, but only this incidental, yet blessed teaching, that Jesus loved this family.[104]

Lacy used his chosen verse into order to craft a topical Argument that described Jesus's love for individuals, families, and friends. While it is true that Jesus loved Mary and Martha and Lazarus, the biblical author used that truth within the narrative for a different purpose than the purpose for which Lacy used it.

Lacy's willingness to craft the Scripture toward his own purpose likewise guided his use of a clause of 1 Kings 20:40, in which an unnamed prophet says, "And as your servant was busy here and there, he was gone." The prophet's words form part of a larger narrative in which Ahab, King of Israel, spared the life of Ben-Hadad, King of Syria, even though the LORD had

101. Dabney, *Sacred Rhetoric*, 77.

102. Lacy, "Home," 115.

103. Dabney, *Sacred Rhetoric*, 77.

104. Lacy, "Jesus Loved Martha," 139.

devoted Ben-Hadad to destruction. The prophet, having disguised himself, told a parable that paralleled Ahab's folly, only revealing to Ahab the point of the story after Ahab had indicted himself. Lacy understood and reviewed this context for his listeners, but considered the prophet's words "the drapery of the story, a necessary detail of the incident."[105] He then suggested that despite the proper place of the text in the larger narrative, he planned to use the text to "teach us lessons not to be overlooked"[106] on the importance of fulfilling one's duties. Lacy's willingness to use the Scripture for a purpose other than the purpose for which the biblical author employed it demonstrates that he, not unlike Dabney and Strickler, was willing to assume the stance of a craftsman rather than that of a herald.

Lacy also demonstrated, however, that he was capable of carefully expounding a text. Preaching on Daniel 12:3, which teaches, "And those who are wise shall shine like the brightness of the sky above; and those who turn many to righteousness, like the stars forever and ever," Lacy's Introduction described the discoveries and fame of German astronomer Johannes Kepler.[107] Moving from Kepler to the stars he studied, Lacy explained the Hebrew parallelism in the text, noting that the latter clause amplified the former. Those deemed wise "shall instruct many," and Lacy argued: "[T]he idea is, they that teach wisely will shine as the general glory of the starry skies, they that teach successfully as the splendid stars, and forever."[108] Lacy's Proposition thus purposed to demonstrate "*The reward of the useful teacher of souls*,"[109] and his Argument worked carefully through the ideas of the text, ultimately culminating in a Conclusion that offered several emotive appeals to his listeners, exhorting them to pursue soul winning. Though his chosen text consisted of but one verse, Lacy accurately unfolded the "meaning of God in that sentence."[110]

Lacy's sermons, like Strickler's, strongly resembled Dabney's. At their best, they faithfully attended to the context and carried forward the biblical author's meaning and purpose. At their worst, they demonstrated the same deformities and inconsistencies that mar Dabney's manuscript collection, while mimicking his stance as a craftsman.

105. Lacy, "First Duties Neglected," 172.

106. Lacy, "First Duties Neglected," 172.

107. Lacy, "Reward," 62–64.

108. Lacy, "Reward," 66.

109. Lacy, "Reward," 66 [emphasis original].

110. Dabney, *Sacred Rhetoric*, 77.

William Lucas Bedinger

The Bookend

If G. B. Strickler won denominational renown and if William Lacy was born to Presbyterian royalty, William Bedinger enjoyed neither advantage. His sermons are instructive, however, for while William Lacy was among the earliest class of students that Robert Dabney trained at Union,[111] and while Givens Strickler studied under Dabney during the middle of Dabney's tenure at the seminary,[112] William Bedinger was a member the second-to-last class of students Dabney trained to preach before he left Union.[113] He therefore serves as something of a bookend to Dabney's tenure as a teacher of preachers. Not unlike Strickler and Lacy, Bedinger's sermons[114] show that Dabney's students, whether trained early or late in his tenure, primarily preached topical sermons on single verses or clauses of text, demonstrating varying degrees of fidelity to the context and meaning of the Scripture.

Bedinger's Sermons

Of the eighteen sermons this paper evaluated, Bedinger composed five on a single clause of a verse of Scripture,[115] seven utilized a single verse,[116] three employed two verses,[117] one used three verses,[118] one embraced two disconnected verses,[119] and one covered two disconnected clauses.[120] None was expository according to Dabney's criteria.

Ten of eighteen sermons made "faithful reference"[121] to the context, primarily during the Exposition. Consider "Particular Redemption," which

111. Lacy entered Union Seminary in 1859. See *Centennial Catalogue*, 75.

112. Strickler entered Union Seminary in 1868. See *Centennial Catalogue*, 85.

113. Bedinger entered Union Seminary in 1880. See *Centennial Catalogue*, 112.

114. Bedinger, *Soul Food*.

115. Bedinger, "Sovereignty," 21–33; Bedinger, "Invincible," 85–98; Bedinger, "Affusion, 2," 203–17; Bedinger, "Reflex," 239–53; Bedinger, "Seeing," 257–69.

116. Bedinger, "Total Depravity," 37–50; Bedinger, "Particular," 69–81; Bedinger, "Perseverance," 101–13; Bedinger, "Justification," 135–48; Bedinger, "Parental," 167–80; Bedinger, "Baptism," 183–99; Bedinger, "Preacher's," 287–300.

117. Bedinger, "Election," 53–66; Bedinger, "Assurance," 151–63; Bedinger, "Constraining," 273–83.

118. Bedinger, "Mediatorial," 303–16.

119. Bedinger, "Imputation," 117–31.

120. Bedinger, "Affusion, 2," 221–36.

121. Dabney, *Sacred Rhetoric*, 77.

Bedinger preached on Romans 5:10, which teaches: "For if while we were enemies we were reconciled to God by the death of his Son, much more, now that we are reconciled, shall we be saved by his life." After a brief Introduction, during which Bedinger reminded his listeners that Jesus's death played out "according to the determinate counsel and foreknowledge of God,"[122] Bedinger's Exposition walked his hearers through the textual and theological context of Romans 5, leading to the assertion: "We hold that Christ died vicariously only for the elect and for them made a penal satisfaction and purchased complete redemption."[123] The remainder of the sermon unfolded topically, defending penal substitution, and Bedinger made little further reference to the context. Nevertheless, his initial work in providing both textual and theological context was sound.

In the same way, Bedinger's sermon, "The Baptism of Infants," which he preached on 1 Corinthians 7:14, offered strong initial context. The Scripture states: "For the unbelieving husband is made holy because of his wife, and the unbelieving wife is made holy because of her husband. Otherwise your children would be unclean, but as it is, they are holy." Bedinger's Introduction described God's wisdom in creating the family, and his Exposition traced the Jewish understanding of uncleanness and holiness in order to provide precise terms for the Argument that followed. Bedinger noted: "This passage is an overwhelming evidence that the standing of children of believers in regard to their right to be included in the covenant was the same as under the Old Testament dispensation."[124] He then shifted into a topical sermon, in which he argued in favor of infant baptism, describing the advantages of the practice for the infant, for the parents, and for the church.[125] Bedinger thus offered strong initial context during the Exposition, but preached a topical sermon, in which the Argument made little further reference to the context.

Not unlike Strickler and Lacy, Bedinger also preached sermons that failed in any significant way to make "constant and faithful reference"[126] to the context. Preaching on Philippians 1:6, which teaches, "And I am sure of this, that he who began a good work in you will bring it to completion at the day of Jesus Christ," Bedinger's Introduction contrasted those who, being mature in Christ, become "unconscious of their goodness," and

122. Bedinger, "Particular," 69. From Acts 2:23.

123. Bedinger, "Particular," 72.

124. Bedinger, "Baptism," 185.

125. Bedinger, "Baptism," 195–99.

126. Dabney, *Sacred Rhetoric*, 77.

"more displeased with themselves,"[127] over against the claims of Christian perfectionism. He then broached the topic of the perseverance of the saints, assuring his hearers that in speaking of such perseverance no "perfection is claimed for them,"[128] teaching instead that God sustains those who persevere. Making no reference to the context of Philippians 1, Bedinger asserted that Philippians 1:6 teaches the doctrine of perseverance, and his Proposition purported to "focus the light of Scripture on this subject."[129] His Argument unfolded topically under five heads, after which he refuted numerous objections. The sermon did not offer any measure of reference to the context, and while he accurately conveyed Calvinist theology, Bedinger failed to offer a "true exposition."[130]

Whereas in ten of eighteen sermons Bedinger offered some form of reference to the context, in only two of eighteen sermons did he faithfully carry forward "the meaning of God in that sentence."[131] Recall that chapter 5 of this paper evaluated a sermon that Robert Dabney preached on Acts 16:30–31,[132] concluding that while Dabney had not preached heterodoxy, he also had not contented himself to discuss the nature of faith as it appears in Acts 16, but instead moved beyond the meaning of the text in order to offer a systematic theology of saving faith. Many of Bedinger's sermons follow this pattern. He did not so much carry forward "the meaning of God in that sentence"[133] as he identified the doctrine or duty in a text, preaching a topical sermon that systematically explored the doctrine or duty he had identified. Bedinger was not heterodox, but neither did he confine himself to offering a true exposition of his text.

Consider "The Reflex Benefits of Giving," which Bedinger preached on Acts 20:35. Paul exhorted the Ephesian elders: "[R]emember the words of the Lord Jesus, how he himself said, 'It is more blessed to give than to receive.'" By way of Introduction, Bedinger noted that Jesus's words are not recorded in the Gospels, and thus canonically represent his last word on giving. After explaining that blessedness is synonymous with happiness, Bedinger's Proposition purposed to "show that giving is more conducive to happiness than receiving."[134] His Argument unfolded topically under five heads, and moved

127. Bedinger, "Perseverance," 101.

128. Bedinger, "Perseverance," 101.

129. Bedinger, "Perseverance," 103.

130. Dabney, *Sacred Rhetoric*, 77.

131. Dabney, *Sacred Rhetoric*, 77.

132. Box 9, File 9/1, Acts 16:30–31 Full Text. See chapter 5 for this evaluation.

133. Dabney, *Sacred Rhetoric*, 77.

134. Bedinger, "Reflex," 240.

well beyond the meaning of the text. Bedinger taught that giving is a key to developing "all the Christian graces,"[135] that giving makes us "coworkers with God,"[136] and that our giving will be "rewarded in heaven."[137] While none of these statements is heterodox, it is also true that none can be derived from the text of Acts 20:35. Bedinger moved beyond the text to offer a systematic treatment of giving rather than confining himself to "the meaning of God in that sentence."[138] He followed the same pattern in "Total Depravity," "Parental Duties," and "The Preacher's Limit."

At other times, Bedinger was less faithful to the meaning of the text. "The Mediatorial Reign," which Bedinger preached on 1 Corinthians 15:24–26, offers an example. The Scripture teaches: "Then comes the end, when he delivers the kingdom to God the Father after destroying every rule and every authority and power. For he must reign until he has put all his enemies under his feet. The last enemy to be destroyed is death." Bedinger offered extensive theological context for his text within a thorough Exposition, demonstrating "the object of Christ's reign as mediator, the vast extent of His power and the certainty of the final triumph of His kingdom."[139] But then Bedinger turned to address a Proposition that seemed *non sequitur* from that which preceded it: "We will now proceed to consider a matter of great importance and practical value, viz: The kingdom of Christ is spiritual."[140] From this Proposition, Bendinger unfolded a topical Argument proving the Reformed doctrine of the "spirituality of the church,"[141] both establishing the doctrine and describing the pitfalls attending its neglect. It appears that Bedinger had previously chosen this topic, found a text he connected to it, and preached a sermon that stood far from "the meaning of God in that sentence."[142]

Yet Bedinger also demonstrated the ability to expound the Scripture carefully, preaching a Narrative sermon on a clause of Hebrews 11:27, which says of Moses: "[H]e endured as seeing him who is invisible." Bedinger's Exposition walked through the narrative of Moses's life, concluding that "God's faithfulness and power . . . made [Moses] steadfast and enabled him

135. Bedinger, "Reflex," 243.

136. Bedinger, "Reflex," 247.

137. Bedinger, "Reflex," 248.

138. Dabney, *Sacred Rhetoric*, 77.

139. Bedinger, "Mediatorial," 308.

140. Bedinger, "Mediatorial," 308.

141. See chapter 1, note 147.

142. Dabney, *Sacred Rhetoric*, 77.

to endure."[143] Stating his Proposition, Bedinger asserted that the "results" of "this endurance . . . will claim our consideration,"[144] and the remainder of the sermon applied lessons from Moses's life to the congregation. Although based on a single clause of a verse, the pattern and purpose clearly followed Dabney's instruction and example for Narrative sermons.

Not unlike Strickler and Lacy, Bedinger also differed from Dabney. He preached a catechetical sermon on Westminster Shorter Catechism 33,[145] which represents a category of preaching Dabney neither taught nor practiced. Bedinger also largely avoided the abuse of texts to which Strickler and Lacy fell prey.[146] Inasmuch as Strickler seemed to prefer Doctrinal sermons, Bedinger appears to have leaned toward Didactic messages, and his sermons frequently defended God—and by extension, sound theology—from misunderstandings and cavils.[147] His stance in reference to the text did not so much bear the mark of a craftsman as it did a systematician, who often moved beyond the plain meaning of the text, but who rarely altered the apparent purpose for which the biblical author employed it. Bedinger's sermons therefore strongly reflected Dabney's influence, but unlike Strickler and Lacy, Bedinger largely avoided the abuses of the text that Dabney's manuscript collection reveals.

Other Students

A Stamp of Influence

During his tenure at Union Seminary, Dabney trained some 325 students to preach.[148] In addition to Strickler, Lacy, and Bedinger, this paper reviewed

143. Bedinger, "Seeing the Invisible," 261.

144. Bedinger, "Seeing the Invisible," 261.

145. See Bedinger, "Justification."

146. The sermon previously mentioned, in which Bedinger moved from the mediatorial reign of Christ to the spirituality of the church, is as near as Bedinger came to abusing the text. But even in this sermon, his Exposition faithfully established the terms and meaning of the text.

147. At least six of Bedinger's sermons devote considerable effort to refuting error and defending God.

148. Dabney taught far more students than this. Homiletics was, however, taught during the middle of a student's three-year course of studies at Union Seminary (see chapter 4, note 3). Several of the students whom Dabney trained studied only one year at Union. These either transferred to or came from another seminary, thereby missing the middle year. Others never completed their studies. Some trained to preach and graduated but were never ordained. Others went into law, medicine, or teaching and never pursued pulpit ministry. One was struck by lightning while on horseback and

twenty-five sermons from eighteen other students whom Dabney trained to preach. A total of seventy-one sermons from twenty-one students is a fragile sample from which to draw conclusions about Dabney's influence, but it is not merely the complete absence of expository messages among his students' sermons that speaks, but also the presence of the same topical form—replete with its inconsistencies and abuses—that comprised ninety-five percent of Dabney's extant sermons, and which featured prominently in his classroom and indirect pulpit pedagogy. Dabney's stamp of influence deeply impresses the pages of his students' sermons.

Their Sermons

Two collections of late nineteenth- and early twentieth-century Southern Presbyterian sermons[149] together feature eleven messages preached by students who had studied homiletics under Dabney, and other sources offer fourteen more sermons. Including the sermons already reviewed, 36 of 71—or roughly fifty percent—included some form of "constant and faithful reference"[150] to the context. Half did not, resulting in the very "sermons without context," which Dabney's expository theory had insisted "should never had had a place in the Church at all."[151]

For a sermon that offered faithful context, consider J. F. Cannon, who preached on Acts 2:24, in which Peter declared: "God raised him up, loosing the pangs of death, because it was not possible for him to be held by it." Cannon began his Introduction by asserting that Jesus's disciples "had no expectation that he would rise from the dead,"[152] and Cannon reminded the congregation how reticent the disciples on the road to Emmaus had been to believe reports of the resurrection. Cannon recalled the context of Peter's Pentecost sermon, walking his hearers through the substance of Peter's address leading up to verse 24. His Proposition, which focused on Peter's assertion that death could not hold Jesus, purported to prove that "*the resurrection of Christ was inevitable and necessary*."[153] The Argument that followed unfolded topically under two heads, and Cannon concluded by promising his hearers

---

died before beginning his ministerial career. Several students fell in Civil War battles before completing their studies. See *Centennial Catalogue*, 71–120.

149. See Kerr, *Southern Presbyterian*, and Nabers, *Southern Presbyterian.*

150. Dabney, *Sacred Rhetoric*, 77.

151. Dabney, *Sacred Rhetoric*, 76.

152. Cannon, "Necessity," 287.

153. Cannon, "Necessity," 290 [emphasis original].

that by faith in Christ they too would rise to imperishable life. Cannon faithfully established the context of his chosen text.

So also did John Alexander Preston, who preached on Mark 15:43,[154] which teaches: "Joseph of Arimathea, a respected member of the council, who was also himself looking for the kingdom of God, took courage and went to Pilate and asked for the body of Jesus." Preston's Introduction explored the importance of burial in all cultures, leading to an Exposition by way of an extended retelling of Joseph's devotion. Preston thereby faithfully referenced and fleshed out the context of his chosen text. His Exposition led to "three pointed truth claims."[155] 1. There is salvation outside of the visible church. 2. Nothing can excuse the neglect of church membership. 3. Fear "prevents confession and destroys Christian testimony."[156] Preston's Conclusion implored his hearers to join the church. While his three points had little do with his chosen text, Preston nevertheless made "faithful reference to the context."[157]

Not so P. D. Stephenson, who preached on Matthew 28:19,[158] in which Jesus taught: "Go therefore and make disciples of all nations, baptizing them in the name of the Father and of the Son and of the Holy Spirit." Stephenson began by noting that society was concerned about the future of the church, suggesting that for the press and pulpit alike this "favorite topic" produced all manner of "discussion and speculation."[159] Offering neither Exposition nor context, Stephenson passed directly to his Proposition, which purposed to address the "double commission"[160] of the church, namely by affirming its responsibilities to go and to teach. The Argument that followed proceeded topically, and Stephenson applied his sermon by warning his congregation not to sacrifice truth for unity,[161] by decrying the "serious menace" of Unitarian hermeneutics,[162] and by lamenting the "growing neglect" of increase in holiness among the churches.[163] In no place did Stephenson address the context of his chosen verse.

154. Preston, "Arimathea," 243–54.

155. Preston, "Arimathea," 248.

156. Preston, "Arimathea," 252.

157. Dabney, *Sacred Rhetoric*, 77.

158. Stephenson, "Go—Teach," 234–46.

159. Stephenson, "Go—Teach," 234.

160. Stephenson, "Go—Teach," 234.

161. Stephenson, "Go—Teach," 240.

162. Stephenson, "Go—Teach," 241.

163. Stephenson, "Go—Teach," 241.

Whereas roughly half of the sermons of Dabney's students made some form of faithful reference to the context, just 27 of 71—or thirty-eight percent—accurately carried forward "the meaning of God in that sentence."[164] As an example of a sermon in which the preacher accurately carried forward the meaning of the text without moving beyond that meaning, consider A. W. Pitzer's sermon on Revelation 1:17–18,[165] in which Jesus declares: "Fear not, I am the first and the last, and the living one. I died, and behold I am alive forevermore, and I have the keys of Death and Hades." Pitzer offered Introduction by way Exposition, recounting the imprisonment of the aged John on Patmos, and described for his congregation the context, writing:

> He was in the spirit on the Lord's day, and in the midst of the seven golden candlesticks he saw one walking like unto the Son of man. He was clothed in full priestly garments, and his countenance was as the sun shineth in his strength. The vision was so majestic, so overpowering, that John fell at his feet as dead; then the glorified Redeemer laid his right hand on his servant, and said unto him, "Fear not."[166]

After noting that Jesus's words of comfort to John apply equally to every believer of every age, Pitzer's Proposition purported to explain from the text why believers should refrain from fear, instead showing "good courage" in Christ.[167] His Argument unfolded under four heads, each of which explained a clause of the text, and concluded with exhortations to trust Jesus. Pitzer faithfully carried forward the "meaning of God in that sentence"[168] confining himself to say that which the text said.

Many of Dabney's students, however, showed little regard for the meaning of the text. James Powers Smith preached on two clauses of 1 Corinthians 16:13,[169] in which the apostle commands: "[A]ct like men, be strong." Addressing cadets at the Virginia Military Institute, Smith began his Introduction by asserting that Paul never forgot his boyhood in Tarsus. Suggesting that he "especially . . . saw the soldiers," Smith imagined that Paul was "one of the boys that followed" when Roman soldiers marched through the streets.[170] Reviewing Scriptures in which Paul employed military imagery, Smith claimed that the present text also bore a military origin in Paul's

164. Dabney, *Sacred Rhetoric*, 77.

165. Pitzer, "Why Believers Should Not Fear," 161–72.

166. Pitzer, "Why Believers Should Not Fear," 161.

167. Pitzer, "Why Believers Should Not Fear," 163.

168. Dabney, *Sacred Rhetoric*, 77.

169. Smith, *Quit*.

170. Smith, *Quit*, 3.

mind,[171] and he used the words of the text as his Proposition. His Argument unfolded under three heads. The first bore no relation to the text, as Smith congratulated the students to whom he spoke on their choice to embrace a "manly life."[172] Smith employed his second head, which was based on the phrase, "[A]ct like men," to command his hearers to "Be a man!"[173] He then offered them several historical examples of manly young men, including Frederick the Great, Alexander the Great, and Galileo,[174] stressing that "the Christian life is the true manhood."[175] Smith's third head, which he based on the phrase, "Be strong," offered manifold exhortations to young men to cultivate strength in "self-respect," in "moral earnestness," in "association with the strong,"[176] and especially in the Lord, whose "divine power will come down to fill the weak places and quicken into new and better life all the elements of your manhood."[177] Powers concluded by recalling the memory of Stonewall Jackson, and encouraged his hearers to serve the "Captain of our Salvation."[178] While his sermon therefore frequently employed the words of the text, he failed to carry forward the text's meaning in the sermon, instead preaching a rousing call to masculine military service.

Other sermons fulfilled both of Dabney's requirements for a "true exposition," offering "constant and faithful reference" to context and faithfully carrying forward "the meaning of the God in that sentence."[179] Consider J. W. Rosebro, who preached on Isaiah 55:6,[180] which urges: "Seek the Lord while he may be found; call upon him while he is near." Rosebro's Introduction asserted that congregants must read and study Isaiah 53–55 together, and he offered brief theological and historical context for his chosen text. His Proposition stated: "Our text gives us a command, a promise and a warning."[181] Three heads of Argument unfolded this threefold Proposition, and through the individual clauses of the text, Rosebro preached the gospel and promised that God would accept every penitent sinner who sought and called upon the Lord. His Conclusion exhorted his hearers to consider

171. Smith, *Quit*, 4.
172. Smith, *Quit*, 5.
173. Smith, *Quit*, 6.
174. Smith, *Quit*, 7–8.
175. Smith, *Quit*, 8.
176. Smith, *Quit*, 9–10.
177. Smith, *Quit*, 11.
178. Smith, *Quit*, 11.
179. Dabney, *Sacred Rhetoric*, 77.
180. Rosebro, "Seeking," 118–27.
181. Rosebro, "Seeking," 119.

the brevity and uncertainty of life, and not to delay obeying the command of the text. Rosebro therefore offered limited but effective reference to context at the beginning of his sermon, and faithfully carried forward the meaning of God in the text.

Abner Crump Hopkins also offered a "true exposition,"[182] preaching an ordination sermon from 1 Timothy 4:14,[183] in which the Scripture teaches: "Do not neglect the gift which you have, which was given you by prophecy when that council of elders laid their hands on you." Hopkins's Introduction proceeded by way of Exposition as he reminded his congregation of Paul's second missionary journey, his initial introduction to Timothy, and of the trust Paul reposed in Timothy when he left him at Ephesus. Stating that the text speaks to Timothy's ordination,[184] Hopkins's Proposition purported to discuss "*ordination to the ministry—its conditions precedent; its divine warrant; its significance; and its mode*."[185] His Argument unfolded under three heads, each rich in biblical citations, which supported and explained the words of the text. Hopkins clearly desired to address the issue of "lay evangelists" within the Presbyterian Church, arguing pointedly against lay evangelism as opposed to the continuing presence of an ordained ministry.[186] But he did this by attending to the faithful exposition of his text rather than abusing it or moving beyond it. His Conclusion asserted that "all persons who are called of God's Spirit to 'preach the word' are required of him to be ordained,"[187] and he finished with a faithful summary, stating:

> Ordination, then, is a sacred thing to be respected by all lovers of the Lord the head of the church, and they who contemn it contemn God's ordinance. And all who receive it should regard it as a high and honorable privilege; they should "not neglect the gift," but with ever-increasing watchfulness and zeal "stir up the gift" which they have received, unto the glory of the Redeemer.[188]

Hopkins made both faithful reference to the context of his text and also accurately carried forward the meaning of the text as he understood it.

182. Dabney, *Sacred Rhetoric*, 77.

183. Hopkins, "Ordination," 235–46.

184. Whether this text addresses the Presbyterian doctrine of ordination is subject to debate. Hopkins, however, believed that it did, and he confined his remarks to carrying forward what he understood to be the meaning of the text.

185. Hopkins, "Ordination," 235 [emphasis original].

186. Hopkins, "Ordination," 238–40.

187. Hopkins, "Ordination," 245–46.

188. Hopkins, "Ordination," 246.

Conversely, some of the sermons that Dabney's students preached neither addressed the context of the Scripture nor carried forward the meaning, thereby failing to offer a "true exposition."[189] Consider Robert Kerr's sermon on Genesis 6:3,[190] which teaches: "And the Lord said, 'My spirit shall not always strive with man, for that he also is flesh: yet his days shall be an hundred and twenty years.'"[191] After describing in his Introduction the wickedness of men, and suggesting that the Holy Spirit had been actively striving against man's descent into that wickedness, Kerr offered a Proposition by way of question: "How did the Spirit strive then, and how does he strive with men to-day?"[192] He answered: 1. Through nature. 2. Through living witnesses. 3. Through the church. 4. Through family life. 5. Through conscience. Kerr then discussed blasphemy against the Holy Spirit, asking and attempting to answer how a person might know if he or she had committed that particular sin.[193] Kerr's Conclusion offered counsel about how to avoid such blasphemy. He thus failed to provide any context for his chosen verse, and used a text that predicts the coming of the Flood as a judgment of God upon the wickedness of the antediluvian generation in order to teach that the Holy Spirit strives to prevent people from sinning so that a Christian can avoid blasphemy against the Holy Spirit. His sermon failed to carry forward the "meaning of God in that sentence," and was by no means a "true exposition"[194] of the text.

Several sermons likewise manifested Dabney's stance as a craftsman, as his students employed the text for their own purposes, rather than pressing the text toward the same purpose for which it was written. Kerr's use of Genesis 6:3 to preach about blasphemy against the Holy Spirit served as a case in point. In the same way, William Murkland used 2 Timothy 1:3 to preach on the "divineness and far-reaching power of [the family] bond,"[195] while John Lyons used Haggai 2:7 and Matthew 1:21 in order to proclaim that the name of Jesus "is the most rugged and resonant name in all the history of God's ancient people,"[196] urging each Christian to be strong like Jesus.

189. Dabney, *Sacred Rhetoric*, 77.

190. Kerr, "Striving," 255–62.

191. Given that much of Kerr's sermon hinged upon the word "strive," this Scripture quotation reflects the King James Version of the Bible.

192. Kerr, "Striving," 256.

193. Kerr, "Striving," 259.

194. Dabney, *Sacred Rhetoric*, 77.

195. Murkland, "Divineness," 146.

196. Lyons, "Christmas," 191.

Consider also Peyton Hoge, who preached on Matthew 10:29, in which Jesus asks: "Are not two sparrows sold for a penny? And not one of them will fall to the ground apart from your Father." Hoge began his Introduction by asserting: "Two theories of the universe contend for the mastery in the world to-day, the mechanical and the paternal."[197] Discussing advances in modern science, Hoge contended that "[f]rom these well known facts of science, men have leaped to the conclusion that the mighty mechanism of nature is *only* a machine,"[198] rightly deducing that in "such a universe, worship is an absurdity."[199] Over against this theory stood the biblical assertion that God "exercises a fatherly care over all his creatures,"[200] and Hoge's Proposition signaled his intent to ask and answer: "What place is there for providence, faith, and prayer in a universe governed by unchanging and inexorable law?"[201] Unfolding under several heads, Hoge's Argument presented a detailed theodicy, crafting a Didactic sermon aimed at convincing non-Christians that providence and science can co-exist. Hoge returned to the text only in his Conclusion, in which he asserted: "The birds, which know only his providential care, may sing in unconscious innocence a Father's praise. But we, his children, may sing a new and nobler song, a song of pardoning, redeeming love."[202] Hoge's sermon reflected the stance of a craftsman, for he used a text that the biblical author intended to encourage believers to trust in God's providential care in order to dispute with non-believers the claims of atheistic science.

Summary

None of the seventy-one sermons Dabney's students preached was Expository according to Dabney's criteria.[203] Fifty-five employed a single verse or a clause of a verse, while one identified no text at all.[204] Half failed to offer "constant and faithful reference" to the context, while nearly two thirds failed to carry

197. Hoge, "Natural," 296.

198. Hoge, "Natural," 297 [emphasis original].

199. Hoge, "Natural," 298.

200. Hoge, "Natural," 298.

201. Hoge, "Natural," 299.

202. Hoge, "Natural," 306.

203. While Dabney rejected "textual" sermons as an independent category of sermon, the sermons of Pitzer and Rosebro fit this category. See Dabney, *Sacred Rhetoric*, 76.

204. Turnbull, "Preaching," 38–44.

forward "the meaning of God in that sentence."[205] Dabney the theorist had written that "[w]here pastors confine themselves . . . to texts of a single sentence, instead of explaining the Scriptures in their connection," or "where they wrest or accommodate the meaning to cover their human speculations" or "where they employ a fragment of the Word as a mere motto," then such preaching had failed, for "[t]he whole authority of [the preacher's] addresses to the conscience depends upon the correspondence evinced between his explanations and inferences and the infallible Word."[206] Nevertheless, Dabney the pedagogue equipped his students to "employ a fragment of the Word as a mere motto,"[207] which his expository theory castigated, while Dabney the preacher modeled for his students how to "wrest or accommodate the meaning to cover their human speculations."[208] It is no surprise therefore that the inconsistencies and defects of Dabney's classroom pedagogy and personal practice stand in clear view in the sermons of the students whom he trained to preach, for Dabney "reproduce[d] himself"[209] in them. His shaping influence upon their homiletical practices was profound.

Reinterpreting Dabney's Legacy

Mixed Evaluations

Lawrence Trotter offered an appraisal of mixed value when he suggested: "Dabney was not strikingly original in his homiletics. Rather, it is more appropriate to see him as one who received a homiletic current and then channeled it and increased its flow."[210] Trotter was correct that Dabney's homiletic offered little that was original. As chapter 5 of this paper has demonstrated, Dabney's homiletical peers expressed the same admiring sentiments in reference to expository preaching that Dabney had,[211] while chapter 2 noted that Dabney's homiletic bore striking similarities to the work of his peer, John Broadus.[212] If, however, J. W. Alexander was correct in his assessment of the absence of expository preaching in American pulpits a generation before

205. Dabney, *Sacred Rhetoric*, 77.

206. Dabney, *Sacred Rhetoric*, 75.

207. Dabney, *Sacred Rhetoric*, 75.

208. Dabney, *Sacred Rhetoric*, 75.

209. Johnson, *Life and Letters*, 554.

210. Trotter, "Blasting Rocks," 302.

211. See chapter 5.

212. Chapter 2, note 65. See also Trotter, *Always Prepared*, 187.

Dabney,[213] then Dabney could not have received an expository "homiletic current,"[214] for no such stream existed. Rather, Dabney made an abortive attempt to restore water to a parched riverbed. Given the arid state of expository preaching in America before Dabney—and given Dabney's failure to equip his students to practice expository preaching—the suggestion that he "channeled and increased its flow"[215] cannot be sustained.

Dabney's Enduring Influence

If the sermons evaluated in this chapter offer any indication of the ordinary homiletical practices of Dabney's students at large, then his students overwhelmingly failed to preach the expository sermons that Dabney theoretically admired. That failure, however, does not indicate Dabney's impotence to influence their homiletical practices. Nor should the blame for their failure to preach expository sermons fall at the feet of Dabney's students. Recall that Trotter contended: "It would seem to take exceptional stubbornness or dullness on the part of the students in order not to be indoctrinated into Dabney's approach to preaching."[216] Ironically, Dabney's students were, more than Trotter realized, "indoctrinated into Dabney's approach to preaching."[217] Trotter failed to see, however, that Dabney's "approach"[218] was, in every practical and measurable way, topical. Dabney's students therefore preached just as his classroom pedagogy trained them to preach and as his personal pulpit example modeled for them. Their failure to preach expository sermons, and their consistent replication of Dabney's topical pedagogy and personal example, stand as evidence that Dabney profoundly influenced their homiletical practices to resemble his own. Trotter's suggestion that Dabney exercised relatively little influence over the homiletical practices of the students whom he trained cannot stand in light of the analysis that this paper has conducted.

If, moreover, Trotter's interpretation of Dabney's legacy is correct, then any future study of Dabney's homiletic possesses relatively little value, for Dabney's homiletical impact died with him. But if the interpretation this paper defends is accurate—that Dabney exercised an enduring shaping influence upon the preaching practices of the students whom he trained,

213. Alexander, "Remarks."
214. Trotter, "Blasting Rocks," 302.
215. Trotter, "Blasting Rocks," 302.
216. Trotter, *Always Prepared*, 203.
217. Trotter, *Always Prepared*, 203.
218. Trotter, *Always Prepared*, 203.

reproducing something of himself in them—then Dabney represents a worthy figure for further study, for his homiletical influence upon the Southern Presbyterian Church has only begun to be explored.

Closing Review

This paper has analyzed Robert Lewis Dabney's expository homiletic, giving special attention to sermon structure, demonstrating that while Dabney crafted a robust expository theory, his weak expository pedagogy and personal neglect of expository preaching united to undermine his robust theory. By so doing, it has shown that Dabney exercised an enduring homiletical influence upon the students whom he trained to preach. Dabney's students failed to preach the expository sermons his theory admired, instead replicating the inconsistencies and defects of his classroom pedagogy and personal practice. Their sermons thus testify to Dabney's profound shaping influence upon them. Dabney's homiletical legacy within the Southern Church offers rich ground for future study, and further examination of the sermons of Dabney and his students seems warranted.

Conclusion

Dabney in Retrospect

As Thomas Cary Johnson concluded his biography of Robert Dabney, he contended: "Dr. Dabney was a great man. We cannot tell just how great yet. One cannot see how great Mt. Blanc is while standing at its foot. One hundred years from now men will be able to see him better."[219] One hundred twenty years have passed since Dabney's death, and history's view of him is not as generous as Johnson had hoped. Dabney no doubt possessed a giant intellect, offered unrivalled literary, theological, and polemical contributions to Southern Presbyterianism, and labored dutifully to preserve Southern Christianity. But Dabney also held tenaciously to an ugly, inveterate racism, bequeathing to his church and to the American South a legacy of unbiblical racial segregation that continues to mar race relations in America today.

Dabney's homiletical legacy is no less mixed. His *Sacred Rhetoric* asserted that all sermons "should be virtually expository, else they are not true sermons,"[220] and while his expository theory offered a robust platform from

219. Johnson, *Life and Letters*, 569.

220. Dabney, *Sacred Rhetoric*, 77.

which to equip his students, Dabney's classroom pedagogy and personal example united to undermine his expository theory. Dabney exerted an enduring shaping influence upon the homiletical practices of the students whom he trained to preach, but his influence consistently led his students to preach the very "sermons without context,"[221] that Dabney's homiletical theory castigated as "vicious,"[222] rather than the "true exposition[s]"[223] of the Scripture that his theory admired. Ultimately, Dabney's homiletical legacy boasts of unfulfilled promise, and his admiration for expository preaching was, in the end, empty.

221. Dabney, *Sacred Rhetoric*, 76.

222. Dabney, *Sacred Rhetoric*, 94.

223. Dabney, *Sacred Rhetoric*, 77.

Bibliography

I. Manuscript Collections

Robert Lewis Dabney Collection. William Smith Morton Library. Union Presbyterian Theological Seminary, Richmond, Virginia.

Robert Lewis Dabney Papers. Albert and Shirley Small Special Collections Library. University of Virginia, Charlottesville, Virginia.

II. Manuscripts Cited

Dabney Papers, University of Virginia:

Dabney, Robert Lewis. Unpublished autobiography. Box 4.

Ramsay, F. P. March 9, 1901 letter to Charles W. Dabney. Box 3, "Material for R. L. Dabney Memorial."

Witherspoon, T. D. "Dr. Dabney's Work in Louisville, KY." Box 4.

Dabney Collection, Union Seminary:

Box 9, File 9/4. 1 Corinthians 9:24–27 Expository Exercise [Not in Dabney's hand].

Box 10, File 10/4. 1 Peter 1:16 Full Text [Not in Dabney's hand].

Box 11, File 11/6. "Class Notes by R. L. Dabney's Students."

Dabney, Robert Lewis. Box 4, File 4/8. "Offered in General Assembly 1878 at Knoxville and Laid on Table."

———. Box 5, File 5/3. "Presbyterianism, with Modern Improvements."

———. Box 6, File 6/3a. "Preface" to Army Sermons.

———. Box 6, File 6/3a. Philippians 4:4–7 Full Text.

———. Box 6, File 6/3b. Matthew 11:28–30 Full Text.

———. Box 6, File 6/3b. Romans 10:6–10 Full Text.

———. Box 6, File 6/4. Genesis 2:17 Skeleton.
———. Box 6, File 6/4. Genesis 4:9 Skeleton.
———. Box 6, File 6/4. Exodus 18:21 Skeleton.
———. Box 6, File 6/4. Exodus 20:8–11 Full Text (#128).
———. Box 6, File 6/4. Exodus 20:8–11 Full Text (#129).
———. Box 6, File 6/4. Exodus 20:12 Full Text.
———. Box 6, File 6/4. Leviticus 19:32 Outline.
———. Box 6, File 6/5. 1 Samuel 24 Narrative Exercise.
———. Box 6, File 6/5. Deuteronomy 32:13–15 Skeleton.
———. Box 6, File 6/5. Numbers 22–24 Narrative Exercise.
———. Box 6, File 6/6. Esther 5:13 Full Text.
———. Box 6, File 6/6. Luke 14:28 Practical Exercise.
———. Box 6, File 6/6. Psalm 23 Full Text.
———. Box 6, File 6/6. Psalm 33:5 Doctrinal Exercise.
———. Box 6, File 6/6. Psalm 33:5 Full Text.
———. Box 6, File 6/6. Psalm 84:11 Skeleton.
———. Box 6, File 6/7. Psalm 35:6 Skeleton.
———. Box 6, File 6/7. Psalm 66:18 Outline.
———. Box 6, File 6/7. Psalm 81:10 Full Text.
———. Box 6, File 6/7. Psalm 85:10 Full Text.
———. Box 7, File 7/1. Psalm 119:18 Full Text.
———. Box 7, File 7/1. Psalm 119:130 Full Text.
———. Box 7, File 7/1. Psalm 139:14 Skeleton.
———. Box 7, File 7/3. Ecclesiastes 1:14 Full Text.
———. Box 7, File 7/3. Ecclesiastes 5:5 Full Text.
———. Box 7, File 7/3. Ecclesiastes 12:1 Practical Exercise.
———. Box 7, File 7/3. Proverbs 29:18 Brief.
———. Box 7, File 7/4. Isaiah 5:1–7 Expository Exercise.
———. Box 7, File 7/5. Jeremiah 2:12–13 Skeleton.
———. Box 7, File 7/5. Jeremiah 3:15 Full Text.
———. Box 7, File 7/5. Jeremiah 9:23–24 Full Text.
———. Box 7, File 7/5. Jeremiah 17:9 Skeleton.
———. Box 7, File 7/5. Jeremiah 29:13 Practical Exercise.
———. Box 7, File 7/6. Daniel 3:8–27 Narrative Exercise.
———. Box 7, File 7/6. Daniel 4:35 Skeleton.
———. Box 7, File 7/6. Habakkuk 1:13 Didactic Exercise.
———. Box 7, File 7/6. Habakkuk 1:13 Outline.
———. Box 7, File 7/6. Habakkuk 2:15 Skeleton.
———. Box 7, File 7/6. Hosea 6:1 [Discarded Draft].
———. Box 7, File 7/6. Malachi 3:6 Doctrinal Exercise.
———. Box 7, File 7/6. Matthew 3:7–12 Expository Exercise.
———. Box 7, File 7/6. Micah 7:18 Skeleton.
———. Box 8, File 8/1. Matthew 5:15 Skeleton.
———. Box 8, File 8/1. Matthew 5:43–44 Exercise.
———. Box 8, File 8/1. Matthew 9:38 Skeleton.
———. Box 8, File 8/1. Matthew 10:29–30 Exercise.
———. Box 8, File 8/2. Matthew 11:28–30 Expository Exercise.
———. Box 8, File 8/2. Matthew 19:16–22 Brief.

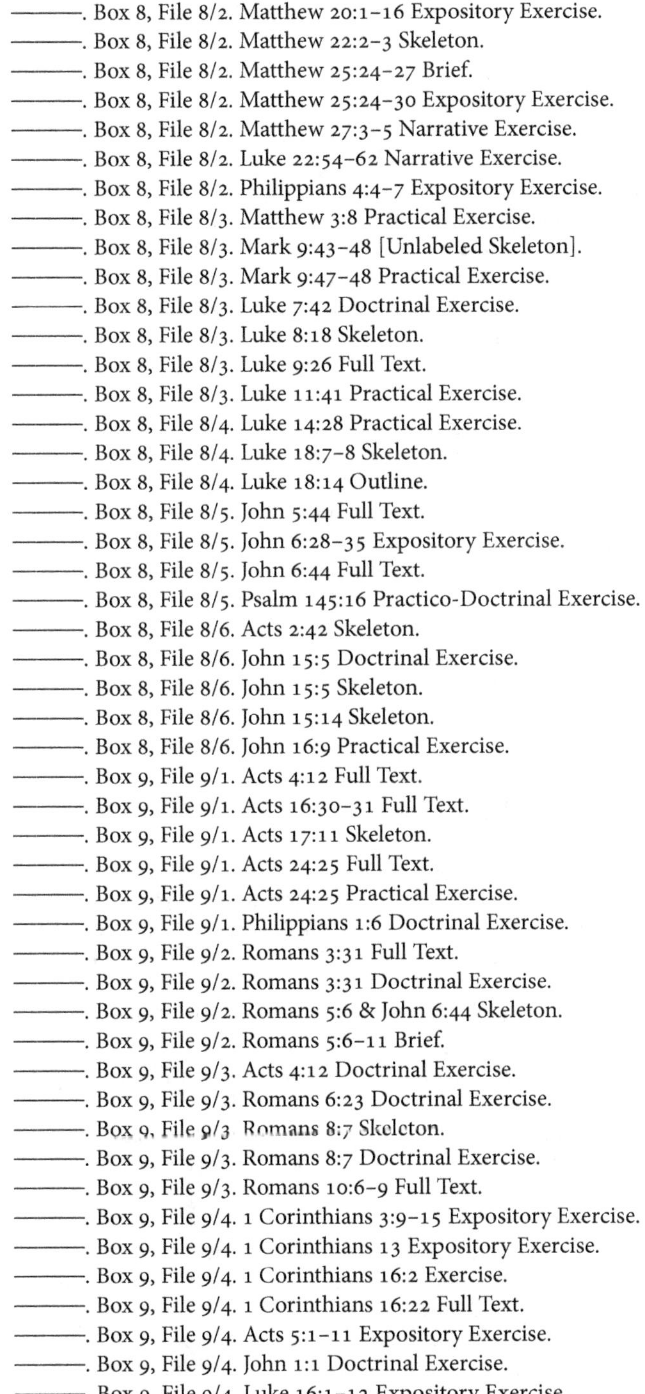

———. Box 8, File 8/2. Matthew 20:1–16 Expository Exercise.
———. Box 8, File 8/2. Matthew 22:2–3 Skeleton.
———. Box 8, File 8/2. Matthew 25:24–27 Brief.
———. Box 8, File 8/2. Matthew 25:24–30 Expository Exercise.
———. Box 8, File 8/2. Matthew 27:3–5 Narrative Exercise.
———. Box 8, File 8/2. Luke 22:54–62 Narrative Exercise.
———. Box 8, File 8/2. Philippians 4:4–7 Expository Exercise.
———. Box 8, File 8/3. Matthew 3:8 Practical Exercise.
———. Box 8, File 8/3. Mark 9:43–48 [Unlabeled Skeleton].
———. Box 8, File 8/3. Mark 9:47–48 Practical Exercise.
———. Box 8, File 8/3. Luke 7:42 Doctrinal Exercise.
———. Box 8, File 8/3. Luke 8:18 Skeleton.
———. Box 8, File 8/3. Luke 9:26 Full Text.
———. Box 8, File 8/3. Luke 11:41 Practical Exercise.
———. Box 8, File 8/4. Luke 14:28 Practical Exercise.
———. Box 8, File 8/4. Luke 18:7–8 Skeleton.
———. Box 8, File 8/4. Luke 18:14 Outline.
———. Box 8, File 8/5. John 5:44 Full Text.
———. Box 8, File 8/5. John 6:28–35 Expository Exercise.
———. Box 8, File 8/5. John 6:44 Full Text.
———. Box 8, File 8/5. Psalm 145:16 Practico-Doctrinal Exercise.
———. Box 8, File 8/6. Acts 2:42 Skeleton.
———. Box 8, File 8/6. John 15:5 Doctrinal Exercise.
———. Box 8, File 8/6. John 15:5 Skeleton.
———. Box 8, File 8/6. John 15:14 Skeleton.
———. Box 8, File 8/6. John 16:9 Practical Exercise.
———. Box 9, File 9/1. Acts 4:12 Full Text.
———. Box 9, File 9/1. Acts 16:30–31 Full Text.
———. Box 9, File 9/1. Acts 17:11 Skeleton.
———. Box 9, File 9/1. Acts 24:25 Full Text.
———. Box 9, File 9/1. Acts 24:25 Practical Exercise.
———. Box 9, File 9/1. Philippians 1:6 Doctrinal Exercise.
———. Box 9, File 9/2. Romans 3:31 Full Text.
———. Box 9, File 9/2. Romans 3:31 Doctrinal Exercise.
———. Box 9, File 9/2. Romans 5:6 & John 6:44 Skeleton.
———. Box 9, File 9/2. Romans 5:6–11 Brief.
———. Box 9, File 9/3. Acts 4:12 Doctrinal Exercise.
———. Box 9, File 9/3. Romans 6:23 Doctrinal Exercise.
———. Box 9, File 9/3. Romans 8:7 Skeleton.
———. Box 9, File 9/3. Romans 8:7 Doctrinal Exercise.
———. Box 9, File 9/3. Romans 10:6–9 Full Text.
———. Box 9, File 9/4. 1 Corinthians 3:9–15 Expository Exercise.
———. Box 9, File 9/4. 1 Corinthians 13 Expository Exercise.
———. Box 9, File 9/4. 1 Corinthians 16:2 Exercise.
———. Box 9, File 9/4. 1 Corinthians 16:22 Full Text.
———. Box 9, File 9/4. Acts 5:1–11 Expository Exercise.
———. Box 9, File 9/4. John 1:1 Doctrinal Exercise.
———. Box 9, File 9/4. Luke 16:1–12 Expository Exercise.

———. Box 9, File 9/5. 2 Corinthians 6:14–18 Full Text.
———. Box 9, File 9/5. 2 Corinthians 6:14—7:1 Practical-Expository Exercise.
———. Box 9, File 9/5. 2 Corinthians 13:5 Full Text.
———. Box 9, File 9/5. 2 Corinthians 13:5 Exercise.
———. Box 9, File 9/5. 2 Corinthians 13:5 Skeleton.
———. Box 9, File 9/6. Galatians 4:24–26 Brief.
———. Box 10, File 10/1. Colossians 1:12 Full Text.
———. Box 10, File 10/1. Colossians 2:10 Full Text.
———. Box 10, File 10/1. Colossians 2:9–10 Outline.
———. Box 10, File 10/1. Philippians 2:12–13 Skeleton.
———. Box 10, File 10/2. Romans 8:7 Doctrinal and Practical Exercise.
———. Box 10, File 10/2. 1 Timothy 3:14–16 Expository Exercise.
———. Box 10, File 10/2. 1 Timothy 3:15 Didactic Exercise.
———. Box 10, File 10/2. 1 Timothy 6:12 Full Text.
———. Box 10, File 10/3. Hebrews 3:13 Practical Exercise.
———. Box 10, File 10/3. Hebrews 11:24–26 Full Text.
———. Box 10, File 10/3. Hebrews 11:24–27 Expository Exercise.
———. Box 10, File 10/3. Hebrews 12:12–13 Skeleton.
———. Box 10, File 10/4. 1 Peter 1:12 Brief.
———. Box 10, File 10/4. 1 Peter 4:12–15 Skeleton.
———. Box 10, File 10/4. James 1:21–25 Brief.
———. Box 10, File 10/4. James 5:20 Skeleton.
———. Box 10, File 10/5. 2 John 10–11 Brief.
———. Box 10, File 10/6. 1 Corinthians 3:8 Skeleton.
———. Box 10, File 10/6. Revelation 6:16 Skeleton.

III. Printed Sources

Alexander, James Waddel. "Remarks on the Disuse of Expository Preaching." *The Biblical Repertory and Princeton Review* 10.1 (January 1838) 33–55.

———. *Thoughts on Preaching: Classic Contributions to Homiletics*. Birmingham, AL: Solid Ground Christian, 2009. Originally published as *Thoughts on Preaching, being Contributions to Homiletics*. New York: Scribner's, 1864.

Annual Catalogue of the Officers and Students of the Union Theological Seminary, 1860–61. Richmond: Ritchie & Dunnavant, 1861.

Armitage, Thomas. *Preaching: Its Ideal and Inner Life*. Philadelphia: American Baptist, 1880.

Arrowood, William Butler. *The Polity of the Presbyterian Church: A Sermon Preached before the Presbytery of Fayetteville, NC*. Richmond: Presbyterian Committee, 1895.

Bedinger, William Lucas. "Affusion vs. Immersion, 1." In *Soul Food: Discourses on Topics from Paul the Apostle*, 203–17. Grand Rapids: Reformed, n.d.

———. "Affusion vs. Immersion, 2." In *Soul Food: Discourses on Topics from Paul the Apostle*, 221–36. Grand Rapids: Reformed, n.d.

———. "Assurance of Salvation." In *Soul Food: Discourses on Topics from Paul the Apostle*, 151–63. Grand Rapids: Reformed, n.d.

———. “The Baptism of Infants.” In *Soul Food: Discourses on Topics from Paul the Apostle*, 183–99. Grand Rapids: Reformed, n.d.

———. “Constraining Love.” In *Soul Food: Discourses on Topics from Paul the Apostle*, 273–83. Grand Rapids, MI: Reformed, n.d.

———. “The Election of Grace.” In *Soul Food: Discourses on Topics from Paul the Apostle*, 53–66. Grand Rapids: Reformed, n.d.

———. “Imputation.” In *Soul Food: Discourses on Topics from Paul the Apostle*, 117–31. Grand Rapids: Reformed, n.d.

———. “Invincible Grace.” In *Soul Food: Discourses on Topics from Paul the Apostle*, 85–98. Grand Rapids: Reformed, n.d.

———. “Justification.” In *Soul Food: Discourses on Topics from Paul the Apostle*, 135–48. Grand Rapids: Reformed, n.d.

———. “The Mediatorial Reign.” In *Soul Food: Discourses on Topics from Paul the Apostle*, 303–16. Grand Rapids: Reformed, n.d.

———. “Parental Duties.” In *Soul Food: Discourses on Topics from Paul the Apostle*, 167–80. Grand Rapids: Reformed, n.d.

———. “Particular Redemption.” In *Soul Food: Discourses on Topics from Paul the Apostle*, 69–81. Grand Rapids: Reformed, n.d.

———. “The Perseverance of the Saints.” In *Soul Food: Discourses on Topics from Paul the Apostle*, 101–13. Grand Rapids: Reformed, n.d.

———. “The Preacher’s Limit.” In *Soul Food: Discourses on Topics from Paul the Apostle*, 287–300. Grand Rapids: Reformed, n.d.

———. “The Reflex Benefits of Giving.” In *Soul Food: Discourses on Topics from Paul the Apostle*, 239–53. Grand Rapids: Reformed, n.d.

———. “Seeing the Invisible.” In *Soul Food: Discourses on Topics from Paul the Apostle*, 257–69. Grand Rapids: Reformed, n.d.

———. *Soul Food: Discourses on Topics from Paul the Apostle*. Grand Rapids: Reformed, n.d.

———. “The Sovereignty of God.” In *Soul Food: Discourses on Topics from Paul the Apostle*, 21–33. Grand Rapids: Reformed, n.d.

———. “Total Depravity.” In *Soul Food: Discourses on Topics from Paul the Apostle*, 37–50. Grand Rapids: Reformed, n.d.

Beecher, Henry Ward. *Lectures on Preaching by the Rev. Henry Ward Beecher, Delivered to the Students of Yale Theological College During the Spring Session, 1874*. London: Clarke, 1874.

Behrends, Adolphus Julius Frederick. *The Philosophy of Preaching*. Lexington, KY: Leopold Classic Library, 2016. Originally published as *The Philosophy of Preaching*. New York: Scribner’s, 1890.

Breed, David Riddle. *Preparing to Preach*. New York: Doran, 1911.

Broadus, John Albert. *Lectures on the History of Preaching*. New York: Armstrong, 1893. Originally published as *Lectures on the History of Preaching*. New York: Sheldon & Company, 1876.

———. *A Treatise on the Preparation and Delivery of Sermons*. 2nd ed. Lexington, KY: University of Michigan Libraries, 2013. Originally published as *A Treatise on the Preparation and Delivery of Sermons*. New York: Sheldon, 1870.

Brooks, Phillips. *Lectures on Preaching, Delivered before the Divinity School of Yale College in January and February, 1877*. New York: Dutton, 1880. Originally published as *Lectures on Preaching, Delivered before the Divinity School of Yale College in January and February, 1877*. New York: Dutton, 1877.

Burton, Nathaniel. *Yale Lectures on Preaching, in Pulpit and Parish*. Edited by Richard E. Burton. London: Forgotten, 2016. Originally published as *Yale Lectures on Preaching, and Other Writings*. Edited by Richard E. Burton. Hartford, CT: Star Printing, 1887.

Campbell, George. *Lectures on Systematic Theology and Pulpit Eloquence. To Which are Added Dialogues on Eloquence by M. De Fenelon, Archbishop of Cambray*. Edited by Henry J. Ripley. Los Angeles: HardPress, 2015. Reprinted from *Lectures on Systematic Theology and Pulpit Eloquence. To Which are Added Dialogues on Eloquence by M. De Fenelon, Archbishop of Cambray*. Edited by Henry J. Ripley. Boston: Lincoln and Edmands, 1832. Originally published as *Lectures on Pulpit Eloquence*. London: Baynes, 1824.

———. *The Philosophy of Rhetoric*. New ed. Los Angeles: HardPress, 2016. Reprinted from *The Philosophy of Rhetoric*. New ed. New York: Harper, 1885. Originally published as *The Philosophy of Rhetoric*. London: n.p., 1776.

Cannon, John Franklin. "The Necessity of Christ's Resurrection." In *The Southern Presbyterian Pulpit: A Collection of Sermons by Ministers of the Southern Presbyterian Church*, 287–95. Richmond: Presbyterian Committee, 1896.

Catalogue of the Officers and Students of the Union Theological Seminary, in Prince Edward County, VA, Under the Care of the Synods of Virginia and North Carolina and the Presbytery of Winchester, 1855–56. Richmond: Wynn, 1856.

Clergy of the Confederate States of America. *An Address to Christians Throughout the World by Clergy of the Confederate States of America Assembled at Richmond, VA., April, 1863*. Harrisonburg, VA: Old South Institute, 2009. Originally published as *An Address to Christians Throughout the World by a Convention of Ministers Assembled at Richmond, VA., April 1863*. London: Strangeway & Walden, 1863.

Cocke, Alonzo Rice. *No Immersion in the Bible; Or, Baptism as Taught and Practiced by Christ and the Apostles*. Richmond: Presbyterian Committee, 1893.

Crosby, Howard. *The Christian Preacher: Yale Lectures for 1879–80*. London: Forgotten, 2015. Originally published as *The Christian Preacher: Yale Lectures for 1879–80*. New York: Randolph, 1879.

Dabney, Charles William, ed. *In Memorium: Robert Lewis Dabney*. Knoxville, TN: University of Tennessee, 1899.

Dabney, Robert Lewis. *Christ Our Penal Substitute*. Harrisonburg, VA: Sprinkle, 1985. Originally published as *Christ Our Penal Substitute*. Richmond: Presbyterian Committee, 1898.

———. *A Defense of Virginia, and Through Her, of the South, in Recent and Pending Contests Against the Sectional Party*. Harrisonburg, VA: Sprinkle, 1977. Originally published as *A Defense of Virginia, and Through Her, of the South, in Recent and Pending Contests Against the Sectional Party*. New York: Hale, 1867.

———. *Discussions*. Vol. 1, *Theological and Evangelical*. Edited by C. R. Vaughan. Harrisonburg, VA: Sprinkle, 1982. Originally published as *Discussions*. Vol. 1, *Theological and Evangelical*. Edited by C. R. Vaughan. Richmond: Presbyterian Committee, 1890.

———. *Discussions*. Vol. 2, *Evangelical*. Edited by C. R. Vaughan. Harrisonburg, VA: Sprinkle, 1982. Originally published as *Discussions*. Vol. 2, *Evangelical*. Edited by C. R. Vaughan. Richmond: Presbyterian Committee, 1891.

———. *Discussions*. Vol. 3, *Philosophical*. Edited by C. R. Vaughan. Harrisonburg, VA: Sprinkle, 1996. Originally published as *Discussions*. Vol. 3, *Philosophical*. Edited by C. R. Vaughan. Richmond: Presbyterian Committee, 1892.

———. *Discussions*. Vol. 4, *Secular*. Edited by C. R. Vaughan. Harrisonburg, VA: Sprinkle, 1994. Originally published as *Discussions*. Vol. 4, *Secular*. Edited by C. R. Vaughan. Mexico, MO: Crescent, 1897.

———. *Discussions*. Vol. 5, *Miscellaneous Writings*. Edited by J. H. Varner. Harrisonburg, VA: Sprinkle, 1999.

———. "The Doctrinal Contents of the Westminster Confession of Faith." In *Discussions: Miscellaneous Writings*, edited by J. H. Varner, 5:119–42. Harrisonburg, VA: Sprinkle, 1999.

———. "The Duty of the Hour." In *Discussions: Secular*, edited by C. R. Vaughan, 4:113. Harrisonburg, VA: Sprinkle, 1994. Originally published as *Discussions, Volume 4: Secular*, edited by C. R. Vaughan. Mexico, MO: Crescent, 1897.

———. *Ecclesiastical Relation of Negroes*. Richmond: Boys and Girls' Monthly, 1868.

———. *The Five Points of Calvinism*. Harrisonburg, VA: Sprinkle, 1992. Originally published as *The Five Points of Calvinism*. Richmond: Presbyterian Committee, 1895.

———. "The Gospel Idea of Preaching." In *Discussions: Theological and Evangelical*, edited by C. R. Vaughan, 1:598–601. Harrisonburg, VA: Sprinkle, 1982. Originally published as *Discussions, Volume 1: Theological and Evangelical*. Edited by C. R. Vaughan. Richmond: Presbyterian Committee, 1890.

———. "The Influence of the German University System on Theological Literature." In *Discussions: Theological and Evangelical*, edited by C. R. Vaughan, 1:444–46. Harrisonburg, VA: Sprinkle, 1982. Originally published as *Discussions, Volume 1: Theological and Evangelical*, edited by C. R. Vaughan. Richmond: Presbyterian Committee, 1890.

———. *Lectures in Systematic Theology*. Grand Rapids, MI: Zondervan, 1976. Originally published as *Syllabus and Notes of the Course of Systematic and Polemic Theology*. St. Louis, MO: Presbyterian of St. Louis, 1878.

———. *The Life and Campaigns of Lieut. Gen. Thomas J. Jackson, (Stonewall Jackson)*. New York: Blelock, 1866.

———. *A Memorial of the Christian Life and Character of Francis Sampson, D. D.* Richmond: Enquirer Book and Job, 1855.

———. "The New South." In *Discussions: Secular*, edited by C. R. Vaughan, 4:1–24. Harrisonburg, VA: Sprinkle, 1994. Originally published as *Discussions, Volume 4: Secular*. Edited by C. R. Vaughan. Mexico, MO: Crescent, 1897.

———. "A Phase of Religious Selfishness." In *Discussions: Theological and Evangelical*, edited by C.R. Vaughan, 1:696. Harrisonburg, VA: Sprinkle, 1982. Originally published as *Discussions, Volume 1: Theological and Evangelical*, edited C. R. Vaughan. Richmond, VA: Presbyterian Committee, 1890.

———. *The Practical Philosophy. Being the Philosophy of the Feelings, of the Will, and of the Conscience, with the Ascertainment of Particular Rights and Duties*. Mexico, MO: Crescent, 1897.

———. *Sacred Rhetoric; Or, A Course of Lectures on Preaching*. New Delhi: Isha, 2013. Originally published as *Sacred Rhetoric; Or, A Course of Lectures on Preaching*. New York: Randolph, 1870.

———. *The Sensualistic Philosophy of the Nineteenth Century Considered.* New York: Randolph, 1875.

———. "A Thoroughly Educated Ministry." In *Discussions: Evangelical,* edited by C. R. Vaughan, 2:659–60. Harrisonburg, VA: Sprinkle, 1982. Originally published as *Discussions, Volume 2: Evangelical.* Edited by C. R. Vaughan. Richmond, VA: Presbyterian Committee, 1891.

———. "Uses and Results of Church History." In *Discussions: Evangelical,* edited by C. R. Vaughan, 2:5. Harrisonburg, VA: Sprinkle, 1982. Originally published as *Discussions, Volume 2: Evangelical.* Edited by C. R. Vaughan. Richmond, VA: Presbyterian Committee, 1891.

———. "What Is a Call to the Ministry?" In *Discussions: Evangelical,* edited by C. R. Vaughan, 2:27–33. Harrisonburg, VA: Sprinkle, 1982. Originally published as *Discussions, Volume 2: Evangelical.* Edited by C. R. Vaughan. Richmond, VA: Presbyterian Committee, 1891.

Dabney, William Henry. *Sketch of the Dabneys of Virginia, with some of their Family Records.* Whitefish, MT: Kessinger, 2015. Originally published as *Sketch of the Dabneys of Virginia, with some of their Family Records.* Chicago: Childs, 1888.

Dale, Robert William. *Nine Lectures on Preaching.* Lexington, KY: University of California Libraries, 2015. Originally published as *Nine Lectures on Preaching.* London: Hodder & Stoughton, 1877.

Etter, John Wesley. *The Preacher and His Sermon: A Treatise on Homiletics.* Dayton, OH: United Brethren, 1893. Originally published as *The Preacher and His Sermon: A Treatise on Homiletics.* Dayton, OH: United Brethren, 1883.

Evans, William. *How to Prepare Sermons and Gospel Addresses.* Chicago: The Bible Institute Colportage Association, 1913.

Fairbairn, Patrick. *Hermeneutical Manual or Introduction to the Exegetical Study of the Scriptures of the New Testament.* Lexington, KY: University of Michigan Libraries, 2014. Originally published as *Hermeneutical Manual or Introduction to the Exegetical Study of the Scriptures of the New Testament.* Philadelphia: Smith, English, 1859.

Fisk, Franklin Woodbury. *Manual of Preaching: Lectures on Homiletics.* 3rd ed. London: Forgotten, 2017. Originally published as *Manual of Preaching: Lectures on Homiletics.* New York: Armstrong, 1884.

Gardiner Spring Resolutions. Transcript of the Minutes of the 73rd General Assembly, 1861. www.pcahistory.org/documents/gardinerspring.html.

Greer, David Hummel. *The Preacher and His Place: The Lyman Beecher Lectures on Preaching, Delivered at Yale University in the Month of February, 1895.* New York: Scribner's, 1904. Originally published as *The Preacher and His Place: The Lyman Beecher Lectures on Preaching, Delivered at Yale University in the Month of February, 1895.* New York: Scribner's, 1895.

Hall, John. *God's Word through Preaching: The Lyman Beecher Lectures before the Theological Department of Yale.* Lexington, KY: Leopold Classic Library, 2015. Originally published as *God's Word through Preaching: The Lyman Beecher Lectures before the Theological Department of Yale.* New York: Dodd & Mead, 1875.

Hervey, George Winfred. *A System of Christian Rhetoric, for the Use of Preachers and Other Speakers.* New York: Harper, 1873.

Hodge, Charles. "The Manner of Preaching." *The Biblical Repertory and Princeton Review* 35.2 (April 1863) 177–206.

———. "The Matter of Preaching." *The Biblical Repertory and Princeton Review* 28.4 (October 1856) 655–88.

———. "Notices of Recent Publications." *The Biblical Repertory and Princeton Review* 43.1 (January 1871) 147–48.

———. "Remarks on the Studies and Discipline of the Preacher." *The Biblical Repertory and Princeton Review* 27.1 (January 1855) 1–24.

Hoge, Moses D. "Regnant Men." In *In Memorium: Robert Lewis Dabney*, edited by Charles W. Dabney, 26. Knoxville, TN: University of Tennessee, 1899.

Hoge, Peyton Harrison. "Natural Law and Divine Providence." In *The Southern Presbyterian Pulpit: A Collection of Sermons by Ministers of the Southern Presbyterian Church*, 296–306. Richmond, VA: Presbyterian Committee, 1896.

———. *The Officers of a Presbyterian Congregation. Three Sermons Preached in the First Presbyterian Church of Wilmington, NC., by Rev. Peyton H. Hoge.* n.p., n.d.

Hogg, Wilson T. *A Hand-Book of Homiletics and Pastoral Theology*. Chicago: Free Methodist, 1895. Originally published as *A Hand-Book of Homiletics and Pastoral Theology*. Chicago: Free Methodist, 1886.

Hooper, Thomas Williamson. "Christ, the Model Preacher." *The Presbyterian Quarterly* 15.2 (April 1901) 238–49.

———. "The Pre-Incarnate Christ." *The Presbyterian Quarterly* 6.3 (July 1892) 399–409.

———. "The Unchangeable Word." *The Presbyterian Quarterly* 2.2 (July 1888) 208–16.

Hopkins, Abner Crump. "Ordination to the Ministry of Christ." *The Presbyterian Quarterly* 8.2 (April 1894) 235–46.

Hoppin, James Mason. *The Office and Work of the Christian Ministry*. New Delhi: Isha, 2013. Originally published as *The Office and Work of the Christian Ministry*. New York: Sheldon, 1869.

Horton, Robert F. *Verbum Dei: The Yale Lectures on Preaching, 1893*. New York: Macmillan, 1893.

Hoyt, Arthur S. *The Work of Preaching: A Book for the Class-Room and Study*. New York: Hodder & Stoughton, 1905.

Johnson, Thomas Cary. "Robert Lewis Dabney—a Sketch." In *In Memorium: Robert Lewis Dabney*, edited Charles W. Dabney, 9. Knoxville, TN: University of Tennessee, 1899.

Kern, John A. *The Ministry to the Congregation: Lectures on Homiletics*. 6th ed. Cincinnati: Jennings & Graham, 1905. Originally published as *Ministry to the Congregation: Lectures on Homiletics*. Nashville: The Methodist Episcopal Church, South, 1897.

Kerr, Robert Pollock. "The Striving Spirit." In *The Southern Presbyterian Pulpit: A Collection of Sermons by Ministers of the Southern Presbyterian Church*, 255–62. Richmond, VA: Presbyterian Committee of Publication, 1896.

Kerr, Robert Pollock, ed. *Southern Presbyterian Pulpit: A Collection of Sermons by Ministers of the Southern Presbyterian Church*. Richmond, VA: Presbyterian Committee, 1896.

Kidder, Daniel Parrish. *A Treatise on Homiletics: Designed to Illustrate the True Theory and Practice of Preaching the Gospel*. New York: Carlton & Porter, 1866. Originally published as *A Treatise on Homiletics: Designed to Illustrate the True Theory and Practice of Preaching the Gospel*. New York: Carlton & Porter, 1864.

Lacy, William Sterling. "Ambassadors for Christ." In *William Sterling Lacy: Memorial, Addresses, Sermons*, 74–88. Richmond, VA: Presbyterian Committee, 1900.

———. "Attestations to Christ's Birth." In *William Sterling Lacy: Memorial, Addresses, Sermons*, 125–36. Richmond, VA: Presbyterian Committee, 1900.

———. "The Choice of Barabbas." In *William Sterling Lacy: Memorial, Addresses, Sermons*, 161–70. Richmond, VA: Presbyterian Committee, 1900.

———. "Christian Courage." In *William Sterling Lacy: Memorial, Addresses, Sermons*, 190–98. Richmond, VA: Presbyterian Committee, 1900.

———. "The City of God." In *William Sterling Lacy: Memorial, Addresses, Sermons*, 89–105. Richmond, VA: Presbyterian Committee, 1900.

———. "First Duties Neglected." In *William Sterling Lacy: Memorial, Addresses, Sermons*, 171–78. Richmond, VA: Presbyterian Committee, 1900.

———. "Home." In *William Sterling Lacy: Memorial, Addresses, Sermons*, 112–24. Richmond, VA: Presbyterian Committee, 1900.

———. "In Remembrance of Me." In *William Sterling Lacy: Memorial, Addresses, Sermons*, 106–11. Richmond, VA: Presbyterian Committee, 1900.

———. "Is the Young Man Safe?" In *William Sterling Lacy: Memorial, Addresses, Sermons*, 179–89. Richmond, VA: Presbyterian Committee, 1900.

———. "Jesus Loved Martha." In *William Sterling Lacy: Memorial, Addresses, Sermons*, 137–48. Richmond, VA: Presbyterian Committee, 1900.

———. "Reward of the Useful Teacher." In *William Sterling Lacy: Memorial, Addresses, Sermons*, 63–73. Richmond, VA: Presbyterian Committee, 1900.

———. *A Sermon Preached at the Buffalo Church, Moore County, January 24th, 1882 on the Occasion of the Death of Walter Temple Jones*. Fayetteville, NC: Garrett, Book and Job, 1882.

———. "What She Could." In *William Sterling Lacy: Memorial, Addresses, Sermons*, 149–60. Richmond, VA: Presbyterian Committee, 1900.

———. *William Sterling Lacy: Memorial, Addresses, Sermons*. Richmond, VA: Presbyterian Committee, 1900.

Lyons, John Sprole. "A Christmas Sermon." In *The Southern Presbyterian Pulpit: Pulpit Addresses by Ministers of the Presbyterian Church in the United States*, edited by Charles Haddon Nabers, 189–94. New York: Revell, 1928.

Martin, S. Taylor. "A Tribute." In *In Memorium: Robert Lewis Dabney*, edited by Charles W. Dabney, 40. Knoxville, TN: University of Tennessee, 1899.

Marye, L. S. "A Light Gone." In *In Memorium: Robert Lewis Dabney*, edited by Charles W. Dabney, 31. Knoxville, TN: University of Tennessee, 1899.

Miller, Samuel. "The Importance of a Thorough and Adequate Course of Preparatory Study for The Holy Ministry." In *Annual of the Board of Education* 1 (1932) 55–95.

Moore, Walter William. "The Three Causes of Salvation." In *The Southern Presbyterian Pulpit: A Collection of Sermons by Ministers of the Southern Presbyterian Church*, 277–86. Richmond, VA: Presbyterian Committee, 1896.

———. *The Whole Man: Baccalaureate Sermon Preached at the University of North Carolina, Chapel Hill, NC., May 31st, 1891*. Wilmington, NC: Steam Printers and Binders, 1891.

Moore, Walter William, and Tilden Scherer, eds. *Centennial General Catalogue of the Trustees, Officers, Professors and Alumni of Union Theological Seminary in Virginia, 1807–1907*. Richmond, VA: Whittet & Shepperson, 1908.

Moore, Walter William, et al., eds. *General Catalogue of the Trustees, Officers, Professors and Alumni of Union Theological Seminary in Virginia, 1807–1924*. Richmond, VA: Whittet & Shepperson, 1924.

Murkland, William Urwick. "The Divineness of the Family Bond." In *The Southern Presbyterian Pulpit: A Collection of Sermons by Ministers of the Southern Presbyterian Church*, 145–60. Richmond, VA: Presbyterian Committee, 1896.

Nabers, Charles Haddon, ed. *The Southern Presbyterian Pulpit: Pulpit Addresses by Ministers of the Presbyterian Church in the United States*. New York: Revell, 1928.

Palmer, Benjamin M. "The Christian Warrior," In *In Memorium: Robert Lewis Dabney*, edited by Charles W. Dabney, 20. Knoxville, TN: University of Tennessee, 1899.

Pattison, T. Harwood. *The Making of the Sermon: For the Classroom and the Study*. Philadelphia, PA: American Baptist, 1898.

Phelps, Austin. *The Theory of Preaching: Lectures on Homiletics*. New York: Scribner's, 1886. Originally published as *The Theory of Preaching: Lectures on Homiletics*. New York: Scribner's, 1881.

Pitzer, Alexander White. "Twenty-fifth Anniversary Sermon." *The Christian Observer*, March 22, 1893, p. 10.

———. "Why Believers Should Not Fear." In *The Southern Presbyterian Pulpit: A Collection of Sermons by Ministers of the Southern Presbyterian Church*, 161–72. Richmond, VA: Presbyterian Committee, 1896.

Porter, Ebenezer. *Lectures on Homiletics and Preaching, and On Public Prayer: Together with Sermons and Letters*. Whitefish, MT: Kessinger, 2013. Reprinted from *Lectures on Homiletics and Preaching, and On Public Prayer: Together with Sermons and Letters*. London: Ward, 1859. Originally published as *Lectures on Homiletics and Preaching, and On Public Prayer: Together with Sermons and Letters*. Andover, MA: Flagg, Gould, & Newman, 1834.

Porter, Ebenezer, ed. *The Young Preacher's Manual*. New Delhi: Isha, 2013. Originally published as *The Young Preacher's Manual; Or a Collection of Treatises on Preaching; Comprising Brown's Address to Students of Divinity. Fenelon's Dialogues on the Eloquence of the Pulpit. Claude's Essay on the Composition of a Sermon, Abridged. Gregory on the Composition and Delivery of a Sermon. Reybaz on the Art of Preaching*. Boston: Flagg & Gould, 1819.

Preston, John Alexander. "Joseph of Arimathea." In *The Southern Presbyterian Pulpit: A Collection of Sermons by Ministers of the Southern Presbyterian Church*, 243–54. Richmond, VA: Presbyterian Committee, 1896.

Proudfoot, J. J. A. *Systematic Homiletics*. Edited by J. A. Turnbull and A. J. MacGillivray. New York: Revell, 1903.

Rice, J. H., Jr. "A Lover of the South." In *In Memorium: Robert Lewis Dabney*, edited by Charles W. Dabney, 33. Knoxville, TN: University of Tennessee, 1899.

Ripley, Henry J. *Sacred Rhetoric: Or, Composition and Delivery of Sermons, to which are added Hints on Extemporaneous Preaching by Henry Ware, Jr.* 4th ed. Charleston, SC: Bibliolife, 2014. Reprinted from *Sacred Rhetoric: Or, Composition and Delivery of Sermons, to which are added Hints on Extemporaneous Preaching by Henry Ware, Jr.* 4th ed. Boston, MA: Gould and Lincoln, 1859. Originally published as *Sacred Rhetoric: Or, Composition and Delivery of Sermons*. Boston, MA: Gould, Kendall & Lincoln, 1849.

Robinson, Ezekiel Gilman. *Lectures on Preaching: Delivered to the Students of Theology at Yale College*. Lexington, KY: Leopold Classic Library, 2016. Originally published as *Lectures on Preaching: Delivered to the Students of Theology at Yale College*. New York: Holt, 1883.

Robinson, Stuart. *The Church of God as an Essential Element of the Gospel, and The Idea, Structure, and Functions Thereof*. New York: Scholar Select, 2017. Originally published as *The Church of God as an Essential Element of the Gospel, and The Idea, Structure, and Functions Thereof*. Philadelphia: Wilson, 1858.

Rosebro, John William. "Seeking the Lord." In *The Southern Presbyterian Pulpit: A Collection of Sermons by Ministers of the Southern Presbyterian Church*, 118–27. Richmond, VA: Presbyterian Committee, 1896.

Sampson, Thornton R. "The Teacher and Friend." In *In Memorium: Robert Lewis Dabney*, edited by Charles W. Dabney, 38. Knoxville, TN: University of Tennessee, 1899.

Scott, William Nelson. "Personal Work for the Master." In *The Southern Presbyterian Pulpit: A Collection of Sermons by Ministers of the Southern Presbyterian Church*, 235–42. Richmond, VA: Presbyterian Committee of Publication, 1896.

Shearer, James B. "The Man and Scholar." In *In Memorium: Robert Lewis Dabney*, edited by Charles W. Dabney, 18. Knoxville, TN: University of Tennessee, 1899.

Shedd, William Greenough Thayer. *Homiletics and Pastoral Theology*. New Delhi: SN Books World, 2015. Originally published as *Homiletics and Pastoral Theology*. New York: Scribner, 1867.

Simpson, Matthew. *Lectures on Preaching*. Lexington, KY: Leopold Classic Library, 2016. Originally published as *Lectures on Preaching*. London: Dickinson, 1879.

Smith, James Powers. "Memorial." In *William Sterling Lacy: Memorial, Addresses, Sermons*, 5–7. Richmond, VA: Presbyterian Committee, 1900.

———. *Quit You Like Men: A Sermon Preached at the Virginia Military Institute June 24, 1906*. Lynchburg, VA: Bell, 1906.

Spurgeon, Charles Haddon. *Lectures to My Students: A Selection from Addresses Delivered to the Students of the Pastor's College, Metropolitan Tabernacle*. Lexington, KY: Leopold Classic Library, 2015. Originally published as *Lectures to My Students: A Selection from Addresses Delivered to the Students of the Pastor's College, Metropolitan Tabernacle*. New York: Sheldon, 1875.

Stalker, James. *The Preacher and His Models: The Yale Lectures on Preaching, 1891*. Lexington, KY: Leopold Classic Library, 2016. Originally published as *The Preacher and His Models: The Yale Lectures on Preaching, 1891*. London: Hodder & Staughton, 1891.

Stephenson, Philip Daingerfield. "Go—Teach; Or, The Church's Double Commission." *The Presbyterian Quarterly* 9.2 (April 1895) 234–46.

Strickler, Given Brown. "Christ's Willingness to Save." In *Sermons by Rev. G. B. Strickler, D. D.*, 251–73. New York: Revell, 1910.

———. "The Christian's Heritage." In *Sermons by Rev. G. B. Strickler, D. D.*, 154–71. New York: Revell, 1910.

———. "The Condemnation." In *Sermons by Rev. G. B. Strickler, D. D.*, 120–36. New York: Revell, 1910.

———."Consecration." In *The Southern Presbyterian Pulpit: A Collection of Sermons by Ministers of the Southern Presbyterian Church*, 220–34. Richmond, VA: Presbyterian Committee, 1896.

———. "The Divine Origin of the Scriptures." In *Sermons by Rev. G. B. Strickler, D. D.*, 9–26. New York: Revell, 1910.

———. "The Doctrines of Calvinism." In *Sermons by Rev. G. B. Strickler, D. D.*, 209–35. New York: Revell, 1910.

———. "Faith." In *Sermons by Rev. G. B. Strickler, D. D.*, 27–48. New York: Revell, 1910.

———. "The Future State." In *Sermons by Rev. G. B. Strickler, D. D.*, 105–19. New York: Revell, 1910.

———. "The Great Salvation." In *Sermons by Rev. G. B. Strickler, D. D.*, 68–86. New York: Revell, 1910.

———. "Our Loss." In *In Memorium: Robert Lewis Dabney*, edited by Charles W. Dabney, 24. Knoxville, TN: University of Tennessee, 1899.

———. "Religion Reasonable." In *Sermons by Rev. G. B. Strickler, D. D.*, 49–67. New York: Revell, 1910.

———. "The Righteous Scarcely Saved." In *Sermons by Rev. G. B. Strickler, D. D.*, 172–89. New York: Revell, 1910.

———. *Sermons by Rev. G. B. Strickler, D. D.* New York: Revell, 1910.

———. "Take Heed How Ye Hear." In *Sermons by Rev. G. B. Strickler, D. D.*, 236–50. New York: Revell, 1910.

———. "The Unpardonable Sin." In *Sermons by Rev. G. B. Strickler, D. D.*, 190–208. New York: Revell, 1910.

———. "What Shall I Do with Christ." In *Sermons by Rev. G. B. Strickler, D. D.*, 87–104. New York: Revell, 1910.

———. "The Word of God." In *Sermons by Rev. G. B. Strickler, D. D.*, 137–53. New York: Revell, 1910.

Taylor, William Mackergo. *The Ministry of the Word.* Los Angeles: HardPress, 2014. Originally published as *The Ministry of the Word.* New York: Randolph, 1876.

Turnbull, Lennox Birkhead. "Preaching with Authority." *The Presbyterian Quarterly* 12.1 (January 1898) 38–44.

Vinet, Alexandre. *Homiletics; Or, The Theory of Preaching.* Translated and edited by Thomas H. Skinner. New York: Ivison & Phinney, 1853.

Watson, John. *The Cure of Souls: Lyman Beecher Lectures on Preaching at Yale University 1896.* Lexington, KY: Leopold Classic Library, 2016. Originally published as *The Cure of Souls: Lyman Beecher Lectures on Preaching at Yale University 1896.* New York: Dodd, Mead & Company, 1896.

Whately, Richard. *Elements of Rhetoric: Comprising an Analysis of the Laws of Moral Evidence and of Persuasion with Rules for Argumentative Composition and Elocution.* Lexington, KY: University of California Libraries, 2016. Reprinted from *Elements of Rhetoric: Comprising an Analysis of the Laws of Moral Evidence and of Persuasion with Rules for Argumentative Composition and Elocution.* New York: Harper & Brothers, 1860. Originally published as *Elements of Rhetoric. Comprising the Substance of the Article in the Encyclopedia Metropolitana: With Additions, etc.* Oxford: Baxter, 1828.

Woods, Neander Montgomery. "Our Redeemer's Prayer for Christian Unity." In *The Southern Presbyterian Pulpit: A Collection of Sermons by Ministers of the Southern Presbyterian Church*, 128–44. Richmond, VA: Presbyterian Committee, 1896.

IV. Secondary Literature

Abernathy, Elton. "Trends in American Homiletic Theory Since 1860." *Speech Monographs* 10.1 (1943) 68–74.

Ahlstrom, Sydney Eckman. *A Religious History of the American People*. 2nd ed. New Haven, CT: Yale University Press, 2004.

Ahlstrom, Sydney Eckman, ed. *Theology in America: The Major Protestant Voices from Puritanism to Neo-Orthodoxy*. New York: Bobbs-Merrill, 1967.

Arthurs, Jeffrey D. *Preaching with Variety: How to Re-create the Dynamics of Biblical Genres*. Grand Rapids, MI: Kregel, 2007.

Baxter, Batsell Barrett. *The Heart of the Yale Lectures*. Grand Rapids, MI: Baker, 1971.

Bradshaw, Herbert Clarence. *History of Prince Edward County, Virginia: From its Earliest Settlements through its Establishment in 1754 to its Bicentennial Year*. Richmond, VA: The Dietz, 1955.

Buck, Paul Herman. *The Road to Reunion 1865–1900*. Boston: Little, Brown, 1937.

Buswell, James Oliver, III. *Slavery, Segregation, and Scripture*. Grand Rapids, MI: Eerdmans, 1964.

Carr, Edward Hallett. *What Is History? The George Mazauley Trevelyan Lectures Delivered in the University of Cambridge January–March 1961*. New York: Knopf, 1964.

Carrigan, William D. "In Defense of the Social Order: Racial Thought among Southern White Presbyterians in the Nineteenth Century." *American Nineteenth Century History* 1.2 (Summer 2000) 31–52.

Carwardine, Richard. *Transatlantic Revivalism: Popular Evangelicalism in Britain and America, 1790–1865*. Westport, CT: Greenwood, 1978.

Cash, Wilbur Joseph. *The Mind of the South*. New York: Knopf, 1941.

Cherry, Conrad. *Hurrying Toward Zion: Universities, Divinity Schools, and American Protestantism*. Bloomington, IN: Indiana University Press, 1995.

Coffin, David Frank. "Reflections on the Life and Thought of Robert Lewis Dabney with Particular Reference to His Views on Divine Sovereignty and Human Free Agency." PhD diss., Westminster Theological Seminary, 2003.

Craddock, Fred Brenning. *As One Without Authority, Revised and With New Sermons*. St. Louis: Chalice, 2001. Originally published as *As One Without Authority*. St. Louis: Chalice, 1971.

Currie, Thomas White. *Austin Presbyterian Theological Seminary: A Seventy-fifth Anniversary History*. San Antonio: Trinity University Press, 1978.

Davenport, R. Dean. "Patriarchy and Politics: A Comparative Evaluation of the Religious, Political and Social Thought of Sir Robert Filmer and Robert Lewis Dabney." PhD diss., Baylor University, 2006.

Duncan, Ligon. "Defending the Faith; Denying the Image—19th Century American Confessional Calvinism in Faithfulness and Failure." http://ligonduncan.com/defending-the-faith-denying-the-image-19th-century-american-confessional-calvinism-in-faithfulness-and-failure.

Edwards, Otis Carl, Jr. *A History of Preaching*. Nashville: Abingdon, 2004.

Ellison, Robert H. *The Victorian Pulpit: Spoken and Written Sermons in Nineteenth-Century Britain*. London: Associated University Presses, 1998.

Farmer, James Oscar. *The Metaphysical Confederacy: James Henley Thornwell and the Synthesis of Southern Values*. Macon, GA: Mercer University Press, 1986.

Fraser, James W. *Schooling the Preachers: The Development of Protestant Theological Education in the United States 1740–1875*. Lanham, MD: University Press of America, 1988.

Garretson, James M. *An Able and Faithful Ministry: Samuel Miller and the Pastoral Office*. Grand Rapids, MI: Reformation Heritage, 2014.

———. *Princeton and Preaching: Archibald Alexander and the Christian Ministry*. Carlisle, PA: Banner of Truth, 2005.

Garth, David Kinney. "The Influence of Scottish Common Sense Philosophy on the Theology of James Henley Thornwell and Robert Lewis Dabney." PhD diss., Union Theological Seminary, 1979.

Gibson, Scott M. "A. J. Gordon and H. Grattan Guinness: A Case Study of Transatlantic Evangelicalism." In *Pilgrim Pathways: Essays in Baptist History in Honour of B. R. White*, edited by William H. Brackney et al., 303–17. Macon, GA: Mercer University Press, 1999.

———. "Critique of the New Homiletic: Examining the link between the new homiletic and the new hermeneutic." In *The Art & Craft of Biblical Preaching*, edited by Haddon Robinson and Craig Brian Larson, 47681. Grand Rapids, MI: Zondervan, 2005.

———. "Defining the New Homiletic." *Journal of the Evangelical Homiletics Society* 5.2 (September 2005) 19–28.

Giles, Kevin. "The Biblical Argument for Slavery: Can the Bible Mislead? A Case Study in Hermeneutics." *The Evangelical Quarterly* 66.1 (1994) 3–17.

Golden, James L., et al. *The Rhetoric of Western Thought*. 4th ed. Dubuque, IA: Kendall/Hunt, 1989.

Groce, William Todd. "Robert Lewis Dabney and the New South Critique." MA thesis, University of Tennessee, 1988.

Hall, David W. "Dabney and the Utility of History." In *The Arrogance of the Modern: Historical Theology Held in Contempt*, 123–31. Oak Ridge, TN: The Covenant Foundation, 1997.

Hart, Darryl Glen, and John R. Muether. *Seeking a Better Country: 300 Years of American Presbyterianism*. Phillipsburg, NJ: P&R, 2007.

Hatch, Nathan Orr. *The Democratization of American Christianity*. New Haven, CT: Yale University, 1989.

Helm, David R. *Expositional Preaching: How We Speak God's Word Today*. Wheaton, IL: Crossway, 2014.

Hettle, Wallace. *Inventing Stonewall Jackson: A Civil War Hero in History and Memory*. Baton Rouge, LA: Louisiana State University Press, 2011.

———. "The Minister, the Martyr, and the Maxim: Robert Lewis Dabney and Stonewall Jackson." *Civil War History* 49.4 (December 2003) 353–69.

Hixon, Stephen Michael. "The Doctrine of Sanctification in the Works of Robert Dabney and Charles Hodge." ThM thesis, Dallas Theological Seminary, 1980.

Hobson, Fred. *Tell About the South: The Southern Rage to Explain*. Baton Rouge, LA: Louisiana State University Press, 1983.

Holifield, E. Brooks. *The Gentlemen Theologians: American Theology in Southern Culture 1795–1860*. Durham, NC: Duke University Press, 1978.

Jenkins, Thomas Ellsworth. "The Character of God in American Theology: 1800–1900." PhD diss., Yale University, 1991.

Johnson, Thomas Cary. *The Life and Letters of Robert Lewis Dabney*. Edinburgh: Banner of Truth Trust, 1977. Originally published as *The Life and Letters of Robert Lewis Dabney*. Richmond, VA: Presbyterian Committee, 1903.

Jones, Edgar Dewitt. *The Royalty of the Pulpit*. New York: Harper, 1951.

Kelly, Douglas Floyd. "Robert Lewis Dabney." In *Southern Reformed Theology*, edited by David F. Wells, 37–60. Grand Rapids, MI: Baker, 1989.

Kennedy, George A. *Classical Rhetoric and Its Christian and Secular Tradition from Ancient to Modern Times*. 2nd ed. Chapel Hill, NC: University of North Carolina Press, 1999.

Lensch, Christopher K. "Presbyterianism in America—The Nineteenth Century: The Formative Years." *Western Reformed Seminary Journal* 13.2 (August 2006) 16–25.

Lewis, Frank Bell. "Robert Lewis Dabney: Southern Presbyterian Apologist." PhD diss., Duke University, 1946.

Loetcher, Lefferts Augustine. *The Broadening Church: A Study of Theological Issues in the Presbyterian Church Since 1869*. Philadelphia: University of Pennsylvania Press, 1954.

Loveland, Anne C. *Southern Evangelicals and the Social Order 1800–1860*. Baton Rouge, LA: Louisiana State University Press, 1980.

Lowry, Eugene L. *The Homiletical Plot: The Sermon as Narrative Art Form, Expanded Edition*. Louisville: Westminster John Knox, 2001. Originally published as *The Homiletical Plot: The Sermon as Narrative Art Form*. Atlanta: John Knox, 1980.

Lucas, Sean Michael. "God and Country American Style." *Westminster Theological Journal* 69 (2007) 185–97.

———. "'Hold Fast to That Which is Good:' The Public Theology of Robert Lewis Dabney." PhD diss., Westminster Theological Seminary, 2002.

———. *Robert Lewis Dabney: A Southern Presbyterian Life*. Phillipsburg, NJ: P&R, 2005.

Marsden, George M. "Introduction: Reformed and American." In *Southern Reformed Theology*, edited by David F. Wells, 1–12. Grand Rapids, MI: Baker, 1989.

Marsden, George M., and Frank Roberts, eds. *A Christian View of History?* Grand Rapids, MI: Eerdmans, 1975.

Matthews, Merrill, Jr. "Robert Lewis Dabney and Conservative Thought in the Nineteenth Century South: A Study in the History of Ideas." PhD diss., University of Texas, 1989.

McAlister, Dennis E. "Old School Presbyterianism and Slavery: A Study in Selective Biblical Literalism and Providential Social Progress." MA thesis, Covenant Theological Seminary, 1982.

Miller, Glenn T. *Piety and Intellect: The Aims and Purposes of Ante-Bellum Theological Education*. Atlanta: Scholar's, 1990.

Miller, Randall M., et al., eds. *Religion and the American Civil War*. Oxford: Oxford University Press, 1998.

Monroe, Haskell M., Jr. "The Presbyterian Church in the Confederate States of America." PhD diss., Rice University, 1961.

Murray, Andrew E. *Presbyterians and the Negro—A History*. Philadelphia: Presbyterian Historical Society, 1966.

Noll, Mark A. *America's God: From Jonathan Edwards to Abraham Lincoln*. New York: Oxford University Press, 2002.

———. *The Civil War as a Theological Crisis*. Chapel Hill, NC: University of North Carolina, 2006.

———. "Theology, Presbyterian History, and the Civil War." *The Journal of Presbyterian History* 89.1 (Spring/Summer 2011) 5–15.

Old, Hughes Oliphant. *The Reading and Preaching of the Scriptures in the Christian Church*. Vol. 6, *The Modern Age*. Grand Rapids, MI: Eerdmans, 2007.

Overy, David Henry. "Robert Lewis Dabney: Apostle of the Old South." PhD diss., University of Wisconsin, 1967.

Parker, Harold M., Jr. *Studies in Southern Presbyterian History*. Gunnison, CO: B & B, 1979.

Robbins, Jerry. "R. L. Dabney, Old Princeton, and Fundamentalism." PhD diss., Florida State University, 1991.

Robinson, Haddon W. *Biblical Preaching: The Development and Delivery of Expository Messages*. 2nd ed. Grand Rapids, MI: Baker Academic, 2001. Originally published as *Biblical Preaching: The Development and Delivery of Expository Messages*. Grand Rapids, MI: Baker, 1980.

Sebesta, Edward H., and Euan Hague. "The US Civil War as a Theological War: Confederate Christian Nationalism and the League of the South." *Canadian Review of American Studies* 32.3 (2002) 253–83.

Simkins, Francis B. "Robert Lewis Dabney, Southern Conservative." *The Georgia Review* 18.4 (1964) 393–407.

———. *The South Old and New: A History 1820–1947*. New York: Knopf, 1948.

Simpson, Barry D. "The Cultural Degradation of Universal Education: The Educational Views of Robert Lewis Dabney." *Journal of Libertarian Studies* 20.3 (Summer 2006) 47–60.

Smith, Morton. "The Southern Tradition." In *Southern Reformed Theology*, edited by David F. Wells, 13–33. Grand Rapids, MI: Baker, 1989.

———. *Studies in Southern Presbyterian Theology*. Phillipsburg, NJ: Presbyterian and Reformed, 1962.

Snay, Mitchell. *Gospel of Disunion: Religion and Separatism in the Antebellum South*. Cambridge: Cambridge University Press, 1993.

Stampp, Kenneth M. *The Peculiar Institution: Slavery in the Ante-Bellum South*. New York: Vintage, 1989. Originally published as *The Peculiar Institution: Slavery in the Ante-Bellum South*. New York: Knopf, 1956.

Stern, Richard C. "Homiletics: A Bibliographic Essay." *Theological Librarianship: An Online Journal of the American Theological Library Association* 6.1 (January 2013) 69–77.

Stitzinger, James F. "The History of Expository Preaching." *The Master's Seminary Journal* 3.1 (Spring 1992) 5–32.

Sweetser, William B., Jr. *A Copious Fountain: A History of Union Presbyterian Seminary, 1812–2012*. Louisville: Westminster John Knox, 2016.

Thompson, Ernest Trice. *Presbyterian Missions in the Southern United States*. Richmond, VA: Presbyterian Committee, 1934.

———. *Presbyterians in the South, Volume One: 1607–1861*. Richmond, VA: John Knox, 1963.

Thompson, Robert Ellis. *A History of the Presbyterian Churches in the United States*. New York: The Christian Literature Company, 1895.

Thompson, William E. *Her Walls Before Thee Stand: The 235-Year History of the Presbyterian Congregation at Hampton-Sydney, Virginia*. n.p., 2010.

Trotter, Lawrence Calvin. *Always Prepared: Robert Lewis Dabney, the Preacher*. Unpublished manuscript.

———. "Blasting Rocks: The Extemporaneous Homiletic of Robert Lewis Dabney." PhD diss., Regent University, 2007.

Turnbull, Ralph G. *A History of Preaching*. Vol. 3, *From the Close of the Nineteenth Century to the Middle of the Twentieth Century*. Grand Rapids, MI: Baker, 1974.

Turner, E. Carter. "Causes Lost and Found: Southern Election in the Life of Robert Lewis Dabney." PhD diss., Iliff School of Theology and University of Denver, 2007.

Watkin, Robert N., Jr. "The Forming of the Southern Presbyterian Minister: From Calvin to the American Civil War." PhD diss., Vanderbilt University, 1969.

Webber, F. R. *A History of Preaching in Britain and America, Including the Biographies of Many Princes of the Pulpit and the Men Who Influenced Them, Part Three*. Milwaukee, WI: Northwestern, 1957.

Wells, David F. "Preface." In *Southern Reformed Theology*, edited by David F. Wells, xi–xii. Grand Rapids, MI: Baker, 1989.

White, Henry Alexander. "Robert Lewis Dabney." In *Southern Presbyterian Leaders, 1683–1911*, 391. Carlisle, PA: Banner of Truth, 2000. Originally published as *Southern Presbyterian Leaders, 1683–1911*. New York: Neale, 1911.

Wilson, Charles Reagan. *Baptized in Blood: The Religion of the Lost Cause 1865–1920*. Athens, GA: University of Georgia Press, 1980.

———. "Robert Lewis Dabney: Religion and the Southern Holocaust." *The Virginia Magazine of History and Biography* 89.1 (January, 1981) 79–89.

Wilson, Howard McKnight. *The Tinkling Spring: Headwater of Freedom*. Fishersville, VA: The Tinkling Spring Presbyterian Church, 1954.

Woods, Henry M. *Robert Lewis Dabney, 1820–1898: Prince Among Theologians and Men. A Memorial Address Delivered before West Hanover Presbytery at it Fall Meeting, 1936, in Stonewall Church, Appomattox County, Virginia, Celebrating the Jubilee Year of the Founding of the Southern Presbyterian Church in 1861*. Richmond, VA: n.p., 1936.

Wyatt-Brown, Bertram, ed. *The American People in the Antebellum South*. West Haven, CT: Pendulum, 1973.

Young, Jonathan M. "Psychology of the South: Robert Lewis Dabney, the Race God, and Sacramental Purity." MA thesis, University of North Carolina, 1993.

Zink-Sawyer, Beverly. "The Pulpit Leads the Seminary." *Interpretation* 66.4 (October 2012) 409–22.